PRAIRIE & PLAINS STATES

GETTING STARTED GARDEN GUIDE

Grow the Best Flowers, Shrubs, Trees, Vines & Groundcovers

First published in 2015 by Cool Springs Press, an imprint of Quarto Publishing Group USA Inc., 400 First Avenue North, Suite 400, Minneapolis, MN 55401 USA

Cool Springs Press titles are also available at discounts in bulk quantity for industrial or sales-promotional use. For details, write to Special Sales Manager at Quarto Publishing Group USA Inc., 400 First Avenue North, Suite 400, Minneapolis, MN 55401 USA. To find out more about our books, visit us online at www.CoolSpringsPress.com.

ISBN: 978-1-59186-639-8

Library of Congress Cataloging-in-Publication Data

Barash, Cathy Wilkinson, 1949- author.
  Prairie & plains states getting started garden guide : grow the best flowers, shrubs, trees, vines & groundcovers / Cathy Wilkinson Barash.
     pages cm
  Other title: Prairie and plains states getting started garden guide
  Includes bibliographical references and index.
  ISBN 978-1-59186-639-8 (sc)
  1. Gardening--United States. I. Title. II. Title: Prairie and plains states getting started garden guide.

  SB453.B346 2015
  635.90973--dc23
                        2015014597

Acquisitions Editor: Billie Brownell
Project Manager: Sherry Anisi
Art Director: Cindy Samargia Laun
Book Designer: Sara Anglin

Printed in China

10 9 8 7 6 5 4 3 2 1

PRAIRIE & PLAINS STATES

GETTING STARTED GARDEN GUIDE

Grow the Best Flowers, Shrubs, Trees, Vines & Groundcovers

Cathy Wilkinson Barash

COOL
SPRINGS
PRESS
Home and Garden Experts™

MINNEAPOLIS, MINNESOTA

Dedication

I dedicate this book to my mother and father, May and Fritz Wilkinson, who instilled in me from a very young age the love of gardening, a respect for all life, the appreciation of the beauty that surrounds us, and the pleasure that comes from enjoying the fruits of the harvest—both ornamental and edible. I only wish they were here to see the gardener and person I am now, and who I will continue to become.

And to my aunt, Toodie (Wilkinson Walt) Powell, who lived and gardened in southern California (Zone 10b) her entire life until 2013, when at age 87, she remarried and moved to the mountains of western North Carolina (Zone 6a). She is enthusiastically learning to garden in an entirely different climate ("there's northing but gray and brown in winter")—and shoveling snow too. What an inspiration! I am looking forward to a family reunion to celebrate her 90th birthday in 2016.

Acknowledgments

There are so many people who have helped me—not only on this book in particular, but also on the road of life-long gardening that led to it. Thank you, all.

The Garden Writers Association (GWA)—as a group and individual members—are always supportive, knowledgeable, and helpful. The network continues to awe me.

My gratitude to the gardeners (who I define as anyone who puts hands in the soil and grows things—no training needed) I've met throughout the Prairie and Plains States. They generously showed me their gardens, taught me how to adapt and garden in this region, introduced me to a whole new world of plants, and shared their experiences and knowledge, which, in turn, have fed and enriched me tremendously.

Special thanks to Susan Howell, Crystal Sikes, Danielle Heltzel, and Tracy Cortez, who helped me keep body and mind together. Without them, I could not have finished this book.

My deepest thanks to Billie Brownell for giving me the opportunity to write this book, continuing and expanding on what I learned writing *Prairie Lands Gardener's Guide* eleven years ago. I am doubly grateful to have Billie as my editor. Her eagle-eye, insight, compassion, and guidance—not to mention excellent editing—have been stellar. Last, but not least, I am eternally grateful for my constant companions, who inspire laughter, provide love, and purrs—Tiarella, Bogart, and Pause.

CONTENTS

WELCOME TO GARDENING
IN THE PRAIRIE & PLAINS STATES

Not being a native to the Prairie & Plains States region, I have a different perspective on gardening here than someone who grew up in this region. I had no idea how spoiled I was living most of my life on Long Island, where the weather is buffered by the warmth of the Gulf Stream. I can count on one hand the times the thermometer dipped below zero. I gardened in comparably tropical Zone 7 (with microclimates of Zone 8), in fairly well-drained, rich, acidic soil.

Moving to Des Moines, Iowa, more than seventeen years ago, I had fifty-five large cartons filled with potted-up outdoor plants accompanied by my furniture in the moving van—in August. How the movers even lifted my cat Sebastian's personal planter—a half whiskey barrel planted with catmint, chives, and dianthus—I'll never know. I am the first to admit that I did not do the basic research I should have. Yet, for me, learning by trial and error often leaves a more indelible impression than reading something online or in a book.

Back then, there were no regional gardening books; in fact, many books had a Northeast bias. That's why I was so excited to write *Prairie Lands Gardener's Guide* in 2003 and share my experiences with other gardeners. In the years that followed, I traveled to all the states covered in the book, giving lectures and holding book signings. I got to meet lots of folks, see their wonderful gardens (as well as fabulous public ones), and learn from their experiences. I spent some time in Oklahoma, too, so when I was given the opportunity to include that state in this book, I felt up to the challenge.

The Unique Prairie & Plains States

When I moved to Iowa, I was warned about the winters, hearing stories of a month with no sun, days on end when the high is in the minus 20s. What no one warned me about were the summers and how unbearably hot and humid (yet dry) they can be. Nor did they mention the wind. These are the basic elements you have to deal with when creating any garden in the Prairie & Plains States. Yes, it can be challenging, but it's so rewarding when it all works. All you need to do is drive around and see the splendid and varied gardens that people have successfully created. And, I'll bet

Native prairie plants, such as black-eyed Susan, purple coneflower, blanket flower, and tickseed, are must-haves.

that those charming small front yard gardens on farms are not molly-coddled. Either it grows or it doesn't.

Many of my Zone 7 plants did not make it through the first (mild) winter. Fortunately, one of the gardening tenets I grew up with was not to bemoan a dead plant. Unless it is diseased, it goes on the compost pile and will become food to nurture the soil for future plants. That was good, because by the next summer, I had a lot of compost in the works.

Learn from Others

One of the best ways to learn what will grow well is to visit friends and neighbors to see what's in their yards. If you're a beginning gardener, and you admire someone's perennials, offer to help divide them when the time comes; you'll likely be rewarded by a division or two for your own garden. Ask questions. Gardeners are the friendliest people, usually willing to share their knowledge. How can anyone resist when you walk up to them as they are working in their garden and you compliment them on their plantings? Ask specific questions about plants that pique your interest. Be prepared to take notes. Not only will they be impressed, you'll remember and do what they suggest. Gardening takes you full circle—and lets you meet the most interesting folks.

When seeking advice, visit your nearest botanical garden or arboretum. Make a day of it. If you don't have a smartphone, bring a camera to take plenty of pictures to refresh your memory later. And by all means go with someone else—to share the beauty *and* help see different things you may not notice.

Your county Cooperative Extension Service (despite budget cuts) offers *lots* of free information, pamphlets, and guidance. It may also offer soil testing and a lab where you can bring samples of plant problems. The Cooperative Extension Service is generally the local authority on what you can successfully grow within your hardiness zone.

Understanding Hardiness Zones

In 1960, after years of studying and recording winter temperatures, the United States Department of Agriculture came up with a remarkable tool for farmers and gardeners alike—the USDA Hardiness Zone Map. The first map listed 10 zones, each with an average annual minimum winter temperature range 10 degrees from one zone to the next. In full color, you could see, if you lived in Zone 4, for example, that the average minimum temperature was between minus 30 and minus 20 degrees Fahrenheit. Zone

3 was 10 degrees chillier—between minus 30 to minus 40, while Zone 5 seemed almost balmy at minus 10 to minus 20.

In 1990, the map was revised (using data collected from 1974 to 1986). In general, demarcations were the same, with the northern half of both Iowa and Nebraska as Zone 4, with the southern sections as Zone 5. However, each zone was divided in half—"a" and "b"—with 5-degree increments between each.

In 2012, the USDA issued a new map based on data collected from 1986 to 2005, and expanded to 13 zones (to include Hawaii and Puerto Rico). What is remarkable to me is how the average minimum temperatures have risen (and the data used is now 10 years old). Most of Iowa is now Zone 5, with only small patches of Zone 4 dotted in the northern regions. All the other states in the book have warmed as well. Considering that recent years have been recorded as the hottest years on record, what changes lie ahead? The new map is interactive: go online, enter your zip code, and get local information. http://planthardiness.ars.usda.gov/PHZMWeb/#

In addition to knowing your hardiness zone, before you plant it is helpful to know the **last frost date**. That is the date in spring after which is it *unlikely* that the temperature will go below 32 degrees Fahrenheit. The **first frost date** is the date in fall before which it is unlikely that the temperature will dip below freezing. Google the National Climatic Data Center Frost Dates on the Internet for the best interactive feature.

Microclimates

You can easily find out your hardiness zone, but that is not the sole determination of what will grow well in your garden. You may have already discovered that some areas are warmer than others—against or near a south-facing wall, protected by a piece of hardscape or large stones. Then there are cooler areas, such as the north-facing side of the house, exposed and open areas, and low-lying spaces. These are *microclimates*.

Use microclimates to your advantage. For example, if a plant is questionably hardy in your zone, site it in one of the warmer spaces. Conversely, if you live in Zone 8 Oklahoma, and the plant you want to grow has a hardiness range to Zone 7 (a zone colder), place it where shade and breezes will keep it cooler. When considering the microclimate, take into account the soil type and drainage before you plant. For a plant to survive is one thing, but you want your plants to thrive!

The Dirt on Soil

The soil in this region is generally on the alkaline side, with a pH of about 7.5. (The pH is the relative measure of acidity and alkalinity, pH of 7 being neutral.) My plants and I were used to more acidic soil in the 5.5 to 6.0 range. Soil varies here from rich loam to clay, with some rocky and even sandy areas. In general though, the soil is rich.

Some people use the words "soil" and "dirt" interchangeably. From my point of view, soil is what is in the garden—the nourishing medium we put our plants into. Soil is a *living* substance with a variety of biological, chemical, and physical forces constantly at work. It is comprised of five major components: air, living organisms (microscopic bacteria, fungi, earthworms, and insects), humus (organic material in varying states of decay), water, and inorganic particles of minerals and rocks. Dirt is the result of a day in the garden—what's smeared on my face and ground in under my nails, in every corrugation of my garden clogs, leaving muddy tracks on the carpet. Whatever you want to call it—dirt or soil—you'll want to know what you're starting with.

You can do a "squeeze test" to determine your soil type right in the garden. Gently squeeze a small amount of lightly moist soil in your hand, release it, and then rub it between your fingers. Sandy soil, made of the largest particles, does not stay together when squeezed, and is gritty to the touch. Sandy soil is easy to work and drains very well. However, water draining through removes most of the nutrients. Clay (sometimes called heavy soil) absorbs and retains moisture. Its particles are so fine that it holds its shape when squeezed. In the ground, air and water cannot move through it. Silt is midway in size between sand and clay, with a smooth texture. Its particles squeeze together but do not remain compacted, especially when they are dry. The ideal garden soil is loam, a mixture of the three types. When you rub loam between your fingers, it breaks up into smaller particles. It holds moisture well and encourages the biological activity necessary for healthy, living soil.

Loam is the ideal garden soil.

Once you know what type of soil you have, it's decision time. Work with what you have and grow plants that thrive in that environment, or amend the soil to make it suit the plants you want to grow. Or, you could do a little of each, making your all-over landscape more varied. Knowing what soil conditions your plant requires allows you to choose the right location. The highest quality, most expensive plant, if grown in the wrong soil conditions, will likely die. Conversely, a so-so plant put in ideal growing conditions will, with some TLC, probably thrive.

Compost—The Gardener's BFF

I am a strong believer in composting—it saves hauling heavy garbage bags and cuts down on what goes to landfills. I am constantly using compost to mix into my soil, which is on the clayey side. Good compost is full of all those wonderful microorganisms that help get the nutrients from the soil to the plant through the plant's rootlets. Some gardeners call compost "black gold"—it certainly pulls its weight.

I add compost to the soil when planting (unless the plant prefers less-fertile soil). Also, each spring I spread a layer of compost around my plants, and it in turn feeds the soil. I cover the compost with organic mulch, such as wood chips, shredded bark, grass clippings (no more than ¾ inch at a time), or shredded leaves. Each spring I renew the mulch, much of which has broken down into compost on its own. If you continue this

Wire mesh lining the compost bin allows air circulation and keeps everything inside.

simple process, you will have healthy soil, which then grows healthy plants, which in turn are less susceptible to pests and diseases.

Planting

If you want only one or two plants of a particular variety, you are better off buying plants locally. They are available in a range of sizes based on the container. A four- or six-cell pack is the smallest. Each cell is about 1-inch square. You can find individual young plants in 3-, 4-, 6-inch pots, or larger. Many full-sized plants are also available in a variety of containers, especially hanging baskets. Obviously, the larger the container, the higher the price. However, if you want instant gratification and need to fill in a hole in the garden, by all means go for the larger pot.

Choose the best plant. When selecting plants, look at the bottom of the container for roots coming out through the holes. Avoid these, as they are rootbound and stressed. Although it is tempting to buy a plant in full bloom, look for one with buds and lots of leaves. While purchasing plants, get a container of liquid transplant/starting solution—invaluable when planting or transplanting. It consists mainly of vitamins in a solution that stimulates root growth. I have found that it can even bring new life to rescued plants that look pitiful (such as those in the sale bin at the end of the season).

Top: Gently pop plants out of the cell packs. *Bottom:* Plant at the same depth they were growing in the pack.

Many plants won't germinate or grow until the soil reaches a certain temperature (indicated in the "When, Where, and How to Plant" section of the plant entry). A soil thermometer is a good investment so you know exactly when to get planting in your garden. Black walnut trees (*Juglans nigra*), common in our region, exude a chemical called juglone from their roots. This chemical inhibits the growth of many plants. It is noted in the "Regional Advice and Care" section if the plant can grow near black walnuts.

The ideal time to plant or transplant is on a cloudy day or late in the afternoon when bright sunlight won't stress the plant. Mix up a batch of transplant solution (following label instructions) in a bucket or container deep enough to set the plant in to absorb the solution. The amount of solution needed depends on how many plants are going in the ground. Allow at least 1½ cups per small plant, 3 cups for 6-inch pots and larger.

Dig a hole the size and depth of the container. Remove any flowers and buds from the plant; you want to stimulate root growth and flowers take energy away from the roots. Dip the container in the transplant solution for about one minute. Gently remove the plant from its pot.

If it is rootbound (there's little visible soil, and the roots are wrapped around each other or coming out of the bottom of the pot), loosen the roots so they can grow:

1. Rip (or cut off) the bottom ½ inch of roots and soil.
2. With both hands on the bottom of the plant, *gently* pull outwards to make a small separation in the middle of the root system.
3. If there are roots that wind around the bottom, gently tease them loose.
4. Cut off any overly long roots.

Pinch off flowers before planting to encourage the roots to grow.

5. Set the plant in the hole so that soil level from the pot is even with the soil level of the surrounding soil. You may need to add or take out soil.
6. Gently firm the plant and surrounding soil with your hands.
7. Water the soil with 1 cup of transplant solution.

If a larger container is rootbound, skip steps 1 and 2. Instead, work your fingers around the plant to loosen its roots. If a large plant is very rootbound (no loose soil comes off the plant), use a knife to make four ½-inch deep slashes down the side of the root mass. Then proceed to step 3 and follow the steps to the end.

The Beauty of Mulch

Mulch is almost as valuable as compost. It moderates soil temperature and helps retain water. Apply at least 3 inches of mulch—at least 1 inch away from the stem. In my travels through our region, I have been surprised at how few gardeners use mulch. Perhaps that is from farm lineage, where the idea of mulching great fields would be outlandish. Yet I constantly hear people complaining about weeds. Mulch solves that problem almost completely. Yes, there are a few noxious weeds that may grow up through the mulch, but very few. In addition, if you plan your garden so there are no large bare spots between plants, weed seeds won't have space or light to germinate.

I generally choose an organic mulch that can break down over time. However, there are exceptions. In particular, Mediterranean herbs that don't tolerate wet soil (as well as some other plants) benefit from a mulch that lets water pass through quickly, such as sand, turkey grit, gravel, pebbles, river rock—it depends on the size of the plant as well as your aesthetic taste. The most unique mulch I've seen was potshards—bits of broken terra-cotta pots surrounding a large shrub. Not only was it eye-catching, it kept critters away—and people as well.

Gravel

Bark

Plants for the Prairie & Plains States

The plants I have included in this book are suited to our tough and variable climate. Especially in the perennials section, native plants abound in this book. Moreover, they are the easiest to grow,

Straw

needing the least care; very few need special attention. The symbols for sunlight indicate how much sun a plant needs (see page 15). But don't just rely on these; look at plants for a clue that you may be doing something wrong. A plant that is leaning toward the sunlight needs to be moved to where it gets more light. Sun-lovers will have more vivid colors with more light. Conversely, some shade-lovers will wilt in the heat of the day, and their colors may fade.

The "When, Where, and How to Plant" section of each plant entry provides you with the information to select the right site for the plant. However, depending on your conditions, you may find that the plant is happier moved to a drier or moister, richer, or poorer soil site. Do not be too quick to give up on a plant. The mere act of putting it in the ground shocks the plant by moving it from its old environment to a new one.

Follow Your Vision

As I have been writing, I have had visions of my great-great-grandmother crossing the Prairie and Plains states in a covered wagon 160 or so years ago. I can't help but wonder what her view was—grasses and perennials taller than she was. And the remarkable thing is I know that on her journey, she either dug some roots, took cuttings, or, more likely, collected seed. The evidence was in my grandmother's garden—these plants were so unique that few people in southern California in the 1940s, '50s, and '60s were at all familiar with them. The vision of my grandmother's garden flashes through my mind and I can see the plants as vividly as if it were yesterday. The property was sold long ago, though I think my aunt kept a few of the plants in her California garden. Yet here am I, starting it all over again, relearning what my ancestor did so many years ago. (And my aunt is relearning as well, having transplanted herself at the ripe age of 87 to the mountains of North Carolina.) And so the tradition of gardening continues.

Even a small backyard can be an oasis with a few carefully chosen plants.

How to Use This Book

Each entry in this guide provides you with information about a plant's particular characteristics, its habits, and its basic requirements for vigorous growth, as well as my personal experience and knowledge of it. I have tried to include the information you need to help you realize each plant's potential. Only when a plant performs at its best can you fully appreciate it. You will find pertinent information including bloom period and seasonal colors (if any), and mature height and spread. The zone information reflects the range of cold (and in some cases heat) tolerance in which the plant can thrive.

Additional Benefits

Symbols represent the "added benefits" provided by a plant:

 Native plant

 Fall or seasonal color

 Resists drought

 Attracts pollinators/butterflies

 Attracts hummingbirds

 Edible for people

 Deer resistant

Sun Requirements

Symbols represent the range of sunlight suitable for each plant. "Full Sun" means a site receiving at least six hours of direct sun daily. "Part Sun" means a site that receives at least four to six hours of direct sun daily. "Part Shade" means a site that receives about four or less hours of direct or dappled sun daily. "Shade" means a site that gets dappled light or less than three hours of sun. Some plants grow successfully in more than one range of sun, which is indicated by more than one sun symbol.

Full Sun   Part Sun   Part Shade   Shade

Detailed planting information, soil preferences, water requirements, fertilizing needs, pruning, care, and pest information are provided for each entry under the sections marked "When, Where, and How to Plant," "Growing Tips," and "Regional Advice and Care."

Companion Planting and Design

In this section, I offer suggestions for different ways to showcase the plant with others for particular style or effect. If plants have a special use, it is noted here.

Try These

In this section, I offer specific cultivars, selections, or hybrids of the featured plant. In some cases I have included closely related plants that are particularly noteworthy. Give them a try. Often these include favorite plants I just couldn't bear to leave out of the book.

USDA Hardiness Zone Maps

Cold-hardiness zone designations were developed by the United States Department of Agriculture (USDA) to indicate the minimum average temperature for an area. A zone assigned to an individual plant indicates the lowest temperature at which the plant can be expected to survive over the winter. Because the hardiness zones within the states covered by this book range from Zone 3 to Zone 8, I have listed the hardiness as a range, as some plants will not grow in the colder regions, while others cannot take the heat of the warmer ones. Zones are not listed when plants will grow in Zones 3 through 8. Hardiness is not an issue for annuals and biennials, so no zone info is listed. You can go online to the interactive map, enter your zip code, and get local information at http://planthardiness.ars.usda.gov/PHZMWeb/#.

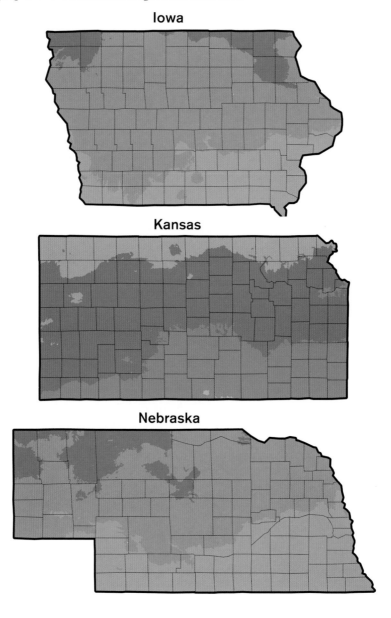

Iowa

Kansas

Nebraska

North Dakota

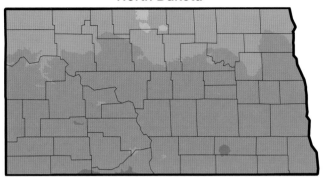

Oklahoma

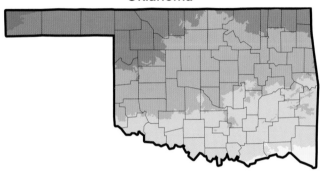

South Dakota

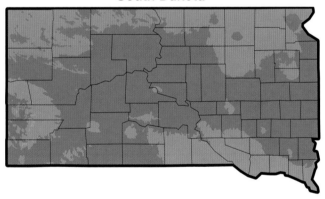

ZONE	Average Minimum Temperature	ZONE	Average Minimum Temperature
3 A	-35 to -40	6 A	-5 to -10
3 B	-30 to -35	6 B	0 to -5
4 A	-25 to -30	7 A	5 to 0
4 B	-20 to -25	7 B	10 to 5
5 A	-15 to -20	8 A	15 to 10
5 B	-10 to -15		

ANNUALS & BIENNIALS

FOR THE PRAIRIE & PLAINS STATES

Although perennials are great and will grow and bloom each year, their bloom period is generally short—sometimes only a week or two, while others may last a month or more.

Annuals and biennials, interspersed among perennials and shrubs or just planted on their own, provide long-lasting color in the garden throughout the summer, right up until frost.

Annuals

In the Prairie and Plains States, annuals are *exactly* what their name says—plants that live one year. You plant annuals in spring (timing depends on the plant), they bloom (many are already in bloom when you buy them), set seed (if you don't deadhead them), and die in autumn, usually with the first frost. For those of you who are snowbirds and travel to warm climates for the winter, you will notice that, in areas with no frost, many annuals will just keep growing. (Indeed, in those climates, some are perennial and may not even go through a period of dormancy.)

Some annuals, such as spring-planted pansies, are not heat tolerant and will die in summer. Fall-planted pansies, however, are extremely cold tolerant and will last through the winter, often blooming when the snow melts, and continue to bloom through spring. They are also surprisingly heat tolerant and may last through the summer, to die in fall. However, these are exceptions to the usual behavior of annuals.

A bench is a focal point to a view with cosmos in the foreground.

Some annuals self-sow, which means that their seeds drop to the ground and germinate the following year. They give the impression of being perennial when, in fact, these annuals were not deadheaded and were allowed to set seed and thus returned.

Pansies and violas, ready for planting; what could say "spring" more than that?

Biennials

By definition, biennials grown from seed put out leaves the first year and often die back in fall. Their roots, however, do not die. Often the leaves remain, looking rather tattered by spring. It is not until their second year that they send out flowers. Reproduction is what a plant's entire life cycle is all about, so once the flowers set seed, the plant dies.

Biennials can be a bit confusing. They are sometimes mistaken for annuals and sometimes for perennials. Generally, when you purchase a biennial plant—such as hollyhock or foxglove—at a nursery, garden center, or home-improvement store, it is already in its second year and is either in bloom or about to bloom. It will bloom in the garden, go to seed, and die.

Here is where the magic of Mother Nature steps in, especially with hollyhocks and foxgloves. Try letting the seedheads remain on the plant. Some of the seeds will fall on the ground near the original plant and germinate that season; therefore, the following year, they will be in their second year and bloom. Since the new plants are in the same general location as the original plant, an erroneous assumption may be made that the plant is perennial when in truth it is a biennial.

Planting

Often when you buy annuals, they are already blooming. Although it is wonderful to have instant color in the garden, the plants will be happier and more lush in the long run if you pinch off the flowers as well as any buds. Pinch or cut down one or two sets of leaves, depending on how tall the plant is. This will do two things. First, and most important, it forces the plant to redirect its energy into root production, growing long, strong roots that can reach deeper into the soil. The result is a plant that needs less water, especially when it is well mulched. Second, the plant will send out two stems wherever it was pinched, and you'll end up with a bushier plant. Just have patience and a new—and better—flush of bloom will appear before long. Follow planting information in the "Planting" section at the front of the book (page 11).

After planting, do not mulch for two weeks. Then use 2 inches of organic matter (compost, well-rotted manure, or leaf mold) around the plant. Keep the mulch 1 inch away from the stem of the plants. Otherwise, you might smother the stem and introduce insects or disease. Do not mulch seeded beds. Wait until the plants are thinned to their proper spacing and have at least four sets of leaves.

Growing From Seed

The seed packet has good instructions on when to plant—indoors or directly in the garden.

You can get a jump-start on the season by starting the seeds inside. Fill flats or containers (I use small peat pots, which I can transplant directly into the ground) with a lightly moistened sterile seed-starting mix. Sprinkle fine seeds on the soil surface. Use a chopstick or pencil to make a planting hole for larger seeds. Plant them at a depth that is about twice their diameter. Cover with soil, and water lightly with a fine mist. Avoid a strong stream of water that can dislodge the seeds. Keep the soil warm and moist to ensure germination (I use heat mats for plants). Cover the containers with plastic to help conserve moisture. Check daily, and water often enough to keep the soil surface moist, *but not wet*. Remove the plastic and move the flat or container to a sunny window or under grow lights as soon as seedlings appear. Place grow lights 6 inches above the plants and keep them on sixteen hours a day. When plants have at least two sets of leaves, thin to one or two plants per peat pot. If you started in a flat, thin or transplant into larger pot. Transplant into the garden according to the timing suggested on the seed packet.

You can also sow seeds directly in the ground where they will be growing as soon as soil temperatures are warm enough. Follow the directions on the seed packet. Put about ½ inch of soil over the seeds. Tamp the soil down firmly and water the area gently to avoid washing away the seeds. When plants are up and growing, thin to recommended spacing.

Self-Sowers

The self-sowers, or self-seeders, as they may be called, are my favorites among both annuals and biennials. Once you plant them, you will continue to have long-lasting bloom for years to come with virtually no effort. With some plants, such as perilla (*Perilla frutescens*), angel's trumpet (*Datura metel*, which many folks in this region call moonflower, confusing others with the night-blooming morning glory cousin [*Ipomoea alba*]; others call it angel's trumpet), and amaranths (*Amaranthus* spp.), this can almost work too well since they are very prolific and can easily overrun a garden within a few years. However, if you are like me and love these plants, you will quickly learn to recognize the seedlings and pull the excess out when they are young.

Here is a list of self-sowing annuals and biennials that you could try. Those with asterisks (*) are included as plant selections in this chapter. Morning glory is on page 70 in the Groundcovers & Vines chapter.

Self-Sowing Annuals & Biennials

Common Name	Botanical Name	Type
*Angel's trumpet	*Datura metel*	Annual
*Bachelor's buttons	*Centaurea cyanus*	Annual
Black-eyed Susan	*Rudbeckia hirta*	Biennial
Calendula	*Calendula officinalis*	Annual
Chinese forget-me-not	*Cyanoglossum amabile*	Biennial
*Cleome	*Cleome hassleriana*	Annual
*Cosmos	*Cosmos bipinnatus*	Annual
*Flowering tobacco	*Nicotiana alata*	Annual
*Four o'clocks	*Mirabilis jalapa*	Annual
Foxglove	*Digitalis* spp.	Biennial
*Hollyhock	*Alcea rosea*	Biennial
*Johnny jump-up	*Viola tricolor*	Annual
Love-in-a-mist	*Nigella damascena*	Annual
*Love-lies-bleeding	*Amaranthus caudatus*	Annual
Money plant	*Lunaria annua*	Biennial
*Morning glory	*Ipomoea tricolor*	Annual
Moss rose	*Portulaca grandiflora*	Annual
Plains coreopsis	*Coreopsis tinctoria*	Annual
Rose mallow	*Lavatera trimestris*	Annual
Sweet William	*Dianthus barbatus*	Biennial

If the plants are cultivated hybrids and they self-sow, it is quite possible that the resulting plants will *not* be the same as the original ones. I enjoy letting these plants go to seed and watching the variations that pop up the following year. If you want the *same* plant from seed, you need to grow species plants (those that occur in nature) or open-pollinated heirloom seeds. Heirloom seeds, which have been passed down from generation to generation, were often part of the few belongings immigrants brought to America. Today, resources like Seed Savers Exchange and other online and mail-order sources make these family seed legacies available to all of us. Their names alone make them tempting to grow—Grandpa Ott's morning glory, Mortgage Lifter tomato, and more.

Space limits me from writing more about the innumerable beautiful and colorful annuals and biennials for Prairie and Plains States gardens. To really explore the tremendous range of plants, visit friends' and family members' gardens, go to a local botanic garden, and, of course, take a trips to nurseries, garden centers, and home-improvement stores. You will be amazed at the diversity and range of plants that can enliven your garden all seasons.

If you *don't* want a self-sower to go to seed, deadhead.

Angel's Trumpet

Datura metel

Botanical Pronunciation
dah-TOOR-uh MET-il

Other Name
Thornapple

Bloom Period and Seasonal Colors
Midsummer to frost, white

Mature Height × Spread
3 to 5 ft. × 3 to 5 ft.

Every garden needs at least one angel's trumpet to herald the night. The upfacing, large (5- to 8-inch), trumpet-shaped white flowers open as the sun goes down, filling the air with their sweet perfume, attracting pollinators like the exotic luna and sphinx moths. Although the blooms generally only last a single night, more are produced as the plant grows so that at full maturity it may be 5 feet wide and tall with dozens of blooms. If the day is cloudy or rainy, the flowers will remain open but scentless. What is a boon to most gardeners (but a bane to a few) is that angel's trumpet readily self-sows and will come back year after year. **Beware:** All parts of this plant are poisonous.

When, Where, and How to Plant

Plants are available locally as well as from online and mail-order sources. Angel's trumpet thrives in rich, humusy, well-drained alkaline soil and full sun but will also grow in poorer soil and part sun. For planting information, see page 11. To grow angel's trumpet from seed, sow seeds indoors (for more on seed planting, see page 20) six to eight weeks before the last frost date. Transplant into the garden two or three weeks after last frost date. It is an excellent container plant. Wear disposable gloves when handling the plant—all parts are toxic.

Growing Tips

Although you do not need to fertilize, it will be more impressive with foliar feeding every three weeks. Do not allow the soil to dry out—wilting leaves are a signal to water immediately.

Regional Advice and Care

Remove the faded flowers and the golf ball-sized, spiky seedheads to promote more blooms. Near the end of the season, allow one or two seedheads to ripen and drop seeds for next year's fragrant delight. If grown in a container, bring it indoors for the winter. Cut it back by one-third. If the there is ample light and warmth, it will continue to grow. Otherwise, let it go dormant by placing it in a cool dark place, watering lightly once a month. Keep an eye on the plant for any sign of mealybugs or spider mites. For spider mites, spray with an insecticidal soap. Use a swab dipped in rubbing alcohol to wipe off the cottony mealybugs. To avoid spreading, throw out the swab after each use.

Companion Planting and Design

When planting, consider how large the plant grows and do not put anything within 2 to 3 feet. The Wave® series of petunias (*Petunia* × *hybrida* The Wave®), which spread to form a lovely carpet of pink, white, or lilac, are beautiful surrounding angel's trumpet. Add some height by planting angel's trumpet in front of a morning glory (*Ipomoea tricolor*). In the daytime, the flowers nod, as seen in the photo above, but perk right up again in the evening.

Try These

'Double Purple' is a showstopper in any garden with 8-inch-long, double purple-and-white flowers.

Bachelor's Buttons

Centaurea cyanus

Botanical Pronunciation
sen-TOR-ee-ah sy-AN-us

Other Name
Cornflower

Bloom Period and Seasonal Colors
Late spring to midsummer, blue, deep red,
lavender, pink, white

Mature Height × Spread
8 to 32 in. × 6 to 12 in.

Bachelor's buttons are grown for the dark sky blue, daisylike flowers, which are borne atop multibranched stems that provide eye-catching bloom in summer. Although you may read that it prefers cool weather, in partial shade (afternoon sun) it thrives from late June through August. Even mowers cannot defeat it, as it will rise up to bloom again, often continuing through the summer. Grown organically in the garden, the petals are edible, with a slightly bitter flavor. Toss them with red tomatoes, fresh mozzarella cheese, and a light dressing of olive oil and white balsamic vinegar for a patriotic Fourth of July salad. Bachelor's buttons are beautiful planted in drifts, mixed with other medium-height flowers that lend support, yet they can sway with the breeze.

When, Where, and How to Plant
Bachelor's buttons are one of the few annuals you can sow in early fall to bloom next spring. I have the same success sowing them atop the snow in late winter as with annual poppies. Most people sow seeds directly in the ground where they will be growing as soon as soil temperatures are at least 55 degrees Fahrenheit (use a soil thermometer). Put about ½ inch of soil over the seeds. Tamp the soil down firmly and water the area gently to avoid washing away the seeds. For a head start, sow the seeds indoors in early spring in peat pots. Bachelor's buttons does not like to have its roots disturbed, so plant the peat pot directly into the ground without disturbing the roots.

Growing Tips
For the first two weeks after sowing the seed, you may have to water several times a day to prevent the soil from drying out. Once the plant is several inches tall, water daily or every other day. As the soil heats up and the days become longer, the sun is brighter, and with the probability of wind, you may have to go back to a daily watering regimen. Water the soil in the root area monthly using compost tea or other liquid fertilizer. Avoid wetting the leaves, as wet leaves are more susceptible to downy mildew.

Regional Advice and Care
To prolong the bloom time, deadhead (cut off spent blooms) down to the next lower branching stems. With high humidity, bachelor's buttons are prone to powdery mildew or downy mildew. Treat with baking soda solution (see page 175). Never spray if the temperature is above 80 degrees Fahrenheit.

Companion Planting and Design
Bachelor's buttons are perfect for a naturalistic, meadow-type garden of poppies (*Papaver* spp.), mallows (*Malva* spp.), tickseed (*Coreopsis* spp.), and tall annuals like zinnias (*Zinnia elegans*) and cosmos (*Cosmos bipinnatus*). My "meadow" is only 3 feet by 6 feet and it's beautiful all summer.

Try These
Florence series (seen in the photo above) has multi-branched, compact plants, with double pink, cherry red, lavender, and white flowers.

Blanket Flower

Gaillardia pulchella

Botanical Pronunciation
gay-LARD-ee-ah pull-KEL-lah

Other Name
Indian blanket

Bloom Period and Seasonal Colors
Summer to frost, red, yellow, yellow-tipped red with purple/maroon center

Mature Height × Spread
8 to 24 in. × 9 to 16 in.

There are both annual and perennial blanket flowers. Both are native to this region. Visit a native or restored prairie in summer, and blanket flower will be among the brightest, most vivid flowers there. The flowerhead is daisylike with a circle of yellow-tipped, bright red flowers (another name is firewheel). Slightly jagged-edged petals surround dark purple disk florets (like white daisy petals surround a center of yellow disk florets) for an impressive flower that is about 2 inches across. Natural variations occur, so solid red or solid yellow blooms are actually the species and not a special cultivated variety. Their cheery colors radiate in the garden from June until frost. Named Oklahoma's official state wildflower in 1986, Indian blanket seeds attract birds and self-sow.

When, Where, and How to Plant
Blanket flower prefers fertile, well-drained soil and full sun. Start seeds in peat pots. Pre-moisten some seed-starting mix, fill the pot within ½ inch of the top, and add three seeds. Barely cover the seeds with mix and press lightly. Cover loosely with plastic wrap to retain moisture. Place the pots in a warm place. Mist and vent daily to keep the soil evenly moist. Once the seeds germinate, remove the plastic. Move pots to a sunny window or under grow lights. When seedlings have two sets of leaves, thin to one plant per pot, keeping the strongest plant by cutting off the weaker stems. After all danger of frost has passed, plant them out in the garden about 8 to 12 inches apart. Gently tear off the top edge of the peat pot and set it so the soil in the pot is level with the ground. Or, sow the seed directly in the ground after the last frost date.

Growing Tips
Keep the plants evenly moist after planting. Once established, they are quite drought tolerant. If leaves droop, water the plant and it will perk right up. Foliar feed monthly.

Regional Advice and Care
Cut off flowers after they fade (down to the next lowest branch without removing any other flower buds) to encourage new blooms. Flowers attract butterflies, bees, and other pollinators. Blanket flower is prone to downy mildew. Treat with a baking soda solution (see page 175). Never spray if the temperature is above 80 degrees Fahrenheit. Leave late season flowerheads; seeds attract birds and self-sow.

Companion Planting and Design
Blanket flower is ideal in a meadow setting with false sunflower (*Heliopsis helianthoides*), tickseed (*Coreopsis lanceolata*), and feather reed grass (*Calamagrostis* × *acutiflora*). It is equally at home in a mixed flowerbed with zinnias (*Zinnia elegans*), asters (*Symphyotrichum* spp.), and goldenrod (*Solidago* spp.).

Try These
Plume series (to 12 inches tall) have double flowers with almost round heads. 'Plume Red' is brilliant brick red. 'Sundance' (to 10 inches) bears double, bicolored mahogany red-and-yellow blooms.

Cleome

Cleome hassleriana

Botanical Pronunciation
klee-OH-mee hass-lur-ee-AY-nuh

Other Name
Spider flower

Bloom Period and Seasonal Colors
Summer to frost, pink, white, purple, bicolors

Mature Height × Spread
3 to 5 ft. × 15 to 24 in.

To me, cleome is a plant that shows Nature's sense of humor. It is quite unusual looking, with descriptions ranging from clouds of blooms to flowers arranged on long racemes, opening from top to bottom. Rather gangly and growing up to 6 feet tall (but doesn't need staking), it comes into its glory when the flowers near the top of the plant start to unroll—another unusual trait. As more blooms are exposed, notice the long protruding stamens, reminiscent of cat whiskers. Along the stem are long narrow seedpods, which easily open, making it readily self-sowing. Cleome is a long-lasting cut flower for dramatic arrangements. It's equally at home at the back of a border, center of an island bed, or in a cottage garden.

When, Where, and How to Plant

Cleome plants are readily available locally. Find seeds through online and mail-order sources. Choose plants in larger pots; they are sturdier and usually not rootbound. As cleome is a single-stemmed plant, do not pinch it back. Cleome prefers light, fertile, very well-drained soil (add sand to loam) and full sun. It tolerates part sun. Plant or sow seeds outside two to three weeks after the last frost date. Allow 1 to 3 feet between plants. See page 11 for planting information.

Growing Tips

Keep well watered until plants are established. Cleome is somewhat drought tolerant; water deeply after a week with no rain. Cleome doesn't require feeding, but I foliar feed once in midsummer (when the temperature is less than 80 degrees Fahrenheit).

Regional Advice and Care

To prevent self-seeding, cut the long seedpods forming along the stem. If you want to save the seed, wait until the pod dries. Carefully cut it off; it easily spills seeds. Alternatively, let Mother Nature take her own course. If you are counting on self-sown cleome, be patient. It germinates in late spring; wait until late June to clean and mulch the area. Allow ample room between plants to lessen stress, which makes them susceptible to pests and diseases. If aphids, small caterpillars, whiteflies, or spider mites are a problem, spray the plant with insecticidal soap weekly. Many cleome varieties are fragrant, attracting butterflies and bees.

Companion Planting and Design

Create a beautiful purple garden with cleome mixed with any of these plants: Blue Vein petunia (*Petunia* × *hybrida* 'Blue Vein'), Lavender Lace cuphea (*Cuphea rosea* 'Lavender Lace'), English lavender (*Lavandula angustifolia*), and tall vervain (*Verbena bonariensis*).

Try These

'Helen Campbell', while not fragrant, is a classic with pure white flowers. Sparkler series (to 4 feet tall) are hybrids, so will not come true from seed: 'Sparkler Blush' (bicolor pink and white), 'Sparkler Lavender', 'Sparkler Rose', and 'Sparkler White'. The Queen series includes 'Rose Queen', 'Violet Queen', and 'White Queen'.

Coleus

Plectranthus scutellarioides

Botanical Pronunciation
pleck-TRAN-thuss skoo-tul-air-ee-oh-EYE-deez

Bloom Period and Seasonal Color
Summer, blue

Mature Height × Spread
6 to 36 in. × 6 to 36 in.

Coleus (formerly *Solenostemon* genus) was all the rage in Victorian times, with innumerable named varieties. It was used in great formal gardens and as a houseplant. As with many fads, its popularity waned, and it is remembered by many of us as the unremarkable, common pale pink, cream, and green houseplant in grandmother's parlor. Since the mid-1990s, coleus has made a huge resurgence, especially with the development of the Sun series that thrives in full sun. Today, there are hundreds of varieties, with leaves that vary from the ½-inch 'Ducksfoot' to the 6-inch 'Japanese Giant'. Coleus leaves take variegation to a whole new level—including every color of the rainbow (except blue) in myriad combinations and permutations. The year 2015 was named "The Year of the Coleus."

When, Where, and How to Plant
Coleus is readily available locally; for the greatest variety, turn to online and mail-order sources. It grows easily from cuttings. Snip a 4- to 6-inch stem. Remove all but the top two to four leaves. Place as many cuttings as you want—even from different plants—in a glass with enough room-temperature water so the stem is underwater and the leaves above. Set in a semi-sunny spot and wait for roots to grow. Once rooted, plant cuttings in pots or in the garden three weeks after last frost date. Coleus grows best in rich, lightly moist, well-drained, humusy soil. Do not grow a shade-loving coleus in full sun; it will burn out. Sun lovers can grow in shade but with muted tones. See page 11 for more on planting.

Growing Tips
Foliar feed twice a month with of a solution of kelp or fish emulsion. Keep the soil very lightly moist. Do not let it dry out.

Regional Advice and Care
Many new varieties are self-branching and pinching out the top set of leaves to produce a bushy plant is unnecessary. At the end of the season, take cuttings to overwinter indoors. Coleus is susceptible to mealybugs. They are difficult to control, so isolate any new plant for a week. If infested, dispose of it.

Companion Planting and Design
Combine 'Kiwi Fern' with toothache plant (*Spilanthes* spp.), with its mustardy eyeball-looking flowerhead, and *Lysimachia* 'Firecracker'—all complementary earth tones. Coleus pairs well with canna (*Canna* spp.), adding color at ground level. An over-the-top design is a 10-foot pinwheel-shape comprised of five contrasting coleus.

Try These
'India Frills' (to 6 × 12 inches) resembles the diminutive Ducksfoot series' footprint: deep pink leaves, edged green, spotted vivid yellow and green. 'Saturn' (to 20 × 24 inches) has otherworldly maroon leaves, bright green central splash, and smaller satellite spots. 'The Line' (to 30 × 30 inches) has burgundy-veined, chartreuse leaves. Under the Sea® series (to 18 × 16 inches) is most unusual with dissected leaves in a range of bi- and tricolored leaves that resemble ocean life.

Cosmos

Cosmos bipinnatus

Botanical Pronunciation
KOZ-mose by-pin-AY-tus

Other Name
Mexican aster

Bloom Period and Seasonal Colors
Summer to frost, white, pink, carmine, bicolors

Mature Height × Spread
1 to 5 ft. × 1 to 3 ft.

With fernlike foliage that appears a month or so before the flowers, cosmos makes itself known relatively early in the season. From dwarfs to giants, the yellow-centered, daisylike flower deserves space in any garden. I put one or two tall, old-fashioned, single pink cosmos near the front of the garden. Like a veil, you can look through the plant and still see the rest of the garden. For mass plantings, consider locations in the middle or back of the garden, depending on the variety's height. Today's cosmos is a far cry from the pink or white ones of my childhood. Whether you grow cosmos that is bicolor pink-and-white, or carmine, or white with a picotee edge, it adds a country charm all its own.

When, Where, and How to Plant
Most nurseries, garden centers, and home-improvement stores carry cosmos in 2- or 4-inch pots or cell packs. A greater selection of seeds is available from online and mail-order sources. Cosmos need full sun and well-drained, slightly acidic, average to poor soil. Get a head start by planting the seeds indoors in peat pots four to six weeks before the last frost date. (Follow seed planting information described on page 20.) Or, sow seeds directly in the garden in in late spring, after the last frost. Whether you sow the seed directly in the ground or plant out transplants, allow 1 to 3 feet between them. See page 11 for more on planting.

Growing Tips
Until the seeds sprout and have several leaves, do not let the soil dry out. When transplanting from pots, use a transplant solution to stimulate root production and growth. Do not fertilize cosmos; in fact that can weaken the plant, making it more prone to insect pests or disease. Since cosmos is drought tolerant, it does not need a lot of watering. If you have an automatic sprinkler system, plant it out of range of the regular watering cycle.

Regional Advice and Care
To prolong the bloom time, deadhead any spent flowers. As cosmos is susceptible to leaf spot and anthracnose (two fungal diseases), avoid overwatering the plant. Allow ample air circulation around the plant to help prevent any fungal problems. Let some flowers go to seed and self-sow. Cosmos attracts butterflies, bees, and other pollinators.

Companion Planting and Design
To me, cosmos and cleome (*Cleome hassleriana*) make perfect partners. The heights and colors are similar, and the large blousy cleome blossoms enhance the dainty air of the cosmos. Cosmos also pairs well with tall vervain (*Verbena bonariensis*), also in the same height and color range. Use dwarf varieties in containers.

Try These
'Sea Shells' (to 5 feet tall) has unique quilled, hollow tube-shaped petals in shades of white, pink, or carmine. Sonata series (to 12 inches) is dwarf plants in white, magenta, and shades of pink.

Flowering Tobacco

Nicotiana alata

Botanical Pronunciation
nih-koe-shee-AY-nah ah-LAY-tah

Other Name
Nicotiana

Bloom Period and Seasonal Colors
Midsummer to frost, white

Mature Height × Spread
3 to 5 ft. × 1 to 2 ft.

Much hybridizing has been done with flowering tobacco, but for me (and my sense of smell) the species is the best. It is one of the stars of an evening garden. Narrow tubular flowers flare at the end to form a five-petaled star. Although the flowers droop somewhat during the day, they perk up when they open at night. Their sweet scent perfumes the garden and attracts their pollinators, including the magnificent luna and sphinx moths. In summer, the central stem quickly grows 4 feet or higher with secondary stems as long as 2 feet. The overall effect is like a giant candelabra with white flowers in graceful sprays. An added bonus is that flowering tobacco self-seeds, so you can enjoy it year after year.

When, Where, and How to Plant
The flowering tobacco plants readily available at nurseries, garden centers, and home-improvement stores are usually the smaller hybrids, which are not fragrant. For the true, old-fashioned flowering tobacco, seeds may be available locally or go to online or mail-order sources. Start seeds indoors in late winter or early spring. (Follow seed planting information described on page 20.) In the garden, it grows best in rich, lightly moist, well-drained soil. It prefers sun but will do fine in partial shade. Transplant outdoors several weeks after the last frost date. Space the plants at least 12 to 15 inches apart.

Growing Tips
Unless it's in a protected location, staking protects the tall stem from breaking in high winds or heavy rain. Pound the stake at least 12 inches into the ground. I use 6-foot, green plastic-covered metal stakes and spray paint them bright colors for interest before the plant shoots up. Unpainted, the stake blends into the garden. The choice is yours. To avoid damaging tender roots, install the stake before you put the plant in. Water regularly. Foliar feed with a solution of kelp or fish emulsion every three to four weeks.

Regional Advice and Care
Flowering tobacco attracts bees and other pollinators. As with most plants, deadheading helps produce new flowers. Instead of removing each individual flower when it has finished blooming, I wait until the spray of flowers has passed its prime. Leave some of the last flowers of the season on the plant to allow it to self-sow.

Companion Planting and Design
Grow flowering tobacco among ornamental grasses (*Miscanthus* spp.). The grasses support the flowering tobacco, and in the evening the sweet scent is a delightful surprise. Plant behind smaller and more colorful—yet scentless—hybrids like the Nikki and Domino series for color (red, pink, chartreuse) and fragrance. Keep it away from tomatoes, eggplants, peppers, and potatoes as they can share diseases.

Try These
Nicotiana sylvestris (to 5 × 2 feet) is very similar, with hanging clusters of night-fragrant, tubular-shaped white flowers that resemble shooting stars—another common name.

Four O'Clocks

Mirabilis jalapa

Botanical Pronunciation
meer-AB-ill-iss jah-LAH-pah

Other Name
Marvel of Peru

Bloom Period and Seasonal Colors
Midsummer to frost, cerise, yellow, white, pink-and-white

Mature Height × Spread
2 to 3 ft. × 2 to 3 ft. or more

More of us have less time to spend enjoying our gardens, so plants that are fragrant and bloom in the evening are important in today's gardens. Evening is often the only time when we can truly relax—especially when we cannot see the weeds. Four o'clocks need to be incorporated into an evening garden for their scent and especially their colors—white, yellow, cerise, and candy-cane—which most night bloomers lack. The plant is bushy, bearing sweet little 1- to 2-inch trumpets that open in late afternoon—thus their common name. In fact, it is not the time that triggers the flowers to open but the concurrent temperature drop. Sit quietly after dusk to see the magnificent luna and sphinx moths that drink its nectar.

When, Where, and How to Plant
Although plants are sometimes available in nurseries, garden centers, and home-improvement stores, they are more readily available as seeds. Find them from online and mail-order resources. Four o'clocks are easy to grow. Start seeds indoors six to eight weeks before the last frost (see page 20 for more on planting) or sow directly in the garden at the same time you plant tomatoes (also the time to transplant seedlings outdoors). Four o'clocks like well-drained, ordinary garden soil and full sun to partial shade. If you enjoy varied, fragrant volunteers, just plant them once. In subsequent years, plants will sprout from mature seeds that dropped on the soil.

Growing Tips
Give them a good drink of water (the equivalent of 1 inch if there is no rain) weekly. Foliar feed monthly with seaweed or kelp emulsion.

Regional Advice and Care
Four o'clocks are close to care-free plants. They are self-cleaning; spent flowers, which bloom for a single night, fall off, so no deadheading is needed. If you do not want to save seed or let it self-sow, remove the spent flowers. Despite the name, here they open later than four o'clock—often at dusk or beyond because they won't open until the heat of the day begins to dissipate. On cloudy days, they open earlier. Four o'clocks are pest and disease free. They attract butterflies, bees, and other pollinators.

Companion Planting and Design
Pair them with night-blooming daylilies (*Hemerocallis* spp.) or day-blooming varieties that close after the four o'clocks open. For vibrant daytime color, add some Peppermint Stick zinnias (*Zinnia elegan*s 'Peppermint Stick') and any of the myriad coleus (*Plectranthus scutellarioides*) that strikes your fancy.

Try These
'High Tea Mix' has blooms in single colors of cerise, pink, and white. 'Jingles' (pictured) has multicolored flowers—solid and striped—in hues of cerise to yellow on one plant. 'Kaleidoscope' bears multi-colored bi- and tricolors that include pink, yellow, cerise, and white. 'Marbles Yellow & White' bears bicolor yellow-and-white flowers in streaked or blotched patterns—each flower is unique.

Globe Amaranth

Gomphrena globosa

Botanical Pronunciation
gom-FREE-nah glo-BO-sah

Other Name
Globe flower

Bloom Period and Seasonal Colors
Summer to frost, red, purple, white, pink

Mature Height × Spread
12 to 24 in. × 6 to 12 in.

Globe amaranth is a wonderful multipurpose flower. With its 1-inch, cloverlike blossoms, it is a great addition to any garden—in a sunny border, formal garden, mixed bed, or cutting garden. Globe amaranth is well named since it resembles a field of tall strawberries when planted *en masse*. With its bright color, it pops out even on a dreary day. The cultivar 'Strawberry Fields' is a long-lasting cut flower and is one of the best flowers for air-drying for dried flower arrangements. Its color is unique among the different globe amaranths and is a real eye-catcher in the garden. Globe amaranth thrives in our hot summers, holds up to high humidity, and is fairly drought tolerant. It is also is an excellent plant for containers.

When, Where, and How to Plant
Some small plants are available locally. A greater variety is available as seeds from online and mail-order sources. Globe amaranths grow best in well-drained, fertile, garden soil in full sun. Sow seeds directly in the garden ¼-inch deep once the soil has warmed. Or start the seeds inside eight to ten weeks before the last frost date, following the seed planting information on page 20. Seeds can take three weeks to germinate. Outdoors, plant or thin to 18 inches apart. Add a 2- to 3-inch layer of organic mulch around the plant—keeping the mulch an inch away from the stem—to keep the soil cool.

Growing Tips
Although globe amaranth is fairly drought tolerant, it requires regular watering until it is established. If cutting it for bouquets or to dry, do not foliar feed.

Instead, put 1 cup of well-rotted manure around the base of the plant and water in. Alternatively, use an all-purpose or high-phosphorus fertilizer, following package directions. In drought conditions, water every ten to fourteen days.

Regional Advice and Care
In damp summers, lightly spray weekly with insecticidal soap to prevent mold or mildew (see page 175). To use globe amaranth as a dried flower, cut a 6-inch-long stem before the flower opens. Stems become brittle, so reinforce with florist's wire. Cut a 10-inch length; bend one end forming a small hook. Push the straight end through the center of flower and along the stem until hook portion is down in the center of the flower. Tie eight to twelve stems together at the base and hang upside-down in a dark, warm, dry space for several weeks. Globe amaranth attracts butterflies, bees, and other pollinators.

Companion Planting and Design
Outstanding companions are purple fountain grass (*Pennisetum setaceum* 'Rubrum') and Russian kale 'Perestroika' for a superb contrast of texture, form, and color.

Try These
'Bicolor Rose' has pink and white blossoms. 'Buddy Purple' is only 8 to 12 inches tall, bearing intensely purple flowers. Gnome series (to 6 inches) has pink, purple, and white blooms. 'Lavender Lady' has bright lavender blooms.

Hollyhock

Alcea rosea

Botanical Pronunciation
al-SEE-ah ROSE-ee-ah

Bloom Period and Seasonal Colors
Early to midsummer, red, pink, white, yellow,
apricot, carmine, deep maroon, lavender-blue,
black, purple

Mature Height × Spread
4 to 8 ft. × 1 to 2 ft.

Standing proud and tall at 5 to 8 feet with single or double flowers spaced around the stem, hollyhocks are iconic for any informal garden—especially cottage gardens. The lowest flowers on the stem open first. Over a period of several weeks or more (depending on the weather), the flowers above open in succession. Although the entire stalk is not in flower at one time, it provides color and a strong vertical accent from early to midsummer. Hollyhocks are biennial yet are often mistaken for perennials since they come back and bloom year after year. The lower flowers have already set seed while the upper ones are blooming. The ripe seeds drop, germinate in summer, put out leaves, and bloom the following year.

When, Where, and How to Plant

Traditionally, hollyhocks are pass-along plants—saved seeds of non-hybrid varieties are passed along to friends and family. I have a pale apricot double hollyhock a friend gave me twenty years ago. She collected seed from her mother's garden, which came from *her* grandmother (four generations and nearly 100 years). Otherwise second-year plants (which will bloom that year) are available locally, and a great variety of seeds are available from online and mail-order sources. Hollyhocks grow best in good to rich, well-drained soil in full sun (but tolerate part sun). If you get pass-along seeds or buy seeds, plant them ½-inch deep in midsummer, and they will bloom the following year. Staking tall varieties prevents them from breaking in strong winds. See page 11 for more on planting.

Growing Tips

Keep the soil evenly moist after sowing seed or setting out a plant. Once you see several sets of leaves, cut down on the watering but do not let the soil dry out. Foliar feed once every two to three weeks during the growing season.

Regional Advice and Care

Label the plant so you don't pull it up accidentally during fall cleanup when it goes dormant. Hollyhocks attract butterflies, bees, and other pollinators. They are prone to rust and both bacterial and fungal leaf spots. Although the leaves may be somewhat unsightly up close, these diseases don't affect the flowers. Slugs are more of a problem, feasting on new young leaves in spring. Sprinkle diatomaceous earth in a 1-inch-wide circle around the base of the plant to deter slugs. Repeat after heavy rains.

Companion Planting and Design

Accentuate the cottage-garden look of hollyhocks by planting with foxgloves (*Digitalis* spp.), delphiniums (*Delphinium* spp.), and Jupiter's beard (*Centranthus ruber*).

Try These

'Chater's Double' has large double flowers in bright and pale colors—usually amix. 'Nigra' has nearly black petals accentuated by a yellow throat. Powder Puff series bears dense double flowers in shades of white, purple, yellow, pink, and red. Summer Carnival series only grows to 4 feet tall with bright, showy blooms.

Johnny Jump Up

Viola tricolor

Botanical Pronunciation
vy-OH-lah TRY-kul-or

Other Name
Heart's ease

Bloom Period and Seasonal Colors
Early spring to summer, purple with white and yellow

Mature Height × Spread
3 to 5 in. × 3 to 6 in.

Johnny jump up is one of the cutest flowers to grow. Looking at its five-petaled, 1-inch flower with its coloration of purple, white, and yellow, resembling a face, always makes me smile. A prolific self-seeder, it pops up in unexpected places in the garden from year to year—hence its name. Its long season of bloom makes it attractive from early spring well into summer (especially in more shaded areas). The flowers (grown organically) are edible with a slight wintergreen flavor. Pick the entire flower (including the green sepals that hold it together) and pop it in your mouth. Johnny jump up is a pretty addition to salads and makes elegant, easy hors d'oeuvres when placed atop a cracker spread with cream cheese.

When, Where, and How to Plant
Johnny jump up is readily available in cell packs at nurseries, garden centers, and home-improvement stores. If you don't want to buy it, friends or neighbors may have extra. If they are willing to share, bring a large pot filled with potting mix lightly moistened with transplant solution. Dig up the plants and place them plants in the pot; it doesn't matter if they are right next to each other, as you will be transplanting them soon. If you purchased the plants in pots, gently remove them from the container and loosen any roots if they have wound around themselves. (See page 11 for more about planting.) Johnny jump up grows in full sun to part shade in most types of well-drained soil except clay. In part shade, where it remains cooler, it will last longer into the summer. Water it in with transplant solution. Remove the first set of flowers on the plant to encourage root growth. When you purchase Johnny jump up in cell packs, it is often rootbound. To avoid this problem, learn when your local sources get deliveries of new plants and visit them that day.

Growing Tips
Keep the soil lightly moist until the plants are established. Water every ten to fourteen days. Do not fertilize.

Regional Advice and Care
Deadhead early flowers as they fade. As it gets later in the season, leave the flowers to set seed. Pests are not a problem.

Companion Planting and Design
Johnny jump up is lovely paired with its larger cousin, the pansy (*Viola × wittrockiana*). It is colorful in rock gardens and good in containers. Include it in a cottage, kitchen, or vegetable garden as a pretty, tasty accent.

Try These
'Bowles' Black' is closer to true black than any other touted flower. Its small, central, golden eye makes it stand out. You can fool your friends because, when you eat it, your tongue will turn black—only from the color. Use it to make an unusually dark-colored, sweet syrup for pancakes and desserts.

Love-Lies-Bleeding

Amaranthus caudatus

Botanical Pronunciation
am-ah-RAN-thus KAW-day-tus

Other Name
Tassel flower

Bloom Period and Seasonal Colors
Summer to frost, red

Mature Height × Spread
3 to 5 ft. × 18 to 30 in.

Love-lies-bleeding is a striking plant and not for those who are faint of heart. Tall (3 to 5 feet) with green, red, or purple stems, its light green leaves are a foil for the main attraction—the flowers. Tiny red flowers are borne on 18- to 24-inch long, cascading, chenille-textured panicles that sway gently with the breeze. As the flowers mature, the brightly colored seeds attract songbirds. While feasting, birds inadvertently spread the seed around the garden, so it self-sows readily. An historic plant, it is included in period gardens including Old Sturbridge Village in Massachusetts. The seeds are edible; it's grown as a nutritious grain crop in South America that's now catching on here. It is stunning in a large arrangement—fresh or dried.

When, Where, and How to Plant

Although you may find potted plants at nurseries, garden centers, and home-improvement stores, love-lies-bleeding is generally grown from seed. There are more varieties available as seed from online and mail-order sources. Love-lies-bleeding thrives in rich, moist, well-drained soil in full sun. Add some organic matter (well-rotted manure or leaf mold) to the soil before sowing the seeds. For a jump-start on the season, start the seeds indoors in peat pots six to eight weeks before the last frost date. See page 20 for seed-starting information, or sow the ½-inch deep directly in the garden after all danger of frost has passed. Allow at least 12 inches between plants. A sheltered location is ideal to keep the wind from battering the plants. Keep the soil evenly moist until the seeds germinate.

Growing Tips

Although it tolerates drought, love-lies-bleeding puts on its best show with regular watering and feeding. Foliar feed every two weeks with a half-strength solution of liquid kelp or fish emulsion, following package directions.

Regional Advice and Care

Love-lies-bleeding retains its color even when dried. Cut it just as the flowers open and hang it upside-down in a warm dry place for several weeks. In addition to the seeds, the leaves are edible, used in salads or sautéed. Although it is susceptible to aphids and some fungal diseases, keeping the plants well fed and well watered can often thwart these problems. It attracts butterflies, bees, and other pollinators.

Companion Planting and Design

Love-lies-bleeding is beautiful in a cottage garden; consider placing it against a white picket fence to provide support and set off its vivid color. In a cottage setting, it consorts well with sweet William (*Dianthus barbatus*), white hollyhocks (*Alcea rosea* 'Chater's Double White'), and old-fashioned pink roses (*Rosa* 'Gertrude Jekyll'). It also makes an outstanding container plant, which limits seed scattering.

Try These

'Fat Spike' (to 4 feet tall) bears 3-inch-wide, upright, deep purplish red spikes that taper to 1 inch. 'Viridis' (to 3 feet) has pendulous, lime-green flower tassels that age to cream.

Mexican Sunflower

Tithonia rotundifolia

Botanical Pronunciation
tih-THO-nee-yah roe-tun-dih-FOE-lee-uh

Bloom Period and Seasonal Colors
Midsummer to frost, orange

Mature Height × Spread
3 to 6 ft. × 1 to 2 ft.

Mexican sunflower, with its bushy form; handsome dark green leaves; 3-inch, orange, daisylike flowers; and impressive size (growing to 6 feet tall), is the perfect plant to bridge the seasons. From midsummer to frost it veritably glows in the garden. As the days grow shorter and start to cool down, its color makes me feel like it's still midsummer. Bees and butterflies are frequent visitors to the flowers that resemble single dahlias. I see hummingbirds visit (but that's not documented in common literature). Mexican sunflower is long lasting as a cut flower. Because of the plant's size, a few are usually enough. Although it isn't touted as a self-seeder, it has returned several years in my gardens.

When, Where, and How to Plant

Find plants at many garden centers, nurseries, and home-improvement stores, but the unusual varieties are only available as seed from online and mail-order sources. Start the seeds indoors about four to six weeks before the last frost date. (Follow seed planting information described on page 20.) Mexican sunflower grows best in average, well-drained soil in full sun. In rich soil, the plants tend to be weak-stemmed and have an excess of leaves with fewer blooms. Choose a space that is sheltered from the wind. Transplant outdoors at the same time you would plant tomatoes (at least two weeks after all danger of frost has passed and soil temperature is above 60 degrees Fahrenheit). You can also sow seeds directly in the garden at the same time. Young seedlings and transplants are temperature sensitive and will turn yellow when

they are exposed to cold. Keep the plants well watered until they are established.

Growing Tips

Once established, Mexican sunflowers require water only during dry spells. Foliar feed monthly.

Regional Advice and Care

Staking the plants keeps them upright no matter what. Slugs feast on new young foliage. Protect transplants and seedlings by pouring a 1-inch-wide circle of garden-grade diatomaceous earth around the base of the plant. This scratches the soft underbellies of slugs and snails, keeping them at a distance. After a heavy rain, renew the circle. Deadhead all spent flowers to prolong the bloom and to make the plant even bushier.

Companion Planting and Design

Mexican sunflower makes a brilliant show with the golden yellow petals of black-eyed Susan (*Rudbeckia fulgida* 'Goldsturm') and the vivid red of montbretia (*Crocosmia* 'Lucifer'). Mix and match it with any of the myriad sunflowers (*Helianthus annuus*).

Try These

'Torch' (to 6 feet tall) is the best cut flower with dramatic, 3½-inch, red-orange flowers. *Tithonia speciosa* varieties include 'Goldfinger' (to 30 × 30 inches), bushier with larger leaves, so the flowers don't appear as prominent. 'Red Torch' (to 40 inches tall) bears 3- to 4-inch-wide red flowers in early summer. 'Yellow Torch' is similar, but with yellow flowers.

Nasturtium

Tropaeolum majus Alaska series

Botanical Pronunciation
troe-pay-OH-lum MAY-jus

Bloom Period and Seasonal Colors
Summer to frost, cream, yellow, mahogany,
red, orange

Mature Height × Spread
6 to 12 in. × 6 to 12 in.

Alaska is one of the most beautiful strains of nasturtium with its handsomely round, variegated leaves (light green accented with creamy white splotches and dots) that set off the delectable flowers that may be cream, yellow, orange, or red. The plant has a nice bushy shape. Enjoy the same peppery flavor of the flowers as with the leaves; both make a savory addition to a salad. Pop an entire flower in your mouth. As you chew it, you first get a sweet sensation from the nectar, and then the peppery flavor comes through. For a show-stopping yet simple hors d'oeuvre, mix chopped nasturtium petals and leaves into whipped cream cheese. Stuff individual flowers with the mixture or put on crackers. Nasturtium is great in containers.

When, Where, and How to Plant
Alaska hybrid plants may be available locally. However, the seed is readily available through online and mail-order sources; it is easy to grow. Start the seeds indoors four to six weeks before the last frost date (follow seed planting information on page 20). Or sow seeds outdoors 1-inch deep, two weeks later. Nasturtiums thrive in poor to sandy, well-drained soil in full sun. In hot summer areas, they benefit from some afternoon shade. Nasturtiums are fairly drought tolerant.

Growing Tips
Do not fertilize nasturtiums or grow in good soil. The result will be large leaves but no flowers. Water regularly until the plant is established, then only once a week or when the leaves start to wilt.

Regional Advice and Care
If you don't keep up with eating the flowers, deadhead them. Nasturtiums attract butterflies and bees. They are susceptible to aphids, but when I intersperse nasturtiums throughout my garden, these insects are not a problem. When I grow a passel of beans, I plant a row of nasturtiums nearby to attract the aphids away from the beans. Do not eat aphid-infested flowers, leaves, or stems. Avoid pesticides if you will be eating any plant parts.

Companion Planting and Design
Nasturtiums were a staple in Victorian gardens. They consort well with moss rose (*Portulaca grandiflora*), love-in-a-mist (*Nigella damascena*), lavender (*Lavandula* spp.), and thyme (*Thymus* spp.). These plants all thrive in the same type of soil. Nasturtiums make good groundcover or edging plants.

Try These
'Empress of India' (to 12 inches tall) is a Victorian heirloom bearing deep purplish green leaves and velvety red, double flowers. 'Jewel of Africa' (to 6 feet tall) is a trailing variety (needs support to climb) that looks like the Alaska strain. 'Peach Melba Superior' (to 12 inches) has bicolored creamy yellow flowers marked with peachy orange throats. Tom Thumb series (to 8 inches) is a semi-trailing plant with yellow, red, orange, and mauve blooms. 'Whirlybird' (to 12 inches) has upward-facing single to semi-double flowers in shades of red, pink, yellow, and orange.

Pansy

Viola × wittrockiana

Botanical Pronunciation
vye-OH-luh wit-ROK-ee-ay-nuh

Bloom Period and Seasonal Colors
Spring to early summer, fall to spring; single, double, or tricolor flowers in red, purple, white, yellow, maroon, blue, pink

Mature Height × Spread
6 to 9 in. × 9 to 15 in.

Pansies have five petals and gives the appearance of a "face." 'Antique Shades' is my favorite pansy because of its semi-muted, delicate colors of pale magenta to lilac blending into white. Its flower is 2 to 3 inches across, borne on stems above attractive, ripple-edged elliptical, dark green leaves. Pansy flowers are edible (grown organically) with a slight wintergreen taste. You can eat the entire flower, including the green sepals that hold it together. Pansies make a flavorful and pretty addition to fruit salads. Place one on top of any hors d'oeuvre to dress it up. Plant pansies for early color in windowboxes, containers, as edging and almost anywhere in the garden. **Warning:** Eating more than ten pansies a day has a diuretic effect.

When, Where, and How to Plant
Pansies are available locally in early spring and fall. More varieties are offered as seed from online and mail-order sources. Pansies prefer slightly moist, fertile, well-drained soil in full sun to part shade. As they are tolerant of light frosts, plant pansies as soon as you get them—provided the ground has thawed. The flowers are edible, but not knowing if they were growing in any soil with additives, I rinse the soil from the plant, cut off any blossoms, and then plant them using transplant solution. Plant pansies in late summer or early fall (six to eight weeks before your first frost date) for fall, winter, and early spring bloom, or as soon as the ground thaws in spring. (See page 11 for more on planting.)

Growing Tips
Keep pansies lightly moist. If eating the flowers, do not foliar feed. Instead, add a layer of compost around the plants monthly. Several varieties have been bred for fall planting, including the Icicle® series. I have been growing fall pansies for nearly twenty years, and they will keep going through the winter. During January thaw, you may even get a flower or two. The pansies perk right back up as soon as the snow melts.

Regional Advice and Care
If you are not eating all the flowers, deadhead any spent blossoms to prolong blooming. Pansies have no major disease or pest problems.

Companion Planting and Design
In spring, pansies—choose a favorite color—are beautiful with pink daffodils, such as *Narcissus* 'Mrs. R. O. Backhouse', blue Siberian squill (*Scilla siberica* 'Spring Beauty'), and hyacinths (*Hyacinthus orientalis*). In fall, they are stunning with New England asters (*Symphyotrichum novae-angliae* 'Purple Dome').

Try These
Freefall series is a "trailing" pansy, which spreads to 15 inches, ideal for hanging baskets—violet, lavender, yellow, and bicolors. 'Frizzle Sizzle' is unusual with double, ruffled flowers in shades of blue, purple, burgundy, yellow, white, and bicolors. 'Jolly Joker' has marvelous coloring—deep purple and bright orange. Majestic Giant series bears huge 4-inch, bicolor "face" flowers in blue, red, purple, white, and yellow.

Petunia

Petunia × hybrida Wave® series

Botanical Pronunciation
peh-TOON-yah HYE-brih-duh

Other Name
Spreading petunia

Bloom Period and Seasonal Colors
Summer to frost, lilac, pink, purple, blue, salmon

Mature Height × Spread
4 to 6 in. × 1 to 4 ft.

When it first arrived on the scene, the Wave® series practically revolutionized the way people grew petunias. Unlike those grown beforehand, which required constant deadheading and got leggy without severe pruning, Wave® petunias are virtually maintenance free. With little attention except watering and fertilizing, a single plant can spread up to 4 feet, making it ideal for large containers, gracefully cascading over the side—almost to the ground. It is equally at home in the garden and makes a super bedding plant. The large size of the flowers is impressive—3 to 4 inches across. The range of hues is broad enough to fit any color scheme. Most important, it thrives in our hot humid summers. Watch for the butterflies, bees, and hummers that visit.

When, Where, and How to Plant
The Wave® series and its relatives are readily available locally as plants. They thrive in well-drained average to poor soil in full sun (rich soil produces leaves, not flowers). Plant after the danger of frost has passed. Wave® petunias come in relatively large pots and are unlikely to be rootbound; check the bottom of the pot to be sure. Plant at the same depth as it was in the pot. Allow at least 2 feet between plants. (See page 11 for more about planting.) Use at least an 18-inch container for a single plant and 24- to 36-inch pots if combined with other plants. When creating container combinations, choose taller plants and let the petunia spill over the edge of the pot. When planting in a hanging basket, line it with a disposable diaper (skin side up) to help retain moisture.

Growing Tips
Keep well watered, and foliar feed every two weeks.

Regional Advice and Care
Dead flowers often fall off by themselves unless there is a lot of rain and they remain wet and stick to the plant. New flowers may cover up those that are spent. There's no need to prune out dead flowers; they readily pull out from the sepals. If necessary, cut the plant back to keep it within a confined area. Pests are rare. These are patented plants; propagation is illegal.

Companion Planting and Design
With the range of colors in both plants, any of the taller coleus (*Plectranthus scutellarioides*) combines well with it. Pair it with zinnias (*Zinnia elegans*).

Try These
Double Wave® (to 8 inches × 2 feet) has double flowers in shades of lavender, pink, purple, white, and rose. Easy Wave® (to 10 inches × 3 feet) blooms earlier than the original Wave® in cherry, shell pink, and white with a more mounding habit. Shock Wave® (to 10 inches × 3 feet) has a mounding, spreading habit in bold and pastel colors. Tidal Wave® (to 22 inches × 3 feet) can grow up (given support); hot pink, cherry, purple-veined silver, and purple.

Sunflower

Helianthus annuus

Botanical Pronunciation
hee-lee-AN-thus AN-yew-us

Bloom Period and Seasonal Colors
Summer to frost, yellow, orange, brown, burgundy with contrasting center

Mature Height × Spread
16 in. to 15 ft. × 6 in. to 3 ft.

Many of us got our first taste of gardening when we were small children growing sunflowers. We planted a sunflower seed in late spring and watched it grow daily until it towered over our heads and kept on growing. We saw the flowerhead (ray florets surrounding disk florets) appear, grow, and set seed. We left the seeds for the birds and squirrels or cut down flowerheads to dry for our own munching. That magic—that a seed less than an inch long can grow into a 15-foot mammoth plant in a couple of months—stays with us forever. Today there are numerous hybrids—from edging plants 2 feet tall to our childhood giants—in single and bicolors in a range of colors. Get growing, again.

When, Where, and How to Plant
Sunflowers need full sun and moist, neutral to alkaline, well-drained soil. After all danger of frost has passed, plant seeds 1 inch deep in full sun. Spacing depends on variety, and can be determined with seed packet information. See page 20 for more planting information. Water sunflowers well at planting.

Growing Tips
Once established, sunflowers tolerate dry soil. However, if the leaves start to droop, water the plant immediately. Foliar feeding is difficult on tall varieties; instead, water bimonthly with compost tea.

Regional Advice and Care
Tall types may need staking in exposed areas. Sunflowers attract butterflies, bees, and other pollinators. If you plan to eat the seeds, cover the flower with bird netting. Cut it down when the seeds are well formed and full sized; put in a warm, dry, well-ventilated space. Otherwise leave it on the plant for birds and other critters to enjoy. Treat powdery mildew on the leaves by spraying weekly with baking soda solution (see page 175) or just accept it. Sunflowers make excellent cut flowers.

Companion Planting and Design
Create a great combination of colors, shapes, and textures with 'Kid Stuff' sunflower planted with black-eyed Susan (*Rudbeckia fulgida* var. *sullivantii* 'Goldsturm'), and creeping zinnia (*Sanvitalia procumbens*). Make a sunflower house (a shelter of sunflowers with a sky blue roof of morning glories). Plant a 6- to 8-foot rectangle of tall sunflowers—the house—spaced 12 inches apart. Leave a "door" opening. Run strings from the sunflowers on one side of the house to those on the other. Plant blue morning glories (*Ipomoea tricolor* 'Heavenly Blue') at the base of the sunflowers on the two sides.

Try These
'Lemon Queen' (to 6 feet tall) has brown-centered, lemon-yellow flowers. 'Music Box Mix' (to 30 inches) bears 4- to 5-inch flowers with bicolor rays from creamy yellow to deep red. 'Sunspot' (to 24 inches) has sunny yellow petals. 'Sunzilla' (to 16 feet) is excellent for eating with golden yellow flowers. 'Teddy Bear' (to 30 inches) resembles 5-inch double, golden yellow chrysanthemums. 'Velvet Queen' (to 5 feet) is a branching sunflower with velvety crimson petals.

Zinnia

Zinnia elegans

Botanical Pronunciation
ZIN-ee-ah EL-eh-ganz

Bloom Period and Seasonal Colors
Summer to frost, red, orange, yellow, green, lavender, pink, rose, single and bicolors

Mature Height × Spread
6 to 48 in. × 6 to 15 in.

Zinnias are must-have plants for any garden. They bring back childhood memories at my grandmother's and parents' gardens, watching the bees and butterflies on the flowers. Flowers range through almost every color of the rainbow. Some zinnias are single with prominent yellow stamens; others are fully double, resembling dahlias. With hybrid varieties in all heights, there's a zinnia for the edge, front, middle, or back of the garden. Zinnias are unsurpassed as cut flowers. As a child, we always had a juice glass in the bathroom with fresh zinnias. I had the responsibility and honor of checking to see how fresh the flowers were each day, trimming ¼-inch off each stem and putting them in fresh water or cutting new zinnias for simple beauty.

When, Where, and How to Plant
Although zinnias are available as potted plants at nurseries, garden centers, and home-improvement stores, seeds (from online and mail-order sources) have more varieties. Plant seeds in rich, well-drained, moist soil in full sun, ¼-inch deep, and 9 inches apart. Keep well watered until they are established. (Follow seed planting information on page 20.)

Growing Tips
Zinnias require regular watering. Avoid wetting the leaves; a soaker hose or drip irrigation system is ideal. Foliar feed once a month.

Regional Advice and Care
Pinch back early flowers to the next lower stem for a bushier plant. Deadhead faded flowers to encourage more blooms. Zinnias are susceptible to powdery mildew. To discourage this, allow ample air circulation between plants. Water early in the day at ground level to keep the leaves dry. Feed regularly; healthy plants are less susceptible to pests and diseases. To fight mildew, spray the tops and bottoms of the leaves (only when temperatures are below 80 degrees Fahrenheit) weekly with a baking soda solution (see page 175). When cutting flowers for bouquets, avoid cutting off more than one set of side stems.

Companion Planting and Design
Zinnias are versatile—equally at home in a cutting garden, cottage garden, mixed border, or as a bedding plant. Grow it in a container alone or in combination with other plants. Go bold with a buttery yellow, container-planted Swizzle zinnia and Purple Wave® petunia (*Petunia × hybrida* Purple Wave®). Interplant mildew-resistant Pinwheel zinnias with curly parsley (*Petroselinum crispum*).

Try These
Benary's Giant series (to 48 inches tall) bears sturdy, long-stemmed (ideal for cutting) 4- to 6-inch wide flowers in rainbow colors. Dreamland series (to 12 inches) features 4-inch-wide double flowers in hues of apricot, ivory, red, yellow, and pink. Profusion series (to 15 inches) is self-cleaning, dropping its 2-inch-wide flowers (white, cherry, orange, and red-orange). Swizzle series (to 12 inches) is a bicolor in circular bands around fully double, 3- to 4-inch-wide flowers. Zowie® 'Yellow Flame' (to 36 inches) bears 3- to 4-inch-wide, semi-double yellow-and-orange daisylike flowers with iridescent magenta centers.

BULBS

FOR THE PRAIRIE & PLAINS STATES

Bulbs have a specialized food storage organ that allows them to have a long period of dormancy and come back yearly. For example, crocus bloom in early spring, the flowers die back, leaves remain for a while, they die down, and then the plant disappears until the following spring. Through photosynthesis, leaves replenish the bulb's food stores. The key to success with bulbs is to let the leaves die back on their own. With spring-bloomers like daffodils and tulips, it's tempting to cut down the foliage, but if you do, the odds of the bulb returning the following year are poor.

Bulbs are categorized as hardy or tender. Spring-blooming bulbs like crocus, daffodils, and snowdrops are hardy, needing a period of cold to induce bloom. Once planted, they remain in the ground for years. Tender summer-blooming bulbs, such as caladiums, cannas, and gladiolas, cannot survive our winters; dig them up in fall.

Planting

Most bulbs need full sun and rich, well-drained soil—exceptions are noted in the individual plant listings. However, early bulbs thrive under deciduous trees when the leaves have yet to emerge. As a rule, bulbs need no fertilizer added at planting time. Feeding is more important during the active growing and flowering season.

Naturalized crocus blooming with early daffodils.

Rules of Thumb for Planting

Depth: Plant a bulb two to three times as deep as its height. For example, plant a 1-inch crocus in 2- to 3-inch deep hole, a 3-inch lily 6 to 9 inches down. **Spacing:** Allow three times the width of the bulb between each bulb—from center to center. Therefore, 1-inch-wide crocus needs 2 inches of soil between bulbs; give 3-inch-wide lilies 6 inches of soil between bulbs.

Make sure to plant bulbs with the pointed end up.

Spring-blooming Bulbs

Bulbs have the most impact in natural-looking clusters, drifts, or swaths. Planting in odd numbers is one of the tenets of gardening. For large bulbs, such as hyacinths or tulips, plant groups of five, seven, or more. Small bulbs like crocus or snowdrops show off best in groups of fifteen, twenty-five, or more.

Interplant spring-blooming bulbs with one another. You can plant them individually, but I prefer to dig a large hole to the depth of the largest bulb. Place the large bulbs first; feel free to put those of the same size in groups at the same level within the hole (like hyacinths, lilies, and large daffodils). Insert plant markers so they show above soil level. Cover bulbs with an inch or two of soil and then add a layer of the next largest bulbs (tulips and species daffodils) with their markers. Add more soil and plant smaller bulbs (like crocus and snowdrops) so that each bulb is at its proper depth. If you start out with large lilies, you may have four layers of bulbs. Try not to put one layer right on top of the bulbs below. In spring, you'll have a riot of color and continuous bloom. Subsequent blooms and leaves hide the ripening foliage of earlier ones. Don't cut off leaves until they brown. I often include several daylilies—even though they are perennials—as they continue the bloom season and hide the ripening foliage of the later bulbs.

In late summer and autumn, squirrels and other critters look upon newly planted bulbs as haute cuisine. An excellent deterrent is pinning chicken wire over the planting. Remove it in late winter before bulbs stick their heads up through the snow. Unless otherwise mentioned, there are no other pest or disease problems affecting the featured plants.

Summer-blooming Bulbs

Plant summer-blooming bulbs in late spring after all danger of frost has passed. Any exceptions are noted in individual entries. They begin growing as soon as you plant them; pest deterrents are not necessary. Include summer-blooming bulbs in perennial beds, mixed borders, and other plantings. Dig up and store for winter, generally after the first frost. Drying and storage vary from plant to plant; store between 40 and 50 degrees Fahrenheit.

Here is a sampling of the best bulbs—spring-, summer-, and fall-blooming—to grow in your garden.

Asiatic Lily

Lilium cvs.

Botanical Pronunciation
LIL-ee-um

Bloom Period and Seasonal Colors
Summer, hues of yellow, red, pink, white, orange, purple, single and bicolors

Mature Height × Spread
1 to 5 ft. × 18 to 30 in.

Zones 4 to 8

In addition to species lilies (dozens that are Nature's creations and the hybrids thereof), there are two main categories of hybrid lilies—Asiatic and Oriental (see page 53 for the Oriental lily). Asiatic lilies bloom in summer with clusters of 3- to 6-inch-wide, six-petaled flowers. They have no scent, but their beauty makes up for any lack of fragrance. Flowers may be upfacing, outfacing, or pendant. 'Connecticut King' is a longtime favorite Asiatic lily. Its up-facing, yellow, 4- to 5-inch, cuplike blooms set the garden aglow at any time of day. A group of flowers blooms at once, making an instant bouquet for cutting and arranging indoors, or on the plant. Blossoms are long lasting, indoors and out, and hold up well in the rain.

When, Where, and How to Plant

Asiatic lilies, unlike most summer-blooming bulbs, are available to plant both in fall and spring locally and from online and mail-order sources. Choose the largest, heaviest, and most solid bulbs. Avoid bulbs with soft spots or signs of mold or mildew. Asiatic lilies grow best in rich, loamy, very well-drained soil in full sun to part shade. In fall, plant bulbs immediately so that the roots have a chance to get established before winter. If moles, voles, or mice are problems, roll the bulb in sulfur before planting. Space 8 to 15 inches apart. Plant with the bottom of the bulb three times as deep as its height. Fill the hole with soil and firm down gently with your hands. Water well. (See page 41 for more planting information.)

Growing Tips

Fertilize at the beginning of the growing season with a bulb booster-type or any well-balanced liquid or granular fertilizer, such as 5-5-5, (following package directions). If there is no rain, water deeply weekly until it begins to flower. Once blooming is over, decrease watering so the bulb can ripen.

Regional Advice and Care

If it's growing in an exposed, windy area, stake the bulb when planting. If you are cutting the flowers for an arrangement, you may want to remove the anthers as the pollen drops off and can stain material. Remove spent blooms. Enjoy the green foliage for an extended period. Mulch with 3 inches of organic matter in winter. At the first sign of aphids, control with insecticidal soap, as aphids transmit the fatal lily mosaic virus.

Companion Planting and Design

'Connecticut King' is handsome in the ground or container combined with yellow evening primrose (*Oenothera biennis*) and periwinkle (*Vinca minor*). Mix several different Asiatic lily varieties together for a riot of color.

Try These

'Enchantment' (2 to 3 feet tall) with deep orange, cuplike petals. 'Lemon Pixie' (to 18 inches) is a dwarf with lemon-yellow flowers and red-speckled centers. 'Magento' (to 4 feet) bears soft pink blooms. 'Red Twin' (to 4 feet) has "double" flaming red flowers.

Autumn Crocus

Colchicum autumnale

Botanical Pronunciation
KOHL-chi-kum aw-tum-NAL-ee

Other Name Meadow saffron

Bloom Period and Seasonal Colors
Late summer to early fall, lavender-pink

Mature Height × Spread
4 to 6 in. × 4 to 6 in.

Zones 4 to 8

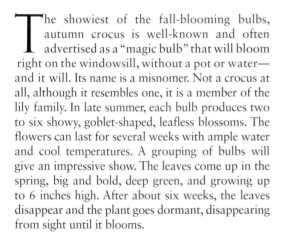

The showiest of the fall-blooming bulbs, autumn crocus is well-known and often advertised as a "magic bulb" that will bloom right on the windowsill, without a pot or water—and it will. Its name is a misnomer. Not a crocus at all, although it resembles one, it is a member of the lily family. In late summer, each bulb produces two to six showy, goblet-shaped, leafless blossoms. The flowers can last for several weeks with ample water and cool temperatures. A grouping of bulbs will give an impressive show. The leaves come up in the spring, big and bold, deep green, and growing up to 6 inches high. After about six weeks, the leaves disappear and the plant goes dormant, disappearing from sight until it blooms.

When, Where, and How to Plant
Choose the largest, firmest bulbs. Avoid ones that have sprouted. Autumn crocus prefers deep, fertile, well-drained soil and full sun, but will grow in part shade. As soon as the bulb arrives, plant it with the top 4 inches below the soil surface. Cluster seven or more bulbs 2 to 3 inches apart for an impressive show. Water well. They will bloom within several weeks (see page 41 for more planting tips). To see their magical quality, place on a sunny windowsill. Watch them send up their goblet-shaped, 2- to 3-inch, lavender-pink flowers. The show will be fleeting, however, from lack of water.

Growing Tips
Keep the soil lightly moist while autumn crocus is in bloom. Allow the soil to dry when it goes dormant. Add 3 inches of organic mulch after the ground freezes. Remove mulch in spring. Foliar feed with liquid kelp or fish emulsion (following package directions) when leaves appear.

Regional Advice and Care
Since it goes dormant until spring and again when the leaves fade, it is important to mark where autumn crocus is. Otherwise, you may inadvertently dig into the area when planting something later in spring or summer, ruining the bulbs before they rebloom in late summer. A small metal marker withstands the test of time; blue jays steal plastic labels, using them in their nests.

Companion Planting and Design
For a sense of a Monet painting, interplant autumn crocus in a sea of periwinkle (*Vinca minor*). It is gorgeous planted with any coleus (*Plectranthus scutellarioides*) with pink in its leaves.

Try These
'Alboplenum' (white meadow saffron) is very striking with large, white, double blossoms that are not knocked down by heavy rains, as are many other cultivars. 'Waterlily' (Zones 4 to 7) is the showiest variety, with large lilac-pink double flowers reminiscent of water lilies on Monet's pond. 'Pleniflorum' bears double rose-pink blooms. *Colchicum atropurpureum* is an interesting species. One bulb can produce as many as twelve flowers, adding a large splash of deep rosy lilac. Unlike the more common autumn crocus, this one sends ups its leaves after the flowers fade in autumn.

Caladium

Caladium bicolor

Botanical Pronunciation
kah-LAY-dee-um BY-kul-or

Other Name Angel wings

Bloom Period and Seasonal Colors
Summer to frost, bi- and tricolor foliage in shades of white, green, pink, red, burgundy

Mature Height × Spread
12 to 30 in. × 12 to 30 in.

Zone 8

Caladiums (formerly *Caladium × hortulanum*) are showy with multicolored (muted or bold), 8- to 18-inch, elongated heart-shaped leaves. Grown for their foliage (I have never seen a bloom), they are prized as plants for livening up any shady area. To me, they are the Dolly Partons of shade plants—big, bold, and beautiful. They are as far from shrinking violets as you can go in the plant world. Color combinations may be simple—the leaf one color with the veins highlighted another—or complex with splashes, dots, edgings, and other permutations of color mixes in shades of red, pink, green, and white. Caladiums make great container plants. Although the tubers are usually dug up and brought in for winter storage, you can keep the plants growing indoors in a container.

When, Where, and How to Plant
Eight to ten weeks before the last frost date, start caladiums indoors in 6-inch pots filled with lightly moistened potting soil or sphagnum moss. Cover with 2 inches of potting soil. Keep it between 80 to 85 degrees Fahrenheit (try a heating mat for plants) and lightly moist. If you plan to grow it in a container outdoors, start it in that pot. Caladiums thrive in rich, slightly acidic, humus-rich, moist, well-drained soil in part to full shade. Transplant outdoors once the soil has reached at least 60 degrees Fahrenheit. Allow 8 to 10 inches between plants. Water well with transplant solution.

Growing Tips
Water well. Never let the soil dry out. Spray leaves frequently during hot, dry weather. Foliar feed monthly with a solution of kelp or fish emulsion (following package directions).

Regional Advice and Care
Cut off faded leaves at soil level. After the first frost, carefully dig the tubers. Place them on a screen in a warm, dry, airy place for about a week to dry. Store the tubers on a shallow tray in a warm, dry place. If you're growing caladiums in a pot, the leaves begin to droop in autumn. Bring the pots inside and water very sparingly until the leaves shrivel and fall off. Store the pots in a warm place, about 70 degrees Fahrenheit. Caladiums are susceptible to tuber rot; check them in the spring before replanting—they should be firm. Otherwise, discard them; do not compost diseased material.

Companion Planting and Design
Caladiums are magnificent in hanging baskets. In moss-lined baskets, plant one on the top and poke several plants into the soil so the outside of the basket is radiant with leaves. In the garden, combine them with hostas (*Hosta* spp.) to enliven a shady spot with their vivid colors. Mix and match caladiums with coleus (*Plectranthus scutellarioides*) for fun color echoes.

Try These
'Miss Muffett' has creamy leaves with strokes of pale green and bright fuchsia spots. 'White Christmas' is pure white with bold green veins. 'Freida Hemple' is a bold fuchsia-red, edged in bright green.

Canna

Canna × generalis

Botanical Pronunciation
KAN-ah gen-uh-RAH-liss

Other Name Indian shot

Bloom Period and Seasonal Colors
Summer, whitish, yellow, orange, red

Mature Height × Spread
1½ to 8 ft. × 1½ to 3 ft.

Zones 7 to 8

Cannas, like coleus and other tropical plants that were held in great esteem in Victorian times, are also enjoying a resurgence of popularity in gardens everywhere. Cannas are favored for their large, lush leaves that accentuate the tropical look (called the "banana-canna craze" by some) enjoyed by many northern gardeners. In fact, some people cut the flower off before it even blooms, preferring just the foliage. Yet, the flower is a colorful accent atop a plant that ranges from 1½ to 8 feet tall. With modern hybridizing, leaves range from varying shades of green to a plethora of variegations—some subtle, some bold. From the colors of a tropical sunset to green and white stripes, there is at least one canna for every garden.

When, Where, and How to Plant
It is easiest to start a canna from a potted plant. Consider it an investment in the future. The following spring, make cuttings from the rhizome for more plants. Cannas thrive in rich soil in full sun. It tolerates very moist soil—growing at the edge of ponds. Plant when the soil temperature is at least 60 degrees; space 18 inches apart. Water well with transplant solution.

Growing Tips
Keep well watered. Foliar feed monthly.

Regional Advice and Care
Deadhead to prolong bloom. After frost blackens the leaves, cut down stems and leaves; lift the rhizomes. Overwinter rhizomes in barely moist peat moss in a cool (above freezing) place. In spring, pot rhizomes (cut them so there are one or two buds per piece) 2 inches deep in 6-inch pots. Water well. Set on a sunny windowsill until planting time. Fungal leaf spot can be a problem; cut off and destroy any suspect leaves.

Companion Planting and Design
Create a tropical look by growing canna with calla lily (*Zantedeschia aethiopica*), summer hyacinth (*Galtonia candicans*), elephant's ear (*Alocasia* spp.), and Burgundy Stem taro (*Colocasia esculenta* 'Burgundy Stem'). There is an old variety with deep purplish green leaves and red flowers growing in neglected gardens and farms—with no attention. I have asked folks what the variety is and they reply, "Canna lilies. They've been here as long as I remember. They just come up each year; I don't do a thing to them." If you see these plants, ask for one or two since they are particularly tough. One came up in my Zone 5 garden unbidden and grows unattended.

Try These
'Australia' (to 5 feet) bears burgundy-black leaves and spikes of bright red flowers. 'Erebus' (to 6 feet) has cream-edged gray-green leaves and pink blossoms. Tropicanna® ('Phaison', to 6 feet) has leaves striated with the colors of a tropical sunset. Plant it where the sun shines through its leaves in early morning or late afternoon like stained glass. 'Bengal Tiger' ('Pretoria', to 6 feet) has dramatic, yellow-and-green-striped leaves and maroon stems topped with bright orange blooms (pictured).

Crocus

Crocus spp.

Botanical Pronunciation
KROW-kus

Bloom Period and Seasonal Colors
Late winter to early spring, late summer to early fall; hues of yellow, white, purple, blue, mauve, in singles and bicolors

Mature Height × Spread
½ to 6 in. × 1 to 6 in.

Although crocus may not be the first bulbs to peek through the snow in late winter, they are the first to show color—true harbingers of spring. There are many species and cultivars of crocus (some fragrant), from the earliest snow crocus that literally peep up and bloom through the snow to the best-known Dutch, or giant, crocus and even some fall-blooming species, including the famous saffron crocus. The colors of crocus can be pure—white, yellow, purple, lilac—bold or muted and even gorgeous bicolors. Some crocus are one color on the inside of the petal that you see in daytime and another when closed at night. Plant crocus by the dozens or hundreds in curving swaths and naturalistic groupings.

When, Where, and How to Plant

Crocus are available locally, but for greatest variety— and fall bloomers—seek out online and mail-order sources. Plant corms when you get them in late summer. Crocus thrive in full sun in humus-rich, lightly moist, well-drained soil, but tolerate most well-drained soils and part shade. Plant 3 to 4 inches deep and 3 inches apart. Water well. (See page 41 for more planting information.)

Growing Tips

Keep the soil lightly moist after planting and during spring growth, watering weekly with compost tea. After that, do not water; allow them to dry.

Regional Advice and Care

Let the leaves remain until they yellow or brown. With crocus planted in the lawn, let the grass grow up to 3 inches high before mowing. Fertilize the lawn only in fall. Spring feeding increases leaf growth at the expense of root growth; if you fertilize in spring, your lawn could be 6 inches high before the crocus ripens! Crocus naturalizes readily.

Companion Planting and Design

Crocus are beautiful in a lawn, giving early color in a sea of green. Use in borders or edging. Let crocus naturalize in a deciduous woodland, on a slope, or beneath a single deciduous tree. Plant snow crocus and Dutch crocus together for a succession of bloom. Mix and match colors.

Try These

Snow crocus (*Crocus tommasinianus*, to 1 inch tall, scented): 'Advance' is lemon-yellow inside, purplish outside; 'Ruby Giant' is deep velvety purple with contrasting orange stigma; and 'Lady Killer' has white petals with bold purple streaks on outsides. Dutch (giant) crocus (*C. vernus*, to 6 inches): 'King of the Stripes' is beautifully striped purple and white; 'Golden Yellow' is outstanding deep sunny yellow; and 'Jeanne d'Arc' is pure white with prominent orange stigmas. Fall bloomers (plant 3 to 4 inches deep in well-drained soil in mid- to late summer) include *C. goulimyi* (to 4 inches) with one to three fragrant lilac-colored flowers per corm blooming simultaneously with narrow green leaves and the true saffron crocus (*C. sativus*, to 6 inches), whose orange-red stigmas are the costly culinary saffron threads.

Daffodil

Narcissus spp.

Botanical Pronunciation
nar-SIS-us

Other Name
Narcissus

Bloom Period and Seasonal Colors
Early to late spring, yellow, white, and bicolors
with pink, orange

Mature Height × Spread
6 to 30 in. × 2 to 8 in.

Sometimes called jonquils, daffodils are the essence of springtime in hues of yellow. Although there are white and bicolors—sometimes accented with pink or orange—daffodils bring to mind sunny yellow, large-trumpeted ones like the classic 'King Alfred'. The *hundreds* of daffodils have been classified into twelve divisions. The main divisions are based on the relative length of the trumpet (cup) to the petal and whether it has a single or double flower. From the earliest species daffodil that grows through the snow (*Narcissus asturiensis*) to the last one that blooms with the peonies (often called pheasant's eye, *N. poeticus* 'Actea'), myriad daffodils can grace any part of your garden. Most naturalize; three to five bulbs becoming a foot-wide cluster in a few years.

When, Where, and How to Plant
When buying bulbs, you get what you pay for—locally or from online or mail-order sources. Great bargains are often small bulbs too immature to flower immediately. However, with patience (for a large area) they are worth it. Otherwise, choose the largest size possible. If you're handpicking them, choose firm, solid bulbs with smaller bulbs growing off the sides. Side bulbs may bloom the first year; if not, they'll bloom the second. The main bulb can produce numerous flowering stems. Daffodils grow best with full sun in average to rich, well-drained soil that is moist in spring, but tolerate less light. Plant at three times its depth, with at least 3 inches of soil covering it. Water well. (See page 41 for more planting information.) Fungal infections can be avoided by inspecting the bulb before planting—discard any with soft, greenish blue, or black areas.

Growing Tips
Keep lightly moist after planting and during spring growth. Water weekly with compost tea during the growing period. After that, do not water.

Regional Advice and Care
Remove the flower stem or deadhead it when the blooms fade so the plant's energy goes to the bulb. Let the leaves remain until they yellow or brown. Do *not* braid or tie them back. If the bulbs don't bloom but have healthy leaves, divide them. Dig up the clump and gently tease the bulbs and roots apart. Replant at their original depth, spaced two to three times the width of the bulb (center to center). Water well with transplant solution.

Companion Planting and Design
Daffodils highlight blue grape hyacinths (*Muscari armeniacum*). Interplant early small yellow daffodils like 'Wee Bee' and 'Small Talk' with blue Siberian squill (*Scilla siberica*) and starry blue-and-white glory-of-the-snow (*Chionodoxa luciliae*). Grow them with tulips (*Tulipa* spp.)

Try These
'Actea' (to 18 inches tall, late-season bloom) has fragrant, broad white petals with a short, red-edged yellow cup. 'Cheerfulness' (to 16 inches, midseason bloom) has fragrant clusters of double white blooms. 'Jack Snipe' (to 10 inches, early bloom, pictured above) has recurved white petals with a short lemon-yellow cup.

Gladiolus

Gladiolus spp.

Botanical Pronunciation
glad-ee-OH-lus

Other Name Sword lily

Bloom Period and Seasonal Colors
Summer, single, bi- and tricolors

Mature Height × Spread
18 to 60 in. × 12 to 24 in.

Zones 8

The elegant stalks of gladiolus shoot from 18 to 60 inches tall, with flowers opening in succession up the stem, clasped by swordlike leaves. Gladioli are classified by the size of the flower—from miniatures less than 2½ inches wide to giants 5½ inches across. Flower spikes range to 3 feet tall with as many as twenty-seven buds—ten open at a time—and are long-lasting cut flowers. Blooms are borne in either a formal style, side-by-side so that when they are open there appears to be no space in between, or less formal with one flower above another, stepladder fashion, so you see the stem. The range of colors, variations, and combinations is not seen in any other flower.

When, Where, and How to Plant
Gladiolus is only available as a corm, locally and from online and mail-order sources. It prefers fertile, well-drained soil in sheltered full sun. Dig a 6- to 8-inch-deep hole, depending on the size of the corm. Add 1 inch of organic material (compost, well-rotted manure, or leaf mold). Top with 1 inch of builder's sand to ensure good drainage. Place the corm. Fill with soil and water well. Space corms 6 inches apart. To extend bloom time, plant some corms every two weeks until ninety days before the first frost date. (See page 41 for more on planting.)

Growing Tips
Once the flower spikes reach one-third of their height, apply a high potash (potassium) fertilizer (following package directions). Water every ten days until they finish blooming.

Regional Advice and Care
Gladiolus is a superb cut flower, lasting at least a week indoors. Pull out faded blooms, cut ½ inch off the stem, and change the water daily. Gladiolus is only hardy to Zone 8. Either grow it as an annual and let it die or dig the corm and store it for winter. When the leaves start to wither, lift the corms. Cut the stem close to the corm, roll the corm in sulfur, and place it on a screen in a well-ventilated area for several days to dry. Separate new corms from the old, discarding the old ones and any that show signs of rot. Store in a cool, dry area.

Companion Planting and Design
Many people grow gladiolus in rows—sensible in a cutting garden. In a mixed border or perennial garden, group glads and intermingle them with other plantings. Grow gladiolus among perennials, annuals, or shrubs. It is lovely with canna (*Canna × generalis*) and calla lily (*Zantedeschia aethiopica*), which emphasize their verticality.

Try These
'Black Swan' (to 48 inches tall) produces brilliant deep red flowers. Glamini® Esther (to 25 inches) has soft purple flowers with lighter centers. 'Pink Lady' (to 34 inches) produces twenty-five to twenty-seven buds—with eight or nine white-throated, deep rose pink flowers open at a time.

Glory of the Snow

Chionodoxa luciliae

Botanical Pronunciation
kye-on-uh-DOCKS-uh loo-SILL-ee-ay

Bloom Period and Seasonal Colors
Early spring, deep sky blue with white centers

Mature Height × Spread
6 to 8 in. × 4 to 6 in.

Glory of the snow adds a touch of magic to my early spring garden. Its upward-facing, star-shaped flowers—bright blue with an almost iridescent white center—always make me smile. It sets seed with abandon and hybridizes freely, so the size of the white center is quite variable. I found a single clump of pure white flowers growing on my hillside. Every year I meant to mark them to propagate but, alas, I never remembered. A single small bulb sends up several flower stems. It is very hardy, starting to bloom before the crocus have finished. Although you might not consider it a cut flower, a group of eight to twelve flowering stems is charming in a small container such as an antique inkwell or saltshaker.

When, Where, and How to Plant

Glory of the snow is readily available locally or through online and mail-order sources. Small, early spring bulbs tend to dry out if you don't plant them within a few weeks of receiving them. Keep them cool and dry until planting. Glory of the snow needs full sun. Think full sun for when it is up and blooming but not at planting time. You can remember this by keeping in mind it may be shady under a deciduous tree or shrub when you are planting in fall, but it will be sunny when the early bulbs bloom because the tree will not have leafed out. Glory of the snow grows in any type of soil as long as it is well drained. Plant the bulbs 3 inches deep and 3 inches apart. Water well. (See page 41 for planting tips.)

Growing Tips

Keep the soil lightly moist during the growing season. Add a 2-inch layer of mulch (compost, leaf mold, or well-rotted manure) after the ground freezes to protect the bulbs from heaving during winter thaws. It also breaks down, providing all the nutrition the bulbs need.

Regional Advice and Care

Don't be disappointed if the first year's bloom is not as spectacular as you hoped. Leave the bulbs in place. Since they self-seed freely, you'll soon have a starry carpet.

Companion Planting and Design

Glory of the snow is magnificent in a low section of a rock garden. Make mass plantings either alone or combined with Siberian squill (*Scilla siberica*) or grape hyacinth (*Muscari armeniacum*) for a blue carpet under forsythia (*Forsythia* spp.), dwarf purpleleaf sand cherry (*Prunus × cisterna* 'Crimson Dwarf'), or star magnolia (*Magnolia stellata*). Add a few early daffodils such as *Narcissus* 'Jack Snipe' or 'Tête-à-Tête'. Mass early bulbs under deciduous trees where it is often difficult to get grass to grow. They get ample sunshine before the trees leaf out.

Try These

'Alba' has large, pure white flowers. 'Pink Giant' has six to ten pale pink flowers with white centers per stem.

Grape Hyacinth

Muscari armeniacum

Botanical Pronunciation
muss-KAR-ee ar-men-ee-AY-kum

Bloom Period and Seasonal Colors
Spring, bright blue with white

Mature Height × Spread
6 to 8 in. × 3 to 6 in.

Zones 4 to 8

Grape hyacinth is aptly named. Growing only 6 to 8 inches high, it resembles a miniature blue hyacinth or a tiny bunch of grapes—depending on your point of view. Look closely at the florets, which are rounded and gathered at the bottom with contrasting white, like the white elastic on old-fashioned 1890s ladies' bloomers. Take a whiff of the flowers; they have a delightful light grapey aroma. It multiplies well and can provide an effective spring groundcover under deciduous trees. It sends up its handsome, straplike leaves in autumn, within weeks of planting, that last through winter. The leaves will die back after the flowers finish blooming. Plant in a raised bed or deep windowbox where you can appreciate the delightful scent.

When, Where, and How to Plant

Whether you purchase grape hyacinth bulbs locally or through online or mail-order sources, get them early (by mid-August) and plant within two weeks. They need time to develop a strong root system and send up their leaves before the weather turns cold. Grape hyacinths grow best in rich, lightly moist, well-drained (but somewhat sandy), soil in full sun (but tolerate part sun). Plant 3 to 4 inches deep, allowing 3 to 4 inches between each bulb. Like other small bulbs, they have the most impact when planted in large numbers. Water well. (See page 41 for more on planting.)

Growing Tips

Keep the soil lightly moist until the ground freezes and during the growing season. Mulch with several inches of organic matter after the ground has frozen in fall to prevent heaving. It will break down, providing all the nutrition the bulbs need.

Regional Advice and Care

Grape hyacinths need little attention and naturalize rapidly. If the planting becomes congested, dig it up in summer when the plants are dormant. Gently tease the bulbs and roots apart. Replant at the original depth and spacing. You will have plenty to start a new area or share with friends. Grape hyacinths are good bulbs for forcing.

Companion Planting and Design

Grape hyacinths are beautiful with tulips of all colors, yet are outstanding in front of red tulips like *Tulipa* 'Red Emperor'. Create a patriotic mix by adding some white tulips (*T.* 'Purissima' or 'Spring Green') or white hyacinths (*Hyacinthus orientalis* 'White Pearl'). Create a blue landscape "river" with hundreds of grape hyacinths.

Try These

'Blue Spike' with its larger, densely bunched, double flowers resemble a miniature lilac. 'Christmas Pearl' is similar to the species, but blooms earlier. 'Fantasy Creation' has a pyramidal head of double flowers that change colors over a span of six to eight weeks—from heavenly blue when they first open, gradually changing to a handsome bluish green, and finally in late spring becoming totally green. 'Saffier', with white-rimmed, dark French blue florets, is the last of the grape hyacinth varieties to bloom.

Hyacinth

Hyacinthus orientalis

Botanical Pronunciation
hye-uh-SIN-thuss or-ee-un-TAY-liss

Other Name Dutch hyacinth

Bloom Period and Seasonal Colors
Midspring, white, pink, yellow, purple, blue, orange

Mature Height × Spread
8 to 12 in. × 3 to 4 in.

Zones 4 to 8

For me, the scent of hyacinth conjures up childhood memories of Easter morning—the Easter basket, jellybeans, and especially the coveted chocolate bunny. Hyacinths were not necessarily blooming outdoors at Easter, but we always had a large pot of 'Delft Blue' hyacinths that we had forced into bloom. We kept them on a sunny windowsill in the coolest room—the living room—and the flowers lasted nearly a month. By then, hyacinths were bursting into bloom outdoors. A hyacinth spike is composed of numerous of closely packed, 1-inch florets around the stem in hues of carmine, pink, purple, blue, white, yellow, and orange—both single and double. They are great show-offs in the garden; their sweet perfume leads you to them.

When, Where, and How to Plant
Hyacinth bulbs are available locally and from online and mail-order sources in late summer. Choose large, firm, weighty bulbs. Reject any with soft spots or skin discoloration. Hyacinths thrive in average to fertile, well-drained soil in full sun. In our region, planting them deeper—6 to 8 inches—allows us to grow them successfully. Space 3 inches apart. Water well (see page 41 for more on planting). You can buy hyacinths in bloom, but it is easy and fun to force them yourself. For a group of hyacinths, use a shallow 12-inch pot (bulb pan); for one bulb use a 4-inch pot. Fill to within an inch of the rim with lightly moistened potting soil. Plant the bulbs close, but not touching, with the tips just above soil level. Refrigerate (no apples in the fridge, they prevent blooming); don't allow the soil to dry out.

After eight to twelve weeks, when the stem is 1 inch high, gradually—over a week—introduce it to warmth and brighter light. Put the container on a sunny windowsill; keep soil lightly moist. Within a few weeks, the hyacinths will bloom. Trying to get flowers by a certain date is challenging. If it is a gift, give it before the hyacinths flower. The recipient can enjoy them even longer. You can slow it down by keeping it cool. Warmer temperatures accelerate blooming, but the flowers fade faster.

Growing Tips
Keep the soil lightly moist until the ground freezes to allow strong root growth. Feeding is not necessary.

Regional Advice and Care
When forced hyacinths finish blooming, plant them outdoors when the ground thaws. They will bloom the following spring. Some hyacinths are magnificent the first year but subsequently have fewer florets. You can move them to a less-prominent area.

Companion Planting and Design
Hyacinths are magnificent with pansies (*Viola × wittrockiana*) in all their hues.

Try These
'Carnegie' has beautiful pure white blooms. 'City of Haarlem' bears soft primrose yellow blooms. 'Delft Blue' has soft violet to flushed purple flowers and is the king of hyacinths. 'Gipsy Queen' created quite a sensation when first introduced with its salmon-orange flowers. 'Queen of the Pinks' produces deep pink flowers.

Magic Lily

Lycoris squamigera

Botanical Pronunciation
lye-KORE-iss skwam-uh-GEER-ah

Other Name Resurrection lily

Bloom Period and Seasonal Colors
Mid- to late summer, lilac pink

Mature Height × Spread
18 to 24 in. × 8 to 14 in.

Zones 5 to 8

Magic lily is one of many names for this unique bulb, including naked lady and surprise lily. It is one of the few bulbs, besides autumn crocus, that blooms one season and leafs out another. Seemingly overnight in mid- to late summer, the flower stalks appear, topped with 4-inch umbels of lilac-pink florets that radiate in all directions, looking very much like a bouquet of miniature lilies. They are beautiful and deceivingly delicate-looking as they stand up to summer storms. As a bonus, they attract butterflies and hummingbirds. The flowers last for several weeks to a month and then die down. In early spring, the deep green, straplike leaves will appear. Magic lilies naturalize and look better year after year. They can be forced indoors like amaryllis.

When, Where, and How to Plant

Magic lilies are available as bulbs, more readily found through online and mail-order sources than locally. As soon as the bulbs arrive in mid- to late summer, get them in the ground. Magic lilies prefer fertile, well-drained soil and full to part sun. Plant them 4 to 6 inches deep and 8 inches apart. They are impressive in groupings of seven or more. (See page 41 for more on planting.) Water well. You can force the bulbs and grow them inside. Choose a deep pot that is 1 to 2 inches wider than the bulb (for a single planting) or a 12-inch pot for multiple bulbs. Fill the pot with a lightly moistened mix of equal parts garden soil, perlite, and compost. Plant the bulb so that the tip is just above soil level. Put it in an area that gets full sun such as a south-facing window. The flowers will soon appear, followed by the leaves. During this growth period, keep watering so that the soil remains lightly moist. Once the leaves die back, cut the watering down to once a month and keep the plant in a warm place.

Growing Tips

After planting, keep the soil lightly moist until the first hard frost hits. Water frequently during the growth cycle; however, when it goes dormant, let it go dry. No fertilizer is necessary.

Regional Advice and Care

Once the ground is frozen, mulch with 3 to 4 inches of organic matter (compost, leaf mold, or well-rotted manure). Remove mulch in spring after the last frost. Once planted, magic lilies do not transplant well.

Companion Planting and Design

Magic lilies are most enchanting when they suddenly appear in the lawn. Mark their space so that they are not accidentally mown down. Include them in a foundation planting or in a perennial bed where they will not be disturbed. Surround them with autumn crocus (*Colchicum autumnale*), which bloom after the lilies fade. Or mix them in with hostas (*Hosta* spp.)

Try These

Grow only the species.

Oriental Lily

Lilium cvs.

Botanical Pronunciation
LIL-ee-um

Bloom Period and Seasonal Colors
Mid- to late summer, shades of white, red, pink,
single color, and bicolor

Mature Height × Spread
1 to 8 ft. × 18 to 24 in.

Zones 5 to 8

Oriental lilies are flowers of mystique—you can sense them at a distance by their sweet scent that perfumes the air during the day and even more in the evening. They are the essence of a romantic evening outdoors. Large and blousy, bigger and more fully open than the earlier-blooming Asiatic lilies (bowl- rather than cup-shape), the flowers are borne in clusters or sprays—an instant bouquet for cutting. Gardeners eagerly await their appearance each year. 'Casa Blanca' (pictured), with its pure white petals and contrasting red-orange anthers, is one of the most popular. The tips of the petals curve back, adding to its exotic look. Like other lilies, it is an excellent cut flower. Remove the anthers since the pollen drops and stains.

When, Where, and How to Plant
Some Oriental lilies, such as 'Casa Blanca' are so popular that potted plants (singly or groups of three to five) are available at nurseries, garden centers, and home-improvement stores. Oriental lilies need full sun and rich, well-drained soil. Take one home and put it—pot and all—in a cachepot or decorative container. Alternatively, dig a hole and plant the pot in the garden. But if you want the lily to come back next year, plant it in the ground. Place the pot in transplant solution for several minutes. Carefully unpot; if it's full grown, avoid breaking the stems. Loosen the roots and plant it. Water with 2 cups of transplant solution. Or, purchase bulbs in spring or fall locally or from online and mail-order sources. Plant bulbs as soon as you get them—the depth three times their height, spaced three times their width apart. Water in well. If they are in an unprotected area, add a stake for support. (See page 41 for more planting information.)

Growing Tips
Keep soil lightly moist. Water weekly when there is no rain. Feed at the beginning of the growing season and then weekly with compost tea.

Regional Advice and Care
After flowering, cut down stems, decrease watering and allow the bulbs to slowly dry. Lilies can be host to many pests and diseases. However, if it is not disfiguring or diminishing the plant, natural enemies will often control a problem. If needed, use insecticidal soap for aphids or small caterpillars. Viruses may be transmitted from plant to plant. To be safe, dig up and destroy any infected plants. The ultimate enemy is the lily beetle, which can quickly decimate a plant. Currently there is no treatment.

Companion Planting and Design
No white or evening garden is complete without 2- to 4-foot-tall 'Casa Blanca'. Grow with David garden phlox (*Phlox paniculata* 'David') and moonflowers (*Ipomoea alba*).

Try These
'Garden Party' (to 18 inches) is a dwarf with white petals with a central golden yellow stripe and a bright green center. 'Star Gazer' (3 to 5 feet) is white-edged, crimson-red with darker spots.

Siberian Squill

Scilla siberica

Botanical Pronunciation
SILL-uh sye-BEER-ih-kuh

Other Name Spring squill

Bloom Period and Seasonal Colors
Early spring, bright blue

Mature Height × Spread
3 to 6 in. × 2 to 4 in.

Zones 4 to 8

Siberian squill is one of the easiest bulbs to grow. Its bright blue, nodding bells push right up through the thawing ground and are not bothered by late snows. It makes quite an impact when planted in large groupings of 50, 100, 250, or more. Like many of the other early bulbs, you wouldn't necessarily consider it as a cut flower, but cut seven or more stems for darling mini-bouquets. The flowers grow in small loose spikes in groups of four or five, opening from bottom to top. Look closely in spring; the pollen is *blue*. Beekeepers always know when it is in flower as the bees come home with blue legs. If you get close, you can detect a slight honeylike scent.

When, Where, and How to Plant

Siberian squill bulbs are available locally, online, and from mail-order sources. As soon as you get the bulbs in late summer or early fall, plant them in well-drained soil in full sun to part shade. Using a spade, dig up the soil 5 inches deep (an ample hole to accommodate the swath of bulbs), reserving the soil in a wheelbarrow or tarp. Add a cupful of bone meal for each cubic foot of soil dug (measurements are not critical) and mix in. Put a 1-inch layer of the amended soil in the hole. Place the bulbs on top, 3 to 4 inches apart, pointed ends up. Gently push them into the soil. If you aren't going for the big display, at least plant a group of seven to eleven bulbs. Cover with the remaining soil, gently firm it with your hands, and water well.

Growing Tips

Keep the soil lightly moist in spring. Fertilizer is not necessary.

Regional Advice and Care

Add 2 to 3 inches of organic mulch when the ground freezes. Be sure to remove it in late winter so the bulbs can push through. You will notice Siberian squill starts to flower almost as it is out of the ground. The stem slowly elongates during flowering. After bloom time, let the leaves die back on naturally. You can leave this plant on its own for years as it naturalizes and will continue to multiply and spread.

Companion Planting and Design

It is a sturdy bulb under trees where grass won't grow—under a dogwood (*Cornus* spp.), star magnolia (*Magnolia stellata*), or cutleaf Japanese maple (*Acer palmatum ornatum* 'Dissectum'). The leaves make an attractive cover of green after the flowers are spent. One of my favorite pairings is with glory of the snow (*Chionodoxa luciliae*) with a few early yellow daffodils (*Narcissus* 'Tête-à-Tête') mixed in to accent the blues.

Try These

'Spring Beauty' is more floriferous, with larger and darker blue flowers than the species. Sterile, it doesn't set seed, but it produces offsets that proliferate. 'Alba' is a white-flowered cultivar.

Snowdrop

Galanthus nivalis

Botanical Pronunciation
gah-LAN-thuss niv-ALL-iss

Other Name Common snowdrop

Bloom Period and Seasonal Colors
Late winter to early spring, white

Mature Height and Spread
3 to 11 in. × 3 to 5 in.

Zones 3 to 7

Snowdrops are the true heralds of spring—the first bulbs to bloom. They have small white nodding flowers, one to a stem. The three inner petals are shorter than the outer three and are tipped with green. They are *extremely* hardy and will push up through the frozen ground and snow in late winter or early spring. However, layers of ice will impede their progress. Snowdrops are greatly influenced by exposure or warm spells, so in a protected nook they may even bloom in late February. Like the other early bulbs, often referred to as "minor bulbs," they are best when they are massed—plant dozens or hundreds. The blooms are lightly fragrant. I like to make an adorable flower arrangement in a 2-inch cobalt blue vase.

When, Where, and How to Plant

Snowdrops are available locally and from online and mail-order sources. Like other early blooming bulbs, they have a tendency to dry out if they are not planted quickly. Plant them within two weeks after you get them. In the meantime, store them in a paper bag in a cool dry space. Snowdrops grow best in part sun to part shade in light, rich, moist, well-drained soil. Plant the bulbs 3 inches deep and 3 inches apart, in groupings of fifteen or more. Water well. (See page 41 for more on planting.)

Growing Tips

Keep the soil lightly moist in spring. Do not let the soil dry out in summer, either. Fertilizer is not necessary.

Regional Advice and Care

Add 1 to 2 inches of fine organic mulch when the ground freezes. Some of the mulch will decay over the winter, and the flowers will grow through it. If you use a coarse mulch, remove it in mid- to late January. You can lay pine boughs over the plantings, which can be easily removed at the appropriate time. Snowdrops naturalize well. If the clumps get too big or you want snowdrops in another area of the garden, dig them up and divide the cluster with a knife or shovel. Replant the divisions at the same level they originally grew. Although it is recommended to divide the plants right after flowering, I have done it successfully just as the plants start to flower.

Companion Planting and Design

Snowdrops pair well with colorful snow crocus (*Crocus tommasinianus* and *C. chrysanthus*). Plant several different species and cultivars of snowdrops together.

Try These

'Flore Pleno' (to 6 inches tall), with slightly upturned double flowers, blooms later than the species. Although its flowers are sterile, it naturalizes well from offsets. Giant snowdrop (*Galanthus elwesii*, to 11 inches) bears 1- to 1½-inch flowers. 'Scharlockii' (to 6 inches) flowers are quite interesting—more slender than the species with the outer petal split in two. 'Viridi-apice' (to 10 inches) has a very long central spathe and green markings on the outer petals.

Tulip

Tulipa spp.

Botanical Pronunciation TEW-lih-pah

Bloom Period and Seasonal Colors
Early to late spring, every color of the rainbow in single, bicolor, or tricolor form

Mature Height × Spread
4 to 28 in. × 5 to 12 in.

Zones 4 to 8

Tulips offer an array of colors, shapes, sizes, and bloom times that no other spring-blooming bulb can match. With hundreds of species and thousands of cultivated varieties, tulips are classified into fifteen divisions by type and/or bloom time. This includes single early, single late, fringed, parrot, viridiflora (with green stripe), double early, lily-flowered, and more. The low-growing species tulips are the first to bloom. *Tulipa biflora*, only 4 inches high, opens fully to a yellow-centered white star shape. Greigii tulips, which bloom a little later, have purple striations on their leaves. Darwin (golden yellow 'Golden Apeldoorn') and Triumph hybrids ('Princess Irene', a gorgeous blend of purple and orange) are midseason bloomers. The tallest and showiest are generally among the last to flower, including peony-flowered 'Angelique'.

When, Where, and How to Plant

You will find tulip bulbs for sale everywhere; the greatest selection is through online and mail-order sources. Tulips thrive in fertile, neutral to slightly acidic, well-drained soil in full or afternoon sun. Tulips have a reputation for being a lot of work (due to lifting and replanting them) or not coming back if left in the ground. Plant the bulbs in early autumn, pointed end up. I plant tulips 3 to 4 inches deeper than recommended (three times the bulb's height) and they come back year after year. Avoid planting them in soldierly rows. Space them 2 to 5 inches apart, depending on the variety. Water well.

Growing Tips

Keep the soil lightly moist until a hard frost. Foliar feed every three to four weeks during the growing season.

Regional Advice and Care

To prevent root and bulb rot, especially in clay soil, add an inch of builder's sand at the bottom of the planting area and then plant the tulips. Deadhead the flowers as they finish blooming. If you are going to dig up the bulbs, do not foliar feed after flowering. Dig the bulbs up six weeks after the leaves turn yellow or when they die back. Put them on a screen to dry for a week. Cut the stem back and store in a warm, dry place until planting time in the fall.

Companion Planting and Design

With the plethora of types and cultivars, plant them with each other. Tulips pair well with daffodils (*Narcissus* spp.). Interplant early bloomers with pansies (*Viola* × *wittrockiana*) and later types with forget-me-nots (*Myosotis sylvatica*).

Try These

'Menton' (to 28 inches) blooms rose pink with pale orange edges outside, white-veined, bright red inside. 'New Design' (to 16 inches) has pale yellow petals melding to pale pink and cream-edged leaves. 'Spring Green' (to 18 inches) blooms ivory white with a central feathery green stripe on the petals. Lady tulip (*Tulipa clusiana* 'Lady Jane', to 14 inches, pictured) has pink candy cane stripes. *Tulipa praestans* 'Unicum' (to 12 inches) bears bouquets of red flowers above cream-edged leaves.

Variegated Dalmatian Iris

Iris pallida 'Variegata'

Botanical Pronunciation EYE-riss PAL-ih-duh

Other Name Variegated orris

Bloom Period and Seasonal Colors
Late spring to early summer, pale lavender-blue

Mature Height × Spread 36 to 48 in. × 8 to 16 in.

Zones 4 to 8

Variegated Dalmatian iris is a welcome addition to any damp or low-lying area. Its blue-green, swordlike leaves with white variegation (striping) grow 8 to 24 inches tall, enlivening a semi-shaded area with their color contrast. It is considered semi-evergreen. In mild winters, the leaves will remain, adding color and architectural interest to the bleak landscape. Branching flower stalks rise above the leaves, each bearing two to six fragrant, 3- to 5-inch, pale lavender-blue flowers with yellow beards. It is an *excellent* cut flower—longer lasting than most iris. The secret is to cut ¼ inch off the bottom of the stem and change the water daily. Orrisroot, which is the ground-up dried rhizome of the species, is used as a fixative in potpourri.

When, Where, and How to Plant

Variegated Dalmatian iris is available as a growing plant at nurseries, garden centers, and home-improvement stores, as well as through mail-order and online merchants. It grows best in rich, moist soil in full sun to part shade. Although you may find the plants in spring, it will perform much better if you plant it in late summer to early fall. In the northern portion of our region, midsummer is the best time to plant it since this iris needs time to establish its roots before the cold weather sets in. If the pot has several plants growing in it, you can simply unpot and put it—soil and all—in the ground. Or, you can remove the soil and plant each (if there is more than one) rhizome separately, spaced 3 inches apart. Plant the rhizome horizontally with the fan of leaves facing up so that the rhizome

is just barely below soil level. Press it gently into the soil. Water well.

Growing Tips

Keep the soil moist; do not let it dry out. Fertilizer is not necessary.

Care and Maintenance

If the clump gets too large or you want more iris in other places in the garden, you can divide the rhizomes either in early spring or late summer to early fall. If you make divisions in spring, the plant may not bloom that season. Variegated Dalmatian iris is relatively pest and disease free, but be on the lookout for soft spots or holes—signs of borers in the rhizomes when you divide the plant. Discard and destroy any infested or suspect rhizomes.

Companion Planting and Design

Variegated Dalmatian iris is beautiful with other bog plants such as Japanese iris (*Iris ensata*), marsh marigold (*Caltha palustris*), and drumstick primrose (*Primula denticulata*).

Try These

Iris pallida 'Aurea Variegata' is quite similar, except its leaves are pale green with golden-yellow striping. The species, *Iris pallida*, has gray-green leaves and is the hardiest of the bunch. The flowers have distinctive silvery, papery bracts.

GROUNDCOVERS & VINES

FOR THE PRAIRIE & PLAINS STATES

Groundcovers and vines are often grouped together because the categories overlap and interlink. Many of the plants can serve dual purposes. Generally, people think of groundcovers as relatively flat plants, growing close to the ground and spreading horizontally, and of vines as climbing plants that grow vertically. Yet many vines can be used as groundcovers if they are trained to grow horizontally.

Groundcovers

Creating a groundcover usually consists of a mass planting of low-growing plants, such as periwinkle, bugleweed, or bearberry, to fill in an area to the exclusion of any

Purple Jackman clematis underplanted with marigolds.

other plants leaving no bare soil. Groundcovers may be utilitarian with the purpose of covering an area of bare earth to prevent soil erosion, especially on slopes. They make attractive "skirts" around large trees—a living mulch. Groundcovers may be evergreen or deciduous. For many gardeners, an evergreen one is more desirable, especially when creating large swaths of plants. However, a deciduous groundcover, such as creeping phlox, is ideal for a small place like between stones on walls or walkways.

Vines

Vines are plants with long stems with a built-in means of supporting themselves as they grow upward. One of their greatest attributes is that they have no genetically preset form, which allows them to fit into the tiniest spaces—provided they have room to root—and then grow vertically and/or horizontally among a bevy of other plants. They can be categorized as clinging and nonclinging. There are several ways clinging vines attach themselves to whatever is nearby on their upward journey.

Hostas make excellent groundcovers and come in a wide range of colors, sizes, and textures.

Boston ivy, for example, has flat adhesive disks at the ends of its branching tendrils. The disks allow it to cling well to most surfaces, so it can easily cover the side of a building or a large area of ground. However, do not let it grow on a wood-shingled building since it can creep between the shingles and even get into the house.

Wintercreeper, on the other hand, has rootlike holdfasts along its stems that cling to rough surfaces. It easily scales trees, stucco, and brick buildings. You can even use these vines to hide an unsightly chain-link fence. If you have an older brick house, do not plant this type of vine as it can send its holdfasts into the mortar. This is not a problem with new mortar since it is not as porous.

Non-clinging vines also have several different ways of being upwardly mobile based on their growth habits. Twining vines circle upward around a support. This spiraling method is called circumnulation and can be clockwise or counterclockwise. No doubt you have had the experience of trying to wrap a morning glory around a trellis. You put it on one way, and the next day it is back on the ground because its natural twining is in the opposite direction. If you curled it one way, it may even uncurl and retwine itself.

Find out how long the vine will grow, whether it is annual or perennial, and herbaceous or woody. If the plant you are growing gets 6 feet tall, you want a support that is a least 7 or 8 feet tall, since at least 12 inches of the support must be underground. Have a support in place—stake, arbor, pergola, trellis, or twine attached to an overhang—before you put the plant in the ground. In the case of a stake, plant both at the same time.

Most of the groundcovers and vines you will grow will come as potted plants. You can follow the basic planting information found in the main introduction on page 11. On rare occasions when you need a large number of plants, it is more cost-efficient to grow them from seed or cuttings. A few large plants can yield dozens of cuttings in a fairly short time. In the meantime, learn how these plants can benefit your garden. Unless otherwise noted in the "Regional Advice and Care" section, there are no significant pest or disease problems for the plant.

Bearberry

Arctostaphylos uva-ursi

Botanical Pronunciation
ark-toe-STAF-il-ohs oo-vah-ER-see

Other Name Kinnikinnick

Bloom Period and Seasonal Colors
Summer, white with pink tinge; late summer into winter, red berries; winter, bronze foliage

Mature Height × Spread 6 to 12 in. × 3 to 6 ft.

Zones 3 to 6

Bearberry, known to the Native Americans as kinnikinnick, is a handsome prostrate groundcover. It is an evergreen branching shrub (woody plant) that only grows to 12 inches tall, with stems up to 6 feet long. One of its unique qualities is that the stems root at the joints, making it easy to propagate. It has thick, leathery green leaves and bears pink-tinged, waxy white flowers in summer. Pea-sized, smooth red fruits accent the plant from August through late winter if they are not eaten. As the name implies, bears like the berries. The leaves turn a beautiful shade of bronze in winter, adding color when there is little or no snow. Native Americans brewed a tea from the leaves and used it as a diuretic.

When, Where, and How to Plant
Bearberry plants can be found at some nurseries and are available through online and mail-order sources. It grows best in sandy or rocky, acidic, well-drained soil in full or part sun. Space plants at least 2 feet apart. Since our soil is likely to be alkaline (test your soil pH), it needs amending for bearberry to thrive. Dig a hole twice the width and depth of the potted plant, putting the soil on a tarp or in a wheelbarrow. Add equal parts of builder's sand and fine sphagnum moss to the reserved soil; mix well. Put enough soil back in the hole so that the plant will be at the same level it was growing in the pot. Loosen roots, if necessary, and place the plant in the hole. Fill in with the remaining amended soil. Water well with transplant solution.

Growing Tips
Keep the plant lightly moist until it is established. Once established, it is fairly drought tolerant, so rains should provide ample water unless there is prolonged drought. Fertilizer is not necessary.

Regional Advice and Care
Bearberry is slightly susceptible to fungal diseases. At the first sign of a problem, spray tops and bottoms of leaves and the entire plant with baking soda spray. (See page 175 for directions on making the solution.) Propagate in spring or late summer by cutting the stem 2 inches long on either side of a rooted node. Carefully dig up the nodes and roots; replant. It does not thrive where summers are hot and humid.

Companion Planting and Design
Bearberry is a good edging plant, alongside a walkway, or between stepping-stones. It can stand up to foot traffic and is very handsome with other low-growing evergreen groundcovers such as mother of thyme (*Thymus serphyllum*) and Corsican mint (*Mentha requienii*). Use as a "skirt" in front of acid-lovers like azaleas (*Rhododendron* spp.).

Try These
'Massachusetts' (to 12 inches tall) has white flowers tinged with pink, is slow growing and vigorous. Birds flock to eat the red berries in autumn.

Bishop's Hat

Epimedium × *versicolor* 'Sulphureum'

Botanical Pronunciation
ep-ih-MEE-dee-um VUR-sih-kull-ur

Other Name Barrenwort

Bloom Period and Seasonal Colors
Mid- to late spring, yellow and white; fall, red foliage

Mature Height × Spread
8 to 12 in. × 24 to 36 in.

Zones 5 to 8

ishop's hat is one of my favorite spring-blooming groundcovers—a little gem that you come across in a partially shaded portion of the garden. In time, it forms a thick, impenetrable matrix of roots, which no weeds can penetrate. The leaves are compound, comprised of nine heart-shaped, 1½- to 2½-inch-long leaflets borne on wiry stems that form a leaf about 12 inches long. When they first open, the semi-evergreen leaflets are coppery red, then turn green, and then red in fall. The flowers on this species are small—1 inch. To me, the blossoms look like a cross between a daffodil and a columbine nestled among the leaves. The common name *bishop's hat* refers to the spurred petals that resemble a bishop's mitre.

When, Where, and How to Plant
In spring, you may be able to find plants at some nurseries, garden centers, and home-improvement stores. However, the greatest selection is available through online and mail-order sources. Bishop's hat grows best in rich, moist, well-drained soil in shade to part shade. Although it tolerates sun and dry shade, it will not grow nearly as well as in its ideal conditions. Plant in spring after danger of frost has passed. Mix several handfuls of compost or other organic matter into the soil before planting. Refer to page 105 for more planting information. Plant it at the same soil level as it was growing in its pot. Space plants 12 inches apart. Water well.

Growing Tips
Keep the soil lightly moist. Do not let the soil dry out. You do not need to fertilize the plant as long as it is growing in rich soil.

Regional Advice and Care
Be patient; it is slow to grow. Add a 3- to 5-inch layer of organic mulch over the plant once the ground freezes. Some of this will break down, enriching the soil. Remove the mulch in early spring. As the new shoots are emerging, cut off any overwintered stems or leaves. It is rabbit resistant.

Companion Planting and Design
Grow bishop's hat in woodland gardens, shady rock gardens, or to edge a shaded walkway. It contrasts nicely with the rounded, shiny leaves of the lower-growing European ginger (*Asarum europaeum*). For added height, include one or more bleeding hearts (*Lamprocapnos spectabilis*), Dutchman's breeches (*Dicentra culcullaria*), or the long-blooming fringed bleeding heart (*D. eximia* 'Snowdrift').

Try These
Other species include longspur barrenwort (*Epimedium grandiflorum*) 'Rose Queen' (to 10 inches tall) with white-spurred, red flowers that reign supreme. 'Lilafee' (to 15 inches) is unusual with its purplish flowers and violet-tinted young leaves. Red barrenwort (*E.* × *rubrum*, to 12 inches) has white-spurred, bright pink to crimson blooms; its foliage turns bronzy purple in fall. Snowy epimedium (*E.* × *youngianum* 'Niveum', to 9 inches) is very showy with late-blooming white flowers held above the wavy foliage.

Bugleweed

Ajuga reptans

Botanical Pronunciation
ah-JEW-gah REP-tanz

Other Name Carpet bugleweed

Bloom Period and Seasonal Colors
Late spring to early summer, blue to purple;
evergreen foliage

Mature Height × Spread 3 to 10 in. × 2 to 3 ft.

Bugleweed, also known as carpet bugle, is a wonderfully hardy perennial that forms a dense, carpetlike mat, even in shady areas. Stems often self-root, so it spreads readily, making it easy to propagate or move to a new area. The dark green leaves are opposite, growing low to the ground, up to 2½ inches long. Much plant breeding has been done in the past decade, and the results are new, mixed colors in the leaves, making the plant even more desirable for a shady area. The 3- to 6-inch flower spikes are composed of blue to lavender, two-lipped, ¼-inch florets in spring or early summer. Cut the flower spikes to use in mini arrangements or put them in a napkin ring for a festive look.

When, Where, and How to Plant
Bugleweed plants are readily available locally; however, the choices are limited. Online and mail-order sources offer a greater range of varieties. Plant bugleweed in spring after all danger of frost is passed. It grows in average, well-drained soil in part sun to shade. It tolerates sun, but the leaves may burn—turning brown. The soil needs no preparation. Plant it at the same level it was growing in the container. Water well with transplant solution. Refer to page 105 for more on planting.

Growing Tips
Bugleweed is a low-maintenance plant that needs regular watering until established. After that, water when the top ½ inch of soil is dry. Fertilizer is not necessary.

Regional Advice and Care
If the plant looks scraggly, mow it down and it will come back looking even more handsome. It is easy to divide as the stems roots. Simply dig up several plants and move them to the new location. Soon they will spread out to form a lovely mat. Rabbits resist eating it. It will grow near black walnuts (*Juglans nigra*). Bugleweed attracts many early butterflies.

Companion Planting and Design
Bugleweed is such a beautiful, mat-forming groundcover that it often does not get the attention it deserves. Use it in a windowbox, container, or raised bed where you can appreciate the loveliness of the flower spires without having to get on your hands and knees. Bugleweed makes a nice transitional plant from lawn into a woodland garden, or an edge to a flagstone walkway. It consorts well with creeping phlox (*Phlox subulata*) and basket-of-gold (*Aurinia saxatilis*).

Try These
All grow to 6 inches tall unless otherwise noted. 'Bronze Beauty' has attractive glossy bronze foliage; it blooms in spring or early summer with spires of very rich, violet-blue flowers. 'Burgundy Glow' (pictured) has tricolor leaves—burgundy, green, and cream—and deep blue flowers. 'Catlin's Giant' (to 10 inches tall) has large (to 6 inches) leaves that are beautiful purplish bronze hue with bright blue flower spikes. 'Chocolate Chip' ('Valfredda', to 3 inches) has narrow chocolate-colored leaves with burgundy highlights. 'Silver Beauty' bears gray-green leaves with irregular cream edges.

Canadian Wild Ginger

Asarum canadense

Botanical Pronunciation
ah-SAR-um kan-ah-DEN-see

Other Name Wild ginger

Bloom Period and Seasonal Colors
Spring, inconspicuous brownish purple;
evergreen foliage

Mature Height × Spread 6 to 8 in. × 6 to 8 in.

Canadian wild ginger is a marvelous perennial groundcover, surviving even in our coldest regions. Shade loving, it is a wonderful accent in a woodland garden. It spreads by rhizomes, and since it spreads rather quickly, you can use it for erosion control on a partially shaded bank. Evergreen, dark matte-green leaves are 2 to 4 inches long and have a rounded heart shape. The leaf stalks are slightly hairy, growing 6 to 12 inches in length. Rhizomes have a pungent gingery smell; however, it is *not* edible—Native Americans used it for birth control. The flowers are inconspicuous, growing under the leaves. In spring, lift up a leaf and look for a bell-shaped, brownish purple flower.

When, Where, and How to Plant

A very hardy woodland perennial, Canadian wild ginger is more likely found through online and mail-order sources. Unfortunately, many nurseries and garden centers tend to carry the more showy European variety rather than the native species. Canadian wild ginger grows best in rich, humusy, moist, neutral to acidic, well-drained soil in part to full shade. Plant it in spring after all danger of frost has passed or in late summer to early fall at the same level it was growing in its container. Space 6 inches apart. Water well with transplant solution.

Growing Tips

Keep the soil uniformly moist; do not let it dry out. Fertilizing is not necessary.

Regional Advice and Care

If slugs appear, let them be as they pollinate the flowers. However, if they are feasting on the leaves, go out at night with a flashlight and handpick and destroy them if you can handle that. Or, put several shingles nearby—their cool shade will attract the critters in the daytime. It's easy to scrape the slugs off the shingles and dispose of them. Canadian wild ginger naturalizes easily, spreading by its creeping rhizomes and from seed. In a few years, it can cover a large area. Control its spread by digging it up if it goes out of bounds.

Companion Planting and Design

Canadian wild ginger belongs in a woodland garden or along a shady path. Its rounded, heart-shaped leaves form a lovely carpet. It mixes well with other woodland wildflowers such as mayapple (*Podophyllum peltatum*), Jack-in-the-pulpit (*Arisaema triphyllum*), and Christmas fern (*Polystichum acrostichoides*).

Try These

Other *Asarum* species include European wild ginger (*Asarum europaeum*, to 6 inches), which is less hardy (Zone 4) and has glossy dark green 2- to 3-inch-long leaves. *A. europaeum caucasicum* has leaf tips that are tapered and more extended than the species. Callaway ginger (*A. shuttleworthii* 'Callaway', to 12 inches, and hardy to Zone 6, but I have grown it in a south-facing, sheltered location in Zone 5) is worth trying for its broadly heart-shaped, 1- to 4-inch, silvery mottled green leaves.

Creeping Juniper

Juniperus horizontalis

Botanical Pronunciation
joo-NIP-er-us hor-ih-zon-TAL-iss

Bloom Period and Seasonal Colors
Evergreen foliage; winter, purplish hues

Mature Height and Spread
6 to 18 in. × 5 to 10 feet

Creeping juniper is one of the more unusual groundcovers as it's a shrub. It is a low-growing bluish gray-green, evergreen shrub that is drought tolerant and will grow in some of the worst soil—rocky and sandy—quickly covering a large area. The branches overlap, so from a distance it looks like a small, wavy ocean. In fall, it takes on a purplish hue. The inconspicuous berries are dark blue. It is *great* for erosion control on hills or banks. Creeping juniper's glaucous gray-green needles are somewhat pointed, making the plant excellent for defining boundaries—at least keeping children and small animals at bay. Deer unfortunately are not deterred but consider it a delicacy. It's an excellent plant where air pollution is a problem.

When, Where, and How to Plant
Potted plants of creeping juniper and some of its cultivars are available at nurseries, garden centers, and home-improvement stores. A greater variety is available through online and mail-order sources. Plant it in spring after danger of frost has passed or in late summer to early fall (look for late season bargains at local stores). Creeping juniper grows best in full sun and thrives in dry, rocky places. If you have rich or clayey soil, add builder's sand to improve drainage. An alternative is to dig a hole about 2 inches larger and deeper than the pot and fill it with cactus potting mix that has been lightly moistened with transplant solution. Plant the juniper in this mix at the level it was growing in the original container. Water well.

Growing Tips
Until the plant is established, do not let the soil dry out completely. Feeding is unnecessary.

Regional Advice and Care
Prune it, if necessary, to keep it within bounds. When pruning, leave its natural overlapping habit; do not try to shape it. Mulch around the plant (within 1 inch of the stem) with sand or gravel to increase drainage and prevent rot.

Companion Planting and Design
Before planting creeping juniper, put in a few daffodils (*Narcissus* spp.) for an interesting color accent in spring. One of the most striking plant combinations I have seen is 'Bar Harbor' juniper with a dwarf bamboo (*Bambusa* spp.) growing up through it. Creeping juniper is lovely trailing over large rocks.

Try These
'Bar Harbor' (to 12 inches × 6 feet) has a dense mat of steely blue needles that turn a lovely silvery purple in winter. 'Blue Chip' (to 10 inches × 10 feet) has cool steely blue foliage; the tips turn purplish in winter. 'Limeglow' (to 12 × 36 inches) forms a vase-shaped mound of chartreuse-yellow foliage that turns shades of coppery bronze in winter. 'Wiltonii' (to 6 inches × 8 feet) is also known as blue rug juniper as it forms a silvery blue carpet; it is one of the best creeping junipers.

Creeping Phlox

Phlox stolonifera

Botanical Pronunciation FLOKS sto-lon-IF-er-ah

Bloom Period and Seasonal Colors
Early spring, blue, lavender, pink, white, single and bicolor; evergreen foliage

Mature Height × Spread
4 to 12 in. × 12 to 36 in.

Zones 5 to 8

Generations of gardeners have grown creeping phlox—a hardy native from the southern Appalachians—for its lustrous foliage and dazzling drifts of color along well-drained woodland slopes and cascading from rock gardens. Named a "Perennial Plant of the Year" by the Perennial Plant Association, it is easy to propagate and share, and even easier to grow. Its mat-forming stems are covered with somewhat narrow leaves most, if not all of the year, and burst into color shortly after spring's first thaw in a cheery profusion of clusters of inch-wide flowers. Underground stems (stolons) spread readily in woodland soils, and aboveground stems root wherever they touch the ground, yet the plant never becomes weedy or invasive. It's lovely covering a bank or in a rock garden.

When, Where, and How to Plant
Creeping phlox is available locally and from online and mail-order sources. Often the best way to acquire the plant is to get some from a friend. It grows best in humusy, well-drained soil in full sun, but will grow in sandy soil and in part shade. Add a moderate amount of organic matter when preparing the soil; when planting between existing plants, loosen soil outside the immediate planting area to help new stems spread. Encourage new roots to grow deep by soaking the area really well, but allow soil to get completely dry before watering again. Mulch lightly to prevent weed seeds from sprouting until phlox begins to cover the area. Feed at half-strength until plants get established.

Growing Tips
Water new plants deeply once a week for several months until they are established. Once they are established, fertilizing is not necessary.

Regional Advice and Care
Creeping phlox thrives in neglected soils, moderate shade, and tolerates summer heat, drought, *and* high humidity. Mulch lightly to keep weeds from taking over while young phlox plants take root and get established. Propagate by removing and immediately replanting well-rooted sections of stems from mature clumps. It has no major insect or disease problems. Rabbits don't like creeping phlox.

Companion Planting and Design
When in full bloom, creeping phlox creates a radiant show all by itself. Out of bloom its radiant green foliage makes a contrasting groundcover for iris (*Iris* spp.), gayfeather (*Liatris spicata*), and other vertical perennials. It is lovely with maidenhair fern (*Adiantum pedatum*) and other taller woodland ferns. Since it needs little water during the summer, it also makes an excellent summer and fall cover for dormant spring-blooming bulbs, such as daffodils (*Narcissus* spp.) and tulips (*Tulipa* spp.), which would rot when planted under fussier summer flowers. Creeping phlox spreads well under small trees.

Try These
'Ariane' has yellow-eyed white flowers. 'Blue Ridge' bears fragrant, yellow-eyed, pale lavender-blue blooms. 'Bruce's White' has white blooms with yellow eyes. 'Home Fires' has fragrant, dark pink blooms. 'Sherwood Purple' bears purple flowers.

Goldflame Honeysuckle

Lonicera × heckrottii 'Goldflame'

Botanical Pronunciation
luh-NISS-ur-uh hek-ROT-ee-eye

Bloom Period and Seasonal Colors
Late spring to summer, rose pink with yellow;
autumn into winter, red berries

Mature Height × Spread 10 to 15 ft. × 2 to 4 ft.

Zones 5 to 8

I first fell in love with 'Goldflame' honeysuckle during an outdoor photography workshop. Wandering around an arboretum, we each had to choose one flower and photograph it from all angles, depths, and distances. I spied the eye-catching clusters of 1½-inch-long tropical-looking flowers and knew it was my choice. The tubular, two-lipped flowers are peachy pink outside and buttery yellow inside, making a cheery display even in the rain. A lightly fragrant plant, I see humming-birds at the flowers, going for their nectar, and bees buzzing around them, too. The leaves are handsome as well—1- to 2½-inch blue-green ovals with whitish undersides. This loosely twining perennial vine looks lovely on a lattice where you can weave it from one side to another.

When, Where, and How to Plant
Container-grown 'Goldflame' honeysuckle plants are readily available at nurseries, garden centers, and home-improvement stores. It thrives in rich, well-drained soil in full sun but will grow in part shade. Plant after all danger of frost has passed, following general planting information on page 105. Grow within 6 inches of a support, using an arbor, trellis, or pergola. Place any supports before you plant the vine.

Growing Tips
Water well at planting and keep lightly moist until the plant is growing. Foliar feed or apply manure tea to the soil monthly during the growing season.

Regional Advice and Care
Loosely tie the stem to the support since it is not a strong twining vine and needs help to keep itself upright. Alternatively, weave it through a lattice or trellis. Deadheading often results in a second, smaller flush of bloom in later summer to early autumn. Spray with baking soda solution (see page 175) if powdery mildew is a problem.

Companion Planting and Design
As a rather delicate-looking vine, it is best left to climb alone; however, you can enliven it by painting its support. It is handsome against white, but cobalt-blue is outstanding, as are sage-green and purple. For a subtle look, paint the support a very pale yellow—too much yellow may not be the right color match for the flowers. Grow one of the yellow and peach lantanas (*Lantana camera*) at the base of this vine for color at ground level.

Try These
Trumpet (or coral) honeysuckle (*Lonicera semper-virens*) grows to 40 feet and is hardy to Zone 4. It is a great hummingbird plant with clusters of 2-inch-long, tubular flowers—bright red-orange outside, yellow inside—from late spring through summer. Winter honeysuckle (*L. fragrantissima*) grows to 6 × 10 feet and is hardy to Zone 5. It has a sweet lemony scent that emanates from pairs of ½-inch, two-lipped, creamy white flowers in late winter and early spring. It is a bushy honeysuckle that is good in the background, as it is not showy.

Hosta

Hosta spp.

Botanical Pronunciation
HOSS-tah

Other Name Plantain lily

Bloom Period and Seasonal Colors
Summer, white, mauve, purple

Mature Height × Spread
2 to 36 in. × 2 to 72 in.

Hostas have been the epitome of perennial shade plants since Victorian times. They are so long-lived that some of the plain green hostas lining walkways of Victorian homes may be the original plants put in when the houses were new, more than 100 years ago. Hosta breeding in recent decades has made great strides. Today, you can find hostas that grow in full sun to full shade—and everything in between. Although hostas are mainly grown for their attractive leaves, they send up flower spikes in summer; some are fragrant, attracting hummingbirds. Plants range from tiny ones 2 inches across to giants over 6 feet wide Leaf colors are phenomenal—in every hue and shade of solid green to chartreuse and blue to variegations including white and cream.

When, Where, and How to Plant
Although container-grown hostas of all types are readily available locally, the greatest selection is from online and mail-order sources. Make sure the light in your planting spot is right for the hosta you choose. Hostas grow best in rich, moist, well-drained soil. Plant after the last frost date. Be sure to allow enough space for its mature size. Water well. Mulch with organic matter to within 1 inch of the crown to keep roots cool and maintain soil moisture. Water the mulch.

Growing Tips
Once established, hostas are fairly drought tolerant, withstanding weeks with no rain. Foliar feed the plant when you first see the flower spikes appear.

Regional Advice and Care
Slugs and snails *love* hostas. Deter them with an inch-wide ring of diatomaceous earth around the plant. Hostas with cross-venation or rippled varieties are less appealing to these slimy pests. Plants will grow in the shade of black walnuts. Divide in spring if the hosta gets too large. Cut flower stalks for fragrant indoor bouquets.

Companion Planting and Design
You can design an entire garden from hostas in all their variations. They make excellent groundcovers. In part shade, they mix well with ferns, bleeding heart (*Lamprocapnos spectabilis*), and heartleaf foamflower (*Tiarella cordifolia*). Line woodland paths with hostas. In sun, put them in cottage gardens, beds, or borders. Variegated hostas glow in evening gardens.

Try These
Sun-loving searsuckered 'August Moon' (to 20 × 42 inches) leaves open chartreuse-green and mature to gold; spikes of pale lavender to white blooms in midsummer. Shade-loving 'Francee' (to 24 × 36 inches) has 9-inch-long, heart-shaped, white-edged, deep green leaves with pale lavender flowers in late summer. 'Shining Tot' (to 3 × 6 inches) has shiny, thick, deep green leaves. *Hosta sieboldiana* (to 36 × 40 inches), "king of the blues" with heart-shaped, thick, puckered, glaucous blue leaves—blue on top, paler on the underside. *H. sieboldiana* 'Frances Williams' (to 24 × 60 inches) yields glaucous blue-green leaves with irregularly wide, greenish yellow margins, white blooms in summer.

Jackman Clematis

Clematis × jackmanii

Botanical Pronunciation
KLEM-uh-tiss jak-MAN-ee-eye

Bloom Period and Seasonal Colors
Summer, deep purple

Mature Height × Spread
8 to 10 ft. × 3 to 6 ft.

Zones
4 to 8

Clematis is often called the queen of the climbers for its regal form and flower. If so, Jackman clematis is the perennial king with its lusciously deep purple, velvety, 4- to 6-inch blooms. It is somewhat historic, as it was the first large-flowered hybrid clematis to be developed. Yet, it still reigns supreme as one of the most popular of all clematis. There are many species and cultivars of clematis, but the large-flowered ones are the overall favorites as they are so showy. Even the seedheads are attractive after they have finished blooming—an interesting-looking whorl. Although most people grow clematis formally on an arbor or trellis, I have seen them supported and still showing off growing through a dogwood, shrub rose, or an evergreen.

When, Where, and How to Plant
Jackman clematis is widely available locally and from online and mail-order sources. Clematis likes its roots shaded with its leaves and flowers in full sun. It grows best in rich, moist, slightly alkaline, well-drained soil. Check the pH; 7.0 is ideal. Dig a hole twice the depth of the roots. Adjust the pH of the reserved soil, if necessary, by adding lime to acidic soil (pH less than 7.0) and bone meal to alkaline soil (pH greater than 7.0). Then amend it with equal parts of organic matter (compost, well-rotted manure, leaf mold); mix well. Put half the amended soil in the hole. Water with 2 cups of transplant solution. Place the support. Plant the clematis so the crown is 2 to 3 inches deep and cover with remaining soil. Firm soil gently with your hands. Water with 2 cups of transplant

solution. Mulch with 3 to 4 inches of organic matter, keeping the mulch at least 1 inch away from stems.

Growing Tips
Water regularly. Foliar feed every six weeks with a solution of kelp or fish emulsion.

Regional Advice and Care
Clematis stems are fragile; handle them gently. Tie them loosely to a support. In the coldest areas, the plant will die down to the ground in late fall but will regrow in spring.

Companion Planting and Design
Jackman clematis is stunning paired with a pink climbing rose (*Rosa* 'Handel', 'New Dawn', or 'Cecile Brunner') growing up white arbor or trellis. Plant a white or pink daylily (*Hemerocallis* 'Sunday Gloves', 'Pink Flirt', 'White Temptation', or 'High Lama') near enough to shade the roots but not steal nutrients. Before planting the daylilies, track the sun so they shade the clematis in the heat of the day—noon to 5 p.m.

Try These
'Jackmanii Superba' has slightly larger (5-inch) flowers that bloom more profusely than the species. Other clematis cultivars include 'Henryi' with stunning, pure white, 8-inch flowers. 'Nelly Moser' bears showy 6- to 8-inch blooms—pale pink petals with darker pink central stripe. Striking 'Niobe' has 7-inch, velvety, deep ruby-red flowers with prominent stamens.

Kamschatka Sedum

Sedum kamtschaticum

Botanical Pronunciation
SEE-dum kam-SHAT-tih-kum

Other Name
Stonecrop

Bloom Period and Seasonal Colors
Summer, yellow; evergreen foliage

Mature Height × Spread
3 to 6 in. × 6 to 9 in.

Kamschatka sedum is a sunny perennial delight in the garden. I first saw it in the garden of a friend who was having trouble with flooding and erosion on a somewhat sandy hillside leading to a Japanese garden. A landscaper had added stone steps, but even they washed away as nothing held the soil. Another friend suggested planting Kamschatka sedum around and between the steps to anchor them—and it worked. It is such a darling plant—much smaller (only 4 inches tall) than common sedums like 'Autumn Joy'. In summer, clusters of pink buds open to reveal ½-inch, yellow star-shaped flowers. It's delightful to see young swallowtail butterflies competing with bees for the flowers' nectar. Showy seedheads follow. Its succulent leaves add year-round interest.

When, Where, and How to Plant
You can readily find Kamschatka sedum locally. Read the tag; some growers are making up common names, so look for the proper botanical name. There are many online and mail-order sources, too. Kamschatka sedum grows best in full to part sun. Good drainage, especially in winter, is extremely important. Unless you have sandy soil, dig the planting hole 2 inches deeper than the container. Put 1 inch of gravel at the bottom of the hole, add 1 inch of builder's sand, and then add soil. Place the plant at the same level it was in its pot.

Growing Tips
Water once a week until the plant is established. Kamschatka sedum is quite drought tolerant, but water if the leaves begin to look puckered. Fertilization is unnecessary.

Regional Advice and Care
Kamschatka sedum needs little care. Propagation of sedum is very easy. If you want fast results, dig up a plant, make divisions, and replant them. If you are patient, remove a leaf, plant it with the cut end one-third of the way into the ground, and in time it will grow a new plant. Kamschatka sedum is rabbit resistant.

Companion Planting and Design
Kamschatka sedum is at home in a rock garden. With the numerous varieties of sedums, you could make an entire rock garden ranging from the larger, familiar *Sedum* 'Autumn Joy' (to 24 inches) to the smallest *S. humifusum* (¼ inch tall), all of which have a wide range of leaf colors, sizes, shapes, and formations. Its dainty size is perfect for the front of a perennial bed or border with earlier-blooming, yellow corydalis or yellow-flowered basket-of-gold (*Aurinia saxatilis*).

Try These
'Ellacombianum' (to 4 inches) has evergreen foliage that turns shades of red in fall; lemon-yellow blooms rise 6 inches above leaves in late spring. 'Variegatum' (to 4 inches) has creamy-edged leaves; yellow flowers in late spring to summer age to crimson. *S. kamtschaticum* var. *floriferum* 'Weinhenstephaner Gold' (to 3 inches) has a more trailing habit, with yellow blossoms that rise 4 to 5 inches above the leaves in summer.

Morning Glory

Ipomoea tricolor 'Heavenly Blue'

Botanical Pronunciation
ip-uh-MEE-uh TRY-kul-or

Mature Height × Spread
10 to 15 ft. × 6 to 15 in.

Bloom Period and Seasonal Colors
Summer to frost, sky blue with white centers

My first childhood garden memory is sky blue 'Heavenly Blue' morning glory with its large, heart-shaped leaves twining its way up a white trellis. On a sunny summer day with a few puffy clouds, it was easy to see how this annual vine got its name. The white in the center of the funnel-shaped 3-inch flowers echoed the clouds in the heavenly sky, with a dash of yellow for the sun. As a small child, watching morning glories grow awed me, as did sunflowers—I could see their progress day by day. When they reached the top of the trellis and wanted to grow taller, my father lifted me up so I could twine the vine to grow across; it eventually filled the entire trellis.

When, Where, and How to Plant
Find morning glory seeds locally or from mail-order and online sources. Morning glory seeds have tough seed coats. For best germination, nick the seeds with a knife and soak overnight in lukewarm water. Morning glories grow best in full sun, in ordinary to dry, even sandy, soil. Plant 1 inch deep and 2 to 6 inches apart once the soil is above 65 degrees Fahrenheit (when you plant tomatoes) in spring. Water well.

Growing Tips
Keep the soil lightly moist until two sets of leaves appear. After that, it is fairly drought tolerant. Drooping leaves signal a need for water. Foliar feed monthly.

Regional Advice and Care
Give morning glory ample support and room to grow, and watch it head for the sky.

Companion Planting and Design
Traditionally, morning glories are trained up a trellis or on strings hung from a gutter to the ground. Try growing on fences and mailboxes, or up walls and lampposts. Let them trail over an unsightly tree stump or ramble across the ground. Combine 'Heavenly Blue' (whose flowers close by noon), cardinal climber (*Ipomoea quamoclit*) with small red blooms that open in the afternoon, and moon-flower (*I. alba*) with luminescent white flowers that open at dusk.

Try These
Other *I. tricolor* hybrids are 'Flying Saucers' (to 15 feet tall) with 5-inch pale blue flowers with darker blue streaks in a pinwheel design. 'Milky Way' (to 15 feet) has white flowers with carmine-rose down the centers of petals; it blooms until midday. 'Pearly Gates' (to 10 feet) has pure white 5-inch blooms. *I. nil* varieties 'Blue Picotee' (to 9 feet) bears 5-inch, white-edged dark blue flowers with a purple star, and 'Chocolate' (to 9 feet) has 5-inch, white-throated, rose to light brown blooms. *I. purpurea* varieties 'Grandpa Ott's' (to 15 feet), an heirloom with 2½ inch, red-throated, deep purple flowers readily self-sows and 'Star of Yelta' (8 to 10 feet), which has 2½-inch purple blooms with central bright pink areas and white dots; it remains open most of the day.

Moss Phlox

Phlox subulata

Botanical Pronunciation
FLOKS sub-yew-LAY-tah

Other Name
Moss pink

Bloom Period and Seasonal Colors
Spring, purple, pink, white; evergreen foliage

Mature Height × Spread
3 to 6 in. × 12 to 24 in.

When I was little, my father created a free-form rock garden on our front lawn (a corner property)—unheard of in the 1960s. The plant selections were fewer then, but the plants that left lasting impressions on me were the moss phlox. (He called it mountain pinks.) We had the three colors—purple, white, and pink—each in its special nook. He planted purple in a hole in the huge top stone so it carpeted the top of the garden and softened the edges. Pink grew in several places between rocks, and white transitioned the garden down into the green carpet of lawn. After blooming, the evergreen perennial creeper added interest and did not hint of its glorious springtime color. It is rabbit resistant.

When, Where, and How to Plant
Container-grown moss phlox is available at garden centers, nurseries, and home-improvement stores, with more varieties from online and mail-order sources. It grow best in average, well-drained soil in full sun. Plant it in the spring one week before the last frost date. Dig a hole the same size as its container. Pour a cup of transplant solution in the hole and then plant so it is growing at the same level it was in the pot. Water with an additional 1 to 2 cups of transplant solution. Allow 8 to 12 inches between plants.

Growing Tips
Keep the soil lightly moist until the plant is established. It is fairly drought tolerant, but water when the top 3 inches of soil is dry. Foliar feed with a solution of fish emulsion or kelp once a month after flowering.

Regional Advice and Care
If you want a denser plant, cut the stems halfway back after they have flowered. This can also encourage a light rebloom. Plants are long-lived. If the center dies out, dig up the entire plant and divide it, discarding the dead part, and replant the divisions. Water early in the day at ground level to prevent powdery mildew.

Companion Planting and Design
Moss phlox grows well in a rock garden or a mixed border. It is impressive planted with airy pasque flower (*Pulsatilla vulgaris*), basket-of-gold (*Aurinia saxatilis*), and species tulips, such as *Tulipa batalini* or *T. bakeri*. Let it grow between stones or railroad ties in a vertical wall—it has a magical effect and softens the look.

Try These
All grow to 6 inches tall. 'Candy Stripe' has white flowers striped pink down the center of each petal. 'Coral Eye' bears pale pink flowers with a dark coral-red eye (center). 'Emerald Blue' ('Emerald Cushion Blue') has deep lavender-blue flowers. 'Emerald Pink' bears vivid pink blooms. 'Laura' bears red-eyed, soft pink blooms. 'McDaniel's Cushion' has vibrant rose-pink flowers. 'Red Wings' produces deep crimson-red flowers with tiny dark red eyes. 'Snowflake' forms a cushion of tiny snowy white flowers.

Periwinkle

Vinca minor 'Bowles'

Botanical Pronunciation VIN-kah MY-nor

Other Name Creeping myrtle

Bloom Period and Seasonal Colors
Lavender-blue in mid-spring; intermittent
rebloom in late summer; evergreen leaves

Mature Height × Spread
3 to 6 in. × indefinite spread

Zones 4 to 8

'Bowles' (or 'Bowles Variety') is one of the larger-flowered varieties of periwinkle. Periwinkle, also called vinca, is one of the "big three" evergreen perennial groundcovers for shade, including ivy (*Hedera helix*) and pachysandra (*Pachysandra terminalis*), but the only one included here as it's the hardiest—thriving in Zone 4—while the others are better for warmer-winter climates. Although there are not as many cultivated periwinkles as ivies, 'Bowles' is my favorite with its five-petaled, 1½-inch, lavender-blue flowers. Its shiny, broadly lance-shaped, deep green leaves grow on thin, wiry stems. Since it's an evergreen, Bowles periwinkle is as attractive in winter as it is in summer. Versatile, it is equally handsome hanging from a deep windowbox as it is a mat-forming groundcover growing at the edge of woodland.

When, Where, and How to Plant
'Bowles' is one of the most popular varieties of periwinkle and is readily found at nurseries, garden centers, and home-improvement stores. As your interest in periwinkles grows, head straight for online and mail-order sources. Although periwinkle tolerates sun (requiring more watering), it grows best in part sun or part shade in rich, moist, well-drained soil. Plant in spring after all danger of frost has passed. You can buy flats of rooted cuttings (good for large areas) or a container-grown plant. Plant at the depth it was originally growing, according to information on page 105. Water well.

Growing Tips
Keep soil lightly moist until plants are well established. Foliar feed once a season.

Regional Advice and Care
Cut back hard in early spring to restrict growth, resulting in a denser plant. Or mow it low after it finishes blooming every few years. Although it roots where the stem touches the ground, it is not considered invasive. Rabbits are not attracted to periwinkle. Very shade tolerant, periwinkle can scorch in too much sun.

Companion Planting and Design
Its trailing, spreading habit makes a fine groundcover, rock garden, border, or container plant. Interplant it with autumn crocus (*Colchicum autumnale*) or daffodils (*Narcissus* spp.) for added interest. For rock garden use, plant it in poor to average, well-drained, gritty soil.

Try These
Unless otherwise noted, all have shiny, deep green leaves and grow up to 6 inches tall. 'Alba' has white flowers. 'Atropurpurea' (also known as 'Purpurea' and 'Rubra') bears dark purplish red flowers. 'Bowles White' pinkish white buds open to white flowers. 'Dart's Blue' bears lovely light blue blooms. 'Double Bowles' has double lavender-blue blooms. 'Golden Bowles' has bright yellow-edged leaves. 'Honeydew' is unique with its chartreuse leaves that contrast with pale blue blossoms; it is outstanding for shade, lighting up even the darkest corner. Illumination® is a patented variety (which means you cannot legally propagate it) with bright golden yellow leaves edged in green with blue flowers. 'Ralph Shugert' has glossy deep green leaves edged in white and bears blue blooms.

Spotted Deadnettle

Lamium maculatum 'White Nancy'

Botanical Pronunciation
LAY-mee-um mak-yew-LAY-tum

Other Name Creeping lamium

Bloom Period and Seasonal Color
White in late spring to early summer;
evergreen foliage

Mature Height × Spread 6 to 8 in. × 2 to 3 ft.

Zones 4 to 8

'White Nancy' is a beautiful perennial groundcover for a shady area. It was discovered as a white-flowering sport of 'Beacon Silver'. Elegant 1- to 2-inch-wide silver leaves have narrow green margins, which show them off well. If the leaves were completely silver, the plant would have the appearance of a silvery carpet; the green edging gives it more definition. In summer, the plant bears spikes of whorled, pure white, two-lipped flowers, each less than ¾-inch long. In general, deadnettles are fast-growing groundcovers, considered invasive by some, because their rhizomes and stolons easily root and spread. 'White Nancy' is more demure, and not an aggressive grower. It is a beautiful woodland plant, eye-catching among evergreens or planted below a canopy of deciduous trees.

When, Where, and How to Plant
'White Nancy' is available at most nurseries, garden centers, and home-improvement stores as are some other cultivars. Many, however, are available only through online and mail-order sources. Plant after the last frost. It prefers moist, well-drained soil and part shade to shade. When buying, check to see if roots are growing through the drainage hole, indicating a rootbound plant. Follow directions on page 105 for planting.

Growing Tips
Keep the soil lightly moist; do not let it dry out. It does not need to be fertilized.

Regional Advice and Care
It is a relatively care-free plant. If it starts growing out of bounds, dig up the unwanted area. You can either replant it elsewhere, divide it and share with friends, or take it to a plant swap. It is slightly susceptible to powdery mildew; use a baking soda spray (see page 175) at the first sign of problems. In hot, humid summers, unsightly bare patches can form ("melting out"). Shear or cut back plant to stimulate new growth.

Companion Planting and Design
Plant 'White Nancy' with low-growing, early-blooming bulbs like species tulips (*Tulipa* spp.), crocus (*Crocus* spp.), and grape hyacinths (*Muscari armeniacum*) in deciduous woodlands. It will not come up until the bulbs have finished blooming and will hide their ripening foliage.

Try These
'Beedham's White' (to 9 × 18 inches) is eye-catching, sporting chartreuse leaves with a white midrib and white flowers. 'Cosmopolitan' (to 6 × 24 inches) has silvery white leaves with narrow green margins and light pink flowers. Golden Anniversary® (to 9 × 18 inches, and patented—you cannot legally propagate) is a showstopper with tricolor leaves of dull green with silvery centers and chartreuse-yellow edges and pinkish lavender blooms. Orchid Frost® (to 8 × 24 inches) is a patented variety with a mounded habit, blue-green edging on silvery green leaves, and vivid orchid-pink flowers. 'Pink Chablis' (to 12 × 18 inches) features green-edged, silvery white leaves and pink blossoms. 'Red Nancy' (to 9 × 24 inches), similar to 'White Nancy', but bears rose-red flowers.

Sweet Autumn Clematis

Clematis terniflora

Botanical Pronunciation
KLEM-ah-tiss ter-nih-FLOOR-ah

Bloom Period and Seasonal Color
Late summer through fall, white

Mature Height × Spread
10 to 20 ft. × 6 to 10 ft.

Zones 4 to 8

Sweet autumn clematis has gone through a number of botanical name changes. Depending on what resource book you use, you can find it listed as *Clematis dioscoreifolia*, *C. maximowicziana*, *C. paniculata* (the name listed in The Royal Horticultural Society Dictionary of Plants, which is my top reference book for plant taxonomy), or *C. terniflora*. This clematis by any name smells delightfully sweet from late summer through fall. Its 1- to 1½-inch flowers nearly cover the mighty vine, which is deceivingly dainty looking. In milder winter areas, it is evergreen. Wonderfully whorled seedpods follow the flowers, then dry and last well into the winter, only displaced by heavy snows. It's a very versatile vine for growing up an arbor, across a fence, or along the ground.

When, Where, and How to Plant

Sweet autumn clematis is available from spring through early fall in nurseries, garden centers and home-improvement stores as well as from online and mail-order sources. In fall, the delicate flowers and sweet aroma entice you to purchase the plant, although it is better to plant it in spring. Like other clematis, it grows best with its roots shaded and the leaves in full sun, but it will tolerate part shade. It prefers slightly alkaline, rich, moist, well-drained soil. Install a support near the planting site. Dig a hole at least twice the depth and width of the container. Put the soil on a tarp or wheelbarrow and mix in equal amounts of organic matter (compost, well-rotted manure, leaf mold, humus). Adjust the pH so it is 7.0 (add lime if the pH is lower, bone meal if it is higher). Fill the hole halfway with the amended soil. Water it with 2 cups of transplant solution. Place the plant so that its crown is 2 to 3 inches below soil level. Fill in around the plant with the amended soil. Firm the soil around the plant. Water with a quart of transplant solution. Add 3 to 4 inches of organic mulch around the plant; be sure to keep it an inch away from the stems. If mulch touches the stems, there is likelihood of rot, disease, or insects getting into the plant.

Growing Tips

Do not let the soil dry out. Foliar feed in late June or early July with a solution of kelp or fish emulsion (mixed according to package directions).

Regional Advice and Care

Loosely tie the stems to the support. You can prune right after it finishes blooming or in spring when the buds swell.

Companion Planting and Design

Sweet autumn clematis is a great cover for a fence, trellis, or arbor, or use it as a groundcover. Plant some fall-blooming bulbs, such as autumn crocus (*Colchicum autumnale*) or saffron crocus (*Crocus sativus*) near its base. Enjoy the attractive swirling seedpods that last into winter.

Try These

There are no cultivars.

Sweet Potato Vine

Ipomoea batatas

Botanical Pronunciation
ip-uh-MEE-uh buh-TAH-tuss

Other Name Ornamental sweet potato

Bloom Period and Seasonal Colors
Summer, green, chartreuse, dark purple foliage

Mature Height × Spread 6 to 12 in. × 8 to 10 ft.

Zones Annual

Sweet potato vine has soared in popularity in the past decade. For northern gardeners, it is part of the "banana-canna craze"—growing a tropical-looking garden in a temperate region. Most people grow it for its large, exotic, colorful leaves, not necessarily realizing what a great groundcover it is (a tender perennial generally grown as an annual). Once, I put out four plants of 'Blackie' in late June, and by early August, they had completely covered a 10-foot by 10-foot area, nearly smothering the existing plants. I had to prune around the roses, dwarf conifers, and coleus in the same bed. When planting there in early September, I discovered the bonus—edible sweet potatoes. Even here, especially with our hot summers, many varieties will produce edible tubers.

When, Where, and How to Plant

Unlike regular sweet potatoes grown from slips, ornamental varieties are easily grown from potted plants. Some cultivars are found at nurseries and garden centers, while others are only available through online and mail-order sources. Sweet potato vine needs full sun and rich, loose, well-drained soil. Amend the area where it will grow—not just the planting hole—with plenty of organic matter. Unpot the plant and unwind the roots (they grow so quickly they easily become rootbound). Dig a hole deep enough for the roots; add 1 cup of transplant solution. Make a cone of soil for the plant, with the roots splaying down so it is growing at the same level it was it the pot. Fill in with soil and gently firm it. Water it with 2 cups of transplant solution. Allow at least 15 to 24 inches between plants.

Growing Tips

Once they are established, which takes less than a week, the plants are fairly drought tolerant. No fertilization is necessary.

Regional Advice and Care

If you have other plants growing in the same bed, you will want to direct the vine (and prune it if necessary) to grow where you want it. To harvest tubers, gently dig them when the vines die back. Cure for two weeks in a warm humid space. Store above 55 degrees Fahrenheit.

Companion Planting and Design

Sweet potato vine is an excellent accent plant in the garden or tumbling out of a container. It's fast-growing as a skirt plant around a tree or shrub. Let it tumble over the edge of a wall or grow it at the edge of a cottage garden.

Try These

'Blackie' ('Blacky') has deeply lobed, 8- to 10-inch, purplish black leaves and large white edible tubers. 'Margarita' ('Marguerite', 'Sulphur') has 5- to 8-inch, deeply lobed, chartreuse leaves. 'Pink Frost' ('Tricolor') has irregularly triangular, 2- to 5-inch, creamy white, pink, and green variegated leaves. 'Sweet Caroline Light Green' is similar to 'Margarita' but leaves are very lightly edged purple.

Virginia Creeper

Parthenocissus quinquefolia

Botanical Pronunciation
par-theh-no-SISS-us kwin-kwih-FOE-lee-uh

Other Name
Woodbine

Bloom Period and Seasonal Colors
Late spring to early summer, greenish white; fall, scarlet foliage

Mature Height × Spread
30 to 50 ft. × 5 to 10 ft.

Virginia creeper is a deciduous, perennial vine that is handsome in summer but really glows in autumn when its leaves turn scarlet. Not a dense vine used to cover a fence or groundcover, its dainty qualities are evident when grown on a wall because you appreciate the vine as well as the bare space. I love its look in winter—it is like seeing the skeleton of the plant, and it's the best time to see how it attaches itself with disk-like suction cups at the ends of the tendrils. It is easily differentiated from its cousin, Boston ivy (*Parthenocissus tricuspidata*), as it is composed of five leaflets, while Boston ivy has three. Birds are attracted to the berries in summer and early fall.

When, Where, and How to Plant

Virginia creeper is readily available at nurseries, garden centers, and home-improvement stores. The recommended varieties can be found through online and mail-order sources. When choosing a plant, look for the sturdiest and most spreading one. Virginia creeper is not fussy, but it will develop more vigorously in moist, fertile, well-drained soil. It will grow in sun or shade but produces the most brilliant fall foliage color when it is growing in full sun. Plant Virginia creeper within 3 to 6 inches of its support. You may need to guide it initially by loosely tying it with a string or with a nail on one side of the stem bent across it, until the suckers have a chance to take hold. After that, it is self-supporting. Allow 6 to 12 inches between plants. Water well with transplant solution. (See page 105 for more on planting.)

Growing Tips

Keep the plant lightly moist until the suckers attach and it's growing well. Fertilization is not necessary, but a 3-inch mulch of compost in the winter will keep the plant nourished.

Regional Advice and Care

Although there are a number of pests and diseases that Virginia creeper can develop, they are uncommon. If you see any evidence of a problem, check with your local Cooperative Extension Service. Prune, if necessary, to keep within bounds.

Companion Planting and Design

Virginia creeper is most handsome growing up a light-colored wall where it can be appreciated year-round. Train it up a tree—evergreen or deciduous—for a natural look. It is especially handsome growing on a crabapple (*Malus* spp.) with the fruits and leaves showing off their fall beauty.

Try These

Red Wall® ('Troki', to 30 feet tall) is a patented variety (illegal to propagate) with bronze-hued spring leaves that mature to dark green and finally turn fire-engine red in autumn. Star Showers® ('Monham', to 35 feet tall) is a patented variety with variegated green leaves that look like white paint is splattered on them. *P. quinquefolia* var. *engelmannii* has smaller leaves than the species that turn bronze-red in autumn.

Wintercreeper

Euonymus fortunei

Botanical Pronunciation
yew-ON-ih-mus for-TOON-ee-eye

Other Name Wintercreeper euonymus

Bloom Period and Seasonal Colors
Evergreen foliage

Mature Height × Spread
1 to 3 ft. × 3 to 5 ft.

Zones 5 to 8

Wintercreeper is an attractive, evergreen vine with shiny green leaves. The leaves cover the spreading stems, almost hiding them completely. Wintercreeper has rootlike holdfasts that enable it to climb on any rough surface; however, it should not be grown on a shingled or brick house as the holdfasts can creep between shingles, loosening them or growing the plant through the wall. The holdfasts can penetrate older mortar, making the bricks unstable. Wintercreeper has two forms—juvenile and mature. As a juvenile, the slender clinging stems have small leaves. Mature branches are bushy in form, have larger leaves, and bear inconspicuous flowers and bright red fruit. If you root a cutting from a mature branch, you will get a shrublike plant.

When, Where, and How to Plant
Wintercreeper is readily available at nurseries, garden centers, and home-improvement stores. Shop mail-order and online sources for some of the recommended varieties. Wintercreeper is not fussy about soil, growing equally well in clay or sandy soil, in full sun to part shade. When purchasing, look carefully to be sure you are getting the vine, as some are sold as mature plants that will be bushy while others are obviously juvenile and vinelike. Allow 1 to 2 feet between plants. Water it well with transplant solution. Mulch with 3 to 4 inches of organic matter, keeping it at least an inch from the stem.

Growing Tips
Once it is established, wintercreeper is fairly drought tolerant, but keep soil lightly moist until then. Fertilizer is not necessary.

Regional Advice and Care
Mulch is essential only until the plant is established. At that time, its dense leaf cover keeps weeds from germinating. It can sunburn in winter from reflected snow and/or ice glare. Cover it lightly with burlap to protect it, removing the burlap in early spring. To maintain an even look, prune out bushy mature branches as soon as they appear. Prune in spring to direct its growth or to keep it within bounds.

Companion Planting and Design
Wintercreeper is ideal for erosion control or growing on a slope as it roots easily along its stem as long as the soil is moist and well drained. It is lovely in a woodland garden. Intersperse spring-blooming bulbs like daffodils (*Narcissus* spp.) when planting wintercreeper for added color.

Try These
'Coloratus' (purple wintercreeper euonymus, to 9 × 36 inches) has dark green leaves that turn dark purple in fall and winter. 'Gracilis' (silver-edge euonymus, to 8 × 36 inches) produces green-and-cream variegated leaves that turn pink as the temperatures drop; it is slow growing. 'Kewensis' (to 3 × 36 inches) has small, $\frac{5}{8}$-inch-long dark green leaves. 'Silver Queen' (to 6 inches × 10 feet) is a favorite with shiny leaves edged in white. 'Variegatus' (to 9 × 48 inches) bears 1- to 2-inch-long, white-variegated green leaves.

HERBS

FOR THE PRAIRIE & PLAINS STATES

B y definition, an herb is a useful plant. Today, herbs are generally divided into three categories: medicinal, culinary, and dye plants. Culinary herbs are the focus of this section. Some have uses that extend beyond the kitchen, which will be noted and discussed. Unless noted in the individual entry, pest and diseases are not problems with most herbs. An added bonus—deer generally don't like herbs.

Growing Herbs

Herbs include annuals, perennials (although our climate dictates that we grow some as annuals or overwinter indoors), and biennials. Most are available as young plants, whether from a nursery, garden center, home-improvement store, online, or mail-order nursery. Some of the most common herbs, such as rosemary, sage, thyme, and oregano, are native to the Mediterranean region and need to be grown differently than parsley, basil, anise hyssop, or chives. What they all have in common is that they like well-drained soil.

Herbs make great container plants.

Mediterranean Herbs

These herbs grow best in full sun and very well-drained, poor to sandy soil. They are well suited for growing in containers. In the garden, consider grouping them together so they can benefit from the soil they need. Mark out the planting area. Dig out the soil—12 inches deep and 6 inches wider than the planting area. Mix the soil with about a gallon each of builder's sand and compost to give it a rougher, more friable texture. Replace the amended soil and then begin planting—one herb at a time.

For a grouping, mix a gallon of transplant solution in a bucket. Place the container-grown herb in

the solution for a minute. Remove the plant from its pot. If it is rootbound, loosen the roots so they hang free. If the plant is in a cell pack, tear off the bottom ½ inch of roots and *gently* loosen the side roots. Dig a hole the size of the plant, pour in a cup of transplant solution, place the plant in the hole, fill in with soil, firm gently, and water with an additional cup of transplant solution.

Include herbs in a flower garden. Here, curly-leafed parsley adds texture with dahlias and celosia.

Add a ½-inch layer of inorganic mulch (sand, gravel, grit, small stones) to within an inch of the stem, and surround the plant extending as far as its mature spread will be. If you are planting individually, follow the same directions, making the hole about 3 inches wider than the existing pot. Water regularly until the plant is established, then once or twice a week as needed (when the top inch of soil is dry).

All Other Herbs

Other herbs also grow best in full sun. Unlike Mediterranean herbs, they generally prefer somewhat fertile, well-drained soil. If you are planting an herb bed, you can do the same thing—dig out the soil for the bed. For these herbs, however, mix in some compost or leaf mold and add a few handfuls of peat moss (to lower the pH of alkaline soil). Mix well, put the soil back in the planting area, and proceed as you would for Mediterranean herbs; do the same for individual plants. However, when it comes to mulching, use organic mulch such as compost, finely shredded bark, pine straw (needles), or small wood chips. Whatever mulch you choose, you want a fine mulch that water can percolate through—not 2-inch wood chips. I prefer dark-colored mulch, but that is an individual choice.

Using Herbs

Even if you don't cook, include herbs in your garden since they are beautiful plants and attract pollinators that other flowers (and veggies) need. I always grow two large containers of mixed herbs—one for Mediterranean herbs and one for others—outside the kitchen door. For me, convenience is the key to edibles from the garden. I can open the kitchen door, snip some basil, sage, rosemary, and chives—even if it is pouring rain. There are more herbs interspersed throughout my garden as well. Experiment; you'll enjoy them too.

Anise Hyssop

Agastache foeniculum

Botanical Pronunciation
ag-ah-STAK-ee foe-NIK-yew-lum

Bloom Period and Seasonal Colors
Late spring to early fall, lavender to purple

Mature Height × Spread
24 to 48 in. × 18 to 24 in.

Zones 4 to 8

Anise hyssop is a handsome perennial that forms stiff, well-branched stalks. In summer when the flower spikes appear, you'll hear softly buzzing bees and whirring hummingbirds and see a variety of butterflies and even sphinx moths in early evening—all seeking the sweet nectar. If you like licorice, anise hyssop is for you. Both the heart-shaped leaves and tiny light purple florets of this native are edible. The leaves are best made into a tasty tea. Pick the florets off the flower spikes; small as they are, they pack a lot of flavor, reminding me of Good 'n' Plenty candies from childhood Saturday movie matinees. The florets are excellent in shortbread and ice cream. Mix them with sugar for use in baking during the off-season.

When, Where, and How to Plant
Potted plants are readily available in spring. Although a mass planting is breathtaking, one or two plants are enough for my needs. Anise hyssop prefers ordinary garden soil and full sun, but grows in part sun. Plant after all danger of frost has passed. Allow 2 feet between plants. Water well. (See page 79 for more planting information.)

Growing Tips
Until the plant is established, keep soil lightly moist. Then water deeply twice a week. Any sign of drooping leaves is a call for water. You can foliar feed in mid-June, but that is probably unnecessary unless your soil is poor.

Regional Advice and Care
If growing in an exposed area, stake to prevent stems from breaking in the wind. Harvest the leaves anytime; younger ones have a fresher licorice flavor. Use fresh, or dry in a dark, warm, well-aired place for several days. When dry, the leaves will crumble easily in your hand. Store in airtight containers for making tea throughout the year. Pluck individual florets off the flower spike; they make delicious custard. Or mix them in with vanilla ice cream for a lovely sweet, light licorice end to the meal. Cut spent flower spikes back to the next-lowest branching stem. New spikes will grow. After a hard frost, cut down completely. A prolific self-sower, it emerges in late spring. Wait to weed until you're sure plants are growing; they transplant or pull out easily. Anise hyssop is pest and disease free. Butterflies, bees, and other pollinators flock to the fragrant blooms.

Companion Planting and Design
Anise hyssop is companionable with sunflower's complementary color. It is eye-catching surrounded with 'Lemon Gem' marigolds in a large container. Include it in an herb, cutting, butterfly, or wildflower garden or perennial border. Plant among vegetables as a pollinator attractant.

Try These
'Alabaster' (24 to 36 inches tall) has white flowers with a musky overtone. 'Golden Jubilee' (12 to 36 inches), with striking chartreuse foliage bears spikes of powder blue flowers. Other anise hyssops are hybrids of other species and have similar benefits, but are not necessarily edible.

Basil

Ocimum basilicum

Botanical Pronunciation
OH-sih-mum bah-SIL-ih-kum

Other Name
Sweet basil

Bloom Period and Seasonal Colors
Summer to frost, white, pink, purple

Mature Height × Spread
8 to 24 in. × 8 to 30 in.

Named an Herb of the Year, basil, an annual, has been used in Asian and European cuisine since ancient times and was even declared the royal herb of France in the 1700s. Its popularity is growing—especially in America—as evidenced by new varieties introduced each year. Both leaves and flowers are edible. There are numerous varieties of basil, each with a distinctive flavor. Some like 'Thai' indicate which cuisine favors its use. Traditionally, leaves are used in pesto (ground with pine nuts, Parmesan cheese, and olive oil). The flowers reflect the flavor of the leaves but in a lighter, sweeter form. Make cream-colored flower pesto. Infuse white wine vinegar with flowers or leaves to make basil vinegar; strain after two weeks.

When, Where, and How to Plant
Potted plants of many basil varieties are available in spring locally and through online and mail-order sources. Some varieties are only available as seed, but look for plants at a farmers' market, plant swap, or botanical garden plant sale. Sow seed indoors in peat pots in lightly moistened seed-starting mix eight weeks before the last frost date. Keep lightly moist. (See page 79 for more planting information.) Grow on a south-facing windowsill or under lights. Plant outdoors at the same time as tomatoes, spacing plants 1 to 2 feet apart depending on variety. Water well.

Growing Tips
Until basil is established, keep the soil lightly moist; then keep it well watered. Water monthly with compost tea.

Regional Advice and Care
Basil thrives in hot weather. Remove the flower stalks to keep the leaf flavor dynamic. Discard or use the florets in cooking and as beautiful, flavorful garnishes.

Companion Planting and Design
Basil pairs well with tomatoes; they are mutually beneficial for keeping pests away. In a container, basil is beautiful with trailing petunias (*Petunia* hybrids) and vervain (*Verbena bonariensis*).

Try These
'Bolloso Napoletano' (to 36 inches tall), an heirloom Italian basil, has huge (up to 6 inch), crinkled leaves. 'Dark Opal' (to 30 inch) has striking, flavorful, dark purple leaves. 'Genovese' (to 24 inches), with its good-sized leaves, is the best for pesto and Caprese salad. Eye-catching, flavorful 'Magical Michael' (to 15 inches, pictured above) has small leaves and beautiful pyramidal clusters of flowers with purple calyxes and white corollas. 'Spicy Globe' ('Greek Dwarf', to 12 inches), with a perfectly rounded shape and ¼-inch leaves is ideal for containers or for edging a formal garden. Thai 'Siam Queen' (to 24 inches) has an anise-basil aroma and taste. Must-have 'Pesto Perpetuo' (*Ocimum × citriodorum* 'Pesto Perpetuo', to 30 inches) is a tasty showstopper with a columnar habit and creamy white-edged, lime-green leaves that's great in containers (and it doesn't flower). Holy basil (*Ocimum sanctum* 'Tulsi', to 18 inches) has a spicy scent of cinnamon, clove, and lemon; it's traditionally used in ceremonies and teas.

Bronze Fennel

Foeniculum vulgare 'Purpureum'

Botanical Pronunciation
fuh-NICK-yew-lum vul-GAIR-ee

Bloom Period and Seasonal Colors
Midsummer to frost, yellow

Mature Height and Spread
2 to 4 ft. × 18 to 30 in.

Zones 4 to 8

Bronze fennel is a must-have plant. The first sign of the leaves reminds me of a 2- to 6-inch-long, light brunette ponytail. As this handsome perennial grows, the ponytails relax, becoming fine-leafed, feathery, purplish bronze leaves. The crowning glory is airy, flat, 4-inch flowerheads composed of delicately spaced yellow florets, followed by fragrant, rice-sized seeds. Bronze fennel is entirely edible—leaves, stems, flowers, and seeds—with a light anise flavor. Cut the leaves and stems for cooking to enjoy this visual feast over and over. Steam or stir-fry the stems as a vegetable. Leaves and florets add pizzazz to salads, pork, vegetables, cheese, and soups. Fennel seeds are a digestive aid, yummy in cookies, stews, and cakes. Black swallowtail butterfly larvae feed on the plant.

When, Where, and How to Plant
Bronze fennel is readily available as plants, but it is easy—and economical—to grow it from seed. It grows best in average, moist, but well-drained soil in full sun. Sow the seed in place in spring after the last frost date. Cover with ¼ inch of soil and water lightly.

Growing Tips
Keep the soil lightly moist until the plant is established. Once it is up and growing well, thin plants to allow 18 to 24 inches between plants (center to center). Use the thinnings (cut off the roots) in a mixed greens salad with the juice of a freshly squeezed orange as the only dressing. Keep the plant well watered with regular deep watering. Foliar feed with a solution of kelp or fish emulsion

(mixed according to package directions) in mid- to late June.

Regional Advice and Care
Bronze fennel is one of the host plants for the black-and-yellow striped caterpillars of black swallowtail butterflies, so grow enough for them to eat and you to enjoy. The caterpillars will feast voraciously for a short time, but the plant bounces back with new growth. Bronze fennel freely self-sows unless you harvest all the seeds. After the first year, you will find it cropping up around the garden. I often let it grow, just to enjoy the ponytails. The plant is easy to identify and weed out if necessary. Cut flowers for fragrant indoor arrangements.

Companion Planting and Design
Those who subscribe to the concept of companion planting (some plants are beneficial to others, while different plants can retard growth) advise keeping fennel *away* from tomatoes, dill, caraway, bush beans, kohlrabi, and coriander. Bronze fennel is beautiful in a container or in the garden with parsley. It makes an airy companion to bold Prairie Fire switchgrass (*Panicum virgatum* 'Prairie Fire') and Gateway Joe-Pye weed (*Eutrochium maculatum* 'Gateway').

Try These
'Smokey' (to 5 feet) has slightly taller, coppery bronze fronds. Like 'Purpureum', the leaves and seeds make a delicious tea, especially soothing after a big meal.

Chives

Allium schoenoprasum

Botanical Pronunciation
AL-ee-um skoy-no-PRAY-sum

Bloom Period and Seasonal Colors
Late spring to early summer, lilac-purple

Mature Height × Spread
12 to 30 in. × 12 to 18 in.

Zones 4 to 8

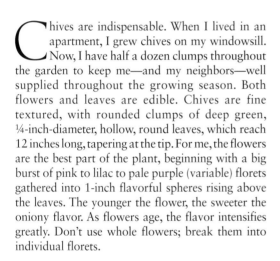

Chives are indispensable. When I lived in an apartment, I grew chives on my windowsill. Now, I have half a dozen clumps throughout the garden to keep me—and my neighbors—well supplied throughout the growing season. Both flowers and leaves are edible. Chives are fine textured, with rounded clumps of deep green, ¼-inch-diameter, hollow, round leaves, which reach 12 inches long, tapering at the tip. For me, the flowers are the best part of the plant, beginning with a big burst of pink to lilac to pale purple (variable) florets gathered into 1-inch flavorful spheres rising above the leaves. The younger the flower, the sweeter the oniony flavor. As flowers age, the flavor intensifies greatly. Don't use whole flowers; break them into individual florets.

When, Where, and How to Plant
Although you can readily buy chive plants or seeds, it is easier to get a piece of someone else's plant. No doubt, you have seen chives growing in a friend or neighbor's garden. Most people are willing to share. Follow your friend's instructions for dividing the plant—everyone has his or her own idiosyncrasies. Immediately put your portion in a pot half-filled with lightly moistened potting soil. Take it home and plant it right away, or put in a shady spot, keep it moist, and plant it within several days. Chives grow best in average to fertile, well-drained soil in full to part sun. Dig a hole the size of the root mass, fill it with transplant solution, and let it drain. Place the plant at the same soil level it was before, filling in with soil if necessary. Water with a cup of transplant solution.

Growing Tips
Keep the soil lightly moist until it is established. Chives need regular watering. No fertilizer needed.

Regional Advice and Care
Keep picking the flowers, and they will keep producing. Shear the plant back to stimulate new growth if necessary. Pick young flowers for cooking, and deadhead older ones; they pack the gustatory wallop of an entire bulb of garlic. In fall, dig up the plant (or divide it into smaller pieces); pot it up, and bring it in to a sunny windowsill and you can enjoy fresh chives all winter.

Companion Planting and Design
My cat Sebastian had his own garden in a whiskey barrel, where he spent many hours, including chives, dianthus (*Dianthus* spp.), sage (*Salvia officinalis*), and catmint (*Nepeta* × *fassenii*).

Try These
'Fine Leaf' (to 20 inches) is prized by chefs and cooks for its slender leaves that don't get tough with age as other chives do. Its lilac-pink blossoms are sweet like a Vidalia onion. 'Forescate' (to 30 inches) is larger than regular chives, with 24-inch-long leaves. Large (to 3 inches across), deep purplish pink blossoms rise up to 6 inches above the foliage.

Dill

Anethum graveolens

Botanical Pronunciation
ah-NEE-thum grav-ee-OH-lenz

Other Name
Dill weed

Bloom Period and Seasonal Colors
Midsummer to frost, deep yellow

Mature Height × Spread
3 to 5 ft. × 3 to 4 ft.

In the garden, dill can be confused with fennel. Both have blue-green stems and threadlike, ferny leaves, but dill (an annual) has domed flower umbels (to 8 inches across) while (perennial) fennel umbels are flat and smaller. The aroma of dill is tangy, while fennel is distinctively anisey. Dill leaves, flowers, and seeds are edible. Try fresh leaves in bread, vinegar, and with chicken or fish. Fresh and dried flowers are eye-catching in arrangements. Pick individual dill florets to use in salads, deviled eggs, flavorful cream cheese dip, and more. For more than 3,000 years, dill seeds have been used as a digestive aid; in addition, they are a natural breath freshener. The seeds are used in pickling cucumbers. Plants attract black swallowtail butterfly larvae.

When, Where, and How to Plant
Dill needs full sun and prefers humus-rich, moist, well-drained, slightly acidic soil. It is best grown from seed. After the last frost date, sow seeds outside ¼-inch deep and thin to 10 inches apart. (See page 79 for more on planting.) Rather than planting in rows, I incorporate dill into my landscape. Keep the soil lightly moist until the plants are up and growing. If you plan to do a lot of pickling, consecutive sowings every three weeks will provide a continuous supply of dill seeds.

Growing Tips
Keep the plants well watered. Feed monthly with compost tea.

Regional Advice and Care
Cut leaves as needed for the kitchen. For flower arrangements, cut the flower stem just as the flower is opening—before it fully opens. For culinary use, pick the flowerheads when fully open. For dried arrangements, allow flowers to dry on the plant and then cut. Collect dry seed for pickling by putting a bag around the flowerhead and shaking it so the seeds fall in the bag. Store seeds in a waterproof container in a cool, dry, dark place. In the caterpillar stage, black swallowtail butterflies feast on dill leaves; let them be. After feeding time, the plant will grow back. Dill readily self-sows, so it will come back year after year.

Companion Planting and Design
Dill is delightful paired with the airy purple flowers of tall vervain (*Verbena bonariensis*) and it makes a handsome backdrop for any of the many brightly colored coleus (*Plectranthus scutellarioides*). It is pretty with pink flowers like purple coneflower (*Echinacea purpurea*) and garden phlox (*Phlox paniculata*). Include it in a butterfly garden.

Try These
'Dukat' (to 5 feet tall), harkening from Denmark, bears an abundance of blue-green, sweetly flavored leaves that last longer than other dills when cut. Slow to bolt, it's a late bloomer that's equally delicious fresh or used for pickling. All-American Selections winner 'Fernleaf' (to 18 inches) is well suited for containers or the front of the garden. Although small, it has all the flavor and fragrance of its larger brethren.

Greek Oregano

Origanum vulgare hirtum

Botanical Pronunciation
uh-RIG-uh-num vul-GAIR-ee HUR-tum

Other Name Oregano

Bloom Period and Seasonal Colors
Summer, white

Mature Height × Spread
12 to 24 in. × 8 to 12 in.

Zones 4 to 8

Greek oregano is the oregano of pizzas and Mediterranean cooking—an aromatic and flavorful herb. There is much confusion when it comes to oregano; some call it marjoram, and vice-versa. The botanical names are a web of disagreement as well. Generally, the best way to guarantee the plant is Greek oregano is to taste it, but it may have been chemically sprayed. Instead, let your nose guide you. Break and rub the leaf, and if the aromatic culinary scent wafts to your nose, you have the right plant. Many named varieties have little flavor, but if looks are what you are after, that is fine. Greek oregano is a compact plant with slightly hairy, green leaves and white flowers, both of which are edible.

When, Where, and How to Plant
Caveat emptor—buyer beware. Read the label carefully; much of the oregano sold is *Origanum vulgare*, which has little or no flavor. You can find plants at specialty nurseries, herb farms, as well as online and mail-order sources. Greek oregano needs average, well-drained soil and full sun. Plant after all danger of frost has passed, following the directions for Mediterranean herbs on page 78. Allow 18 inches between plants (center to center), or plant closer for a matlike effect. It makes a good container plant.

Growing Tips
Water when the top inch of soil is dry. Feeding is not required.

Regional Advice and Care
Cut whole stems for flower arrangements and drying. Cut leaves as needed for culinary use. For maximum harvest, cut the entire plant to 3 inches above the crown before it blooms. Cut the flower stalks and pull off individual florets for cooking. Mulch with pine boughs in early winter to improve its survival rate.

Companion Planting and Design
With its spreading habit, Greek oregano is an excellent plant for patio planting—in the French style—between bricks, pavers, or flagstones. Do *not* plant it between steppingstones. I did that one year and had to leap over its flower stalks—dangerous in wet weather. In the garden, create a low-growing contrast of textures, leaf colors, and long season of bloom by growing it with maiden pinks (*Dianthus deltoides*), sea thrift (*Armeria maritima*), and Silver Posie thyme (*Thymus vulgaris* 'Silver Posie'). I plant Greek oregano in a lower side pocket of a large strawberry pot near my kitchen. It trails downward to the ground, hiding the edge of the pot and thus integrating it into the garden. Strawberry pots will crack in our winters, so plant these hardy herbs in early fall or pot them up and overwinter indoors under lights.

Try These
'Variegatum' (also known as 'Gold Tip') has yellow-tipped leaves, which add a glow to the evergreen plant in winter. It has a tendency to spread more than the species. 'Viride' has white flowers with green bracts.

Lavender

Lavandula angustifolia 'Hidcote'

Botanical Pronunciation
lah-VAN-dew-lah an-gus-tih-FOE-lee-ah

Other Name English lavender

Bloom Period and Seasonal Colors
Summer, dark purple; evergreen foliage

Mature Height × Spread
12 to 18 in. × 12 to 18 in.

Zones 5 to 8

'Hidcote' is one of the hardiest lavenders and is low growing, perhaps accounting for its hardiness. The beautiful dark purple florets, with the delightfully clean, floral scent associated with the herb, grow along velvety, silver spikes. The narrow silvery foliage gives it a dainty look, perfect for the front of a border or a container. The fresh flowers are edible and add unique flavor to tea, ice cream, and other desserts. **Caution:** a little lavender goes a long way; too much and the flavor is soapy. Pick spikes of lavender as they open for fresh or dried arrangements. Let them dry and weave them into wands, or pull off the flowers and put them in a sachet bag to freshen sheets and lingerie.

When, Where, and How to Plant

Potted plants are readily available locally or through online and mail-order sources. All lavenders need full sun and average to sandy, well-drained, alkaline soil. In our region, plant the lavender "high" rather than trying to create ideal soil conditions. After the last frost date, form a 3- to 4-inch-high (and 1 inch wider than the pot) mound of soil in the garden. Plant the lavender in the mound, with the plant at the same soil level *atop* the mound as it was in its pot. Water-in with a cup of transplant solution. Mulch with ¾ inch of turkey grit, sand, gravel, or small stones to increase drainage, keep the mound intact, and drain water away from the plant.

Growing Tips

Water regularly until the plant is established. By then, it is quite drought tolerant, as are most silver- or gray-leafed plants. Do not fertilize.

Regional Advice and Care

In late spring, prune back any shoots that froze over the winter; they will look dead. For continuing bloom, cut back spent flower stalks. Cut flower spikes for drying or using in arrangements when the flowers start to open. For culinary use, cut them when the flowers are fully open. Prune the plant if it gets leggy. Do not prune after mid-August, as any new growth will die back in winter.

Companion Planting and Design

Lavender and red or pink old-fashioned roses, such as 'Gertrude Jekyll', make a delightfully fragrant pairing. Grow lavender with other herbs with the same soil requirements, including sage, rosemary, and thyme. It is lovely in a large container surrounded by clove pinks (*Dianthus caryophyllus*).

Try These

'English Munstead' or 'Munstead' (to 12 inches) is equally hardy and compact with spikes of lavender-blue flowers. 'Jean Davis' ('Rosea', to 18 inches) bears pale pink flowers. 'Lady' (to 16 inches), an AAS winner, blooms the first year when grown from seed—an advantage in the coldest areas, where it can be grown as an annual. 'Twickle Purple' (to 24 inches) has highly fragrant flowers arranged in a fanlike cluster on the spikes.

Parsley

Petroselinum crispum

Botanical Pronunciation
pet-ro-seh-LYE-num KRIS-pum

Bloom Period and Seasonal Colors
Second summer, yellow-green

Mature Height × Spread
8 to 36 in. × 8 to 18 in.

Parsley is a beautiful biennial grown for its edible green leaves. For decades, curly parsley garnished millions of dishes in restaurants—from diners to 5-star restaurants. It usually went back to the kitchen untouched. Finally, we discovered that parsley is more than just a pretty embellishment—it's quite tasty. Perhaps we had to get past eating Iceberg lettuce salads, changing to mixed greens with arugula and mesclun mixes (often with Italian parsley) with more complex flavors before we dared eat the garnish. In the garden, it is an exceptional edging plant, lining the pathway to a front or kitchen door. Its magnificent emerald foliage is lovely skirting taller plants. Swallowtail butterfly larvae, which feed on the leaves, can defoliate plants. Just grow enough to share.

When, Where, and How to Plant
Parsley plants and seeds are now readily available locally in spring. Even grocery stores now carry plants year-round. Go to online and mail-order sources for specific varieties. Parsley grows best in rich, moist, well-drained soil in full to part shade but will tolerate average soil. Follow the planting directions on page 79. Soak the seeds overnight in hot water before planting ½-inch deep in peat pots filled with lightly moistened seed-starting medium. Keep it lightly moist. Slowly harden the plants off before planting. Tear the sides off the peat pot to just below the soil level and plant the whole thing. If a peat pot sticks out of the soil, it will wick moisture from the soil. Water-in well with transplant solution.

Growing Tips
Keep plants evenly moist. Feed by watering at ground level with compost tea once a month.

Regional Advice and Care
Cut stems as needed for the kitchen. It is best to harvest early in the day as the dew dries. In the second year, cut off the flowerheads as they appear since they are not edible. This will prolong leaf production. Parsley is beautiful in small flower arrangements.

Companion Planting and Design
Grow tall, late summer-, and fall-blooming plants such as dahlias (*Dahlia* spp.), Japanese anemone (*Anemone hupehensis* var. *japonica*), or snakeroot (*Actea simplex* 'Brunette') through parsley.

Try These
Italian or flat-leaf parsley (*Petroselinum crispum* var. *neapolitanum*), pictured above, may not be as showy in the garden as the better-known curly parsley, but its flavor is exceptional. Don't waste it as a garnish; use it in soups, stews, with potatoes, and with other vegetables. Add it to a greens salad for some extra zing. 'Gigante Italian' is an heirloom with extra large, shiny green leaves and a mellow, slightly sweet taste. For a great show in the garden, as well as exceptional flavor for curly leafed parsley (*P. c.* var. *crispum*), 'Crispum' is the standard with its crinkled leaves. 'Sweet Curly', an introduction from France, has double-curled leaves and a unique nutty sweetness.

Peppermint

Mentha × piperita

Botanical Pronunciation
MEN-thuh pih-pur-EE-tah

Bloom Period and Seasonal Colors
Summer, lilac-pink

Mature Height × Spread
12 to 24 in. × 12 to 24 in.

Zones 5 to 8

Peppermint brings back fond childhood memories. A patch grew in a friend's garden—contained in a small raised bed. My treat was to pick a single leaf. I slowly chewed and savored its distinctive aromatic oils as they infused my mouth and nasal passages. While the grownups had cocktails outdoors, I had iced ginger ale—each cube encased a mint leaf— garnished with a spray of mint flowers. I picked the tiny florets one by one, savoring their lighter, sweeter flavor, while watching bees and butterflies around the plants. Peppermint is recognized for its mood-elevating quality and is used in aromatherapy. A handsome plant growing an average of 2 feet tall with purple-tinged stems, it bears 2-inch, dark green leaves and spikes of lilac-pink florets.

When, Where, and How to Plant

Potted peppermint plants are readily available in spring. It is invasive, so unless you want a minty hillside, contain it. Peppermint thrives in rich moist soil and full sun. In poorer, drier soil with less sun, it is less invasive. If you want mint to spread, plant it as you would any other herb, allowing 2 feet between plants. Whichever method you choose, water the plant well. To control it in the garden, grow peppermint in an 8- to 10-inch pot. Cover the drainage hole with fine screening. Add an inch of builder's sand and plant the mint in potting mix. Dig a hole 1 inch shallower than the pot. Sink it so that the height of the rim is above ground. Or, plant it within a 12-inch-deep surrounding barrier. The easiest deterrent is to grow it in a decorative pot placed on a deck or patio—not on soil, as roots will grow through.

Growing Tips

When the top inch of soil is dry, give the plant a deep drink of water. Fertilization is unnecessary.

Regional Advice and Care

When mint gets gangly, mow it down. It will return even more lush and healthy. Pick the tender upper leaves for cooking (essential in mint juleps). A flavorful complement to lamb, potatoes, peas, and oranges, peppermint makes great jelly too. Use the flowers (pull the florets off the stem) in fruit salads and chocolate desserts. Peppermint tea is a traditional stomach calmative.

Companion Planting and Design

It is believed that peppermint improves the growth of tomatoes and cabbage. It is striking planted with purple cabbage or red lettuces. Peppermint makes an excellent groundcover in a damp area and is well suited to a rain garden.

Try These

Chocolate mint (*Mentha × piperita* f. *citrate* 'Chocolate', to 24 inches) tastes like the chocolate-mint Girl Scout® cookie and is good in baking, desserts, and garnishes. Lemon mint (*M. × p.* f. *citrate*, to 24 inches), also known as orange mint, has a delightful minty orange fragrance; it's excellent for making tea, garnishing, and in making potpourri.

Rosemary

Rosmarinus officinalis

Botanical Pronunciation
roz-muh-RYE-nus oh-fi-shi-NAH-lis

Bloom Period and Seasonal Colors
Late winter to early spring (indoors), pale blue to white; evergreen foliage

Mature Height × Spread
2 to 6 ft. × 2 to 4 ft.

Zones 6 to 8

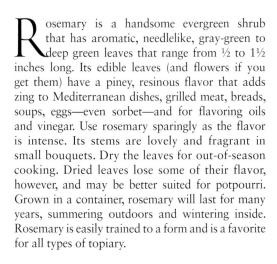

Rosemary is a handsome evergreen shrub that has aromatic, needlelike, gray-green to deep green leaves that range from ½ to 1½ inches long. Its edible leaves (and flowers if you get them) have a piney, resinous flavor that adds zing to Mediterranean dishes, grilled meat, breads, soups, eggs—even sorbet—and for flavoring oils and vinegar. Use rosemary sparingly as the flavor is intense. Its stems are lovely and fragrant in small bouquets. Dry the leaves for out-of-season cooking. Dried leaves lose some of their flavor, however, and may be better suited for potpourri. Grown in a container, rosemary will last for many years, summering outdoors and wintering inside. Rosemary is easily trained to a form and is a favorite for all types of topiary.

When, Where, and How to Plant

Plants are available locally, but for variety, go to online and mail-order sources. Although most rosemary is not hardy in much of our area (lucky Okies!), you can grow it as an annual (follow directions for Mediterranean herbs on page 78) in full to part sun. Harden it off and plant after the last frost date. Rosemary thrives in a container.

Growing Tips

Water regularly. Feed with compost tea every two weeks during the growing season.

Regional Advice and Care

Cut stems as needed for culinary use. Bring potted rosemary inside after the first frost into a cool bright room (at least six hours of sun or use grow lights)

to overwinter. Avoid overwatering—let the soil stay fairly dry. Keep an eye out for any pests (aphids, spider mites, mealybugs). Spray immediately with insecticidal soap, drenching the plant, including the tops and bottoms of leaves. (Do not eat for a week or more after spraying.) Do any hard pruning in early spring, before setting it back outside. Take it back outdoors on the last frost date in spring.

Companion Planting and Design

Planted near carrots, rosemary reportedly deters carrot flies. Include rosemary with other Mediterranean herbs like lavender, sage, and thyme. If you grow herbs in a strawberry pot, plant rosemary at the top. Grow rosemary in a container and you can move it around the garden depending on your whims. Unlike most other garden herbs, we get to enjoy and use it year-round—indoors and out.

Try These

'Arp' (2 to 4 feet tall and wide) is hardy to Zone 6—but may survive in Zone 5 in a sheltered location against a south-facing wall. It has handsome, light gray-green leaves and blue flowers. 'Tuscan Blue' (to 6 × 4 feet), hardy to Zone 7, has a columnar form with short thick, deep green leaves that are extremely flavorful—my favorite for cooking. 'Well-Sweep Golden' (to 18 × 36 inches), a trailing variety hardy to Zone 7, has gold-hued new leaves that mature to light green.

Sage

Salvia officinalis

Botanical Pronunciation
SAL-vee-ah oh-fi-shi-NAH-lis

Other Name Garden sage

Bloom Period and Seasonal Colors
Late spring through early summer, purplish blue;
evergreen foliage

Mature Height × Spread
24 to 30 in. × 24 to 30 in.

Zones 4 to 8

I savor sage more for its flowers than its leaves. Perhaps growing up in a seaside town eating clam chowder overseasoned with dry sage (a gray powder in a tin) prejudiced me. Even when I "discovered" sage's fresh leaves, the flavor was good but a bit strong for my taste. In the flowers, I found a lighter, sweeter taste, and I was hooked. Sage brochettes (4- to 6-inch flower stalks with leaves, dipped in a light tempura batter and quickly fried) are an addiction throughout the flowering season, shared by my friends. Sage is semi-evergreen with gray-green leaves and gorgeous spikes of purplish blue blossoms. It is a natural phytoestrogen (no hot flashes when it's blooming). Sage makes a lovely addition to a perennial garden.

When, Where, and How to Plant
Plants are readily available locally in spring. Look for specialized cultivars through online and mail-order sources. Sage needs full sun and average, well-drained soil. Grow near the south-facing wall of your house to protect the plant and provide a warmer microclimate. Plant sage after the last frost date, following the information for planting Mediterranean herbs on page 78.

Growing Tips
Water when the top inch of soil is dry. Feed with compost tea every two weeks during its flowering season to encourage bloom.

Regional Advice and Care
In spring, cut stems as needed to shape the plant. Dry leaves for later use. Cut flower spikes as needed for culinary use; cut down to the next set of branching stems to stimulate rebloom. Even if you don't eat the blossoms, prune off faded flowers. In Zones 4 and 5, protect by covering the plant loosely with straw after the first hard frost. Remove mulch in early spring and cut back any dead or broken stems.

Companion Planting and Design
Grow sage with other Mediterranean herbs such as rosemary, lavender, and thyme. In the garden, the color contrast of its purplish blue flowers with yellow pot marigolds (*Calendula officinalis*) is brilliant. Its gray-green foliage is versatile in a mixed border, cooling down hot colors, highlighting whites, and separating contrasting plants. It is also effective in an evening garden. Combine it in the garden or in a container with more colorful sages described below.

Try These
'Berggarten' (to 2 feet tall and wide) is a charmer with broader, rounded, bluish green leaves but is less flavorful than the species; hardy to Zone 5. The colored and bicolored sages are generally grown for their beauty, as their flavors are variable; all are hardy to Zone 6 and won't flower. Golden sage ('Aurea', to 24 × 18 inches) has broad, irregular gold edges on light green leaves. Purple sage ('Purpurascens', to 24 × 18 inches) bears wrinkled purplish green leaves. Tricolor sage ('Tricolor', to 18 inches tall and wide) has outstanding variegation of white, purple to pink, and green.

Thyme

Thymus spp.

Botanical Pronunciation
TY-mus

Other Name Garden thyme

Bloom Period and Seasonal Colors
Summer, white, lilac, purple; evergreen foliage

Mature Height × Spread
3 to 12 in. × 6 to 18 in.

Zones 5 to 8

One of the most versatile and varied herbs, with dozens of species and hundreds of cultivated varieties, thyme is another one of my garden must-have plants. It is perennial, often with woody stems (termed a "subshrub"). Garden thyme, highlighted here, has a bushy, cushion-forming habit, growing no more than 12 inches high. Look closely at its small (¼- to ½-inch) aromatic leaves to see the fine hairs. It bears whorls of tiny white to deep purple florets, depending on the variety. Many gardeners use thyme as an insect repellant; planted near members of the cabbage family, it deters cabbage moths. Indoors, it is a moth repellant for pantries and clothes closets. Thyme is essential in cooking—both the leaves and flowers are edible.

When, Where, and How to Plant
You can find many varieties of thyme locally. Before buying, break a leaf to determine its scent. Or order from online or mail-order sources. Not all thymes are edible; they are not toxic, they just have an unpleasant taste. Flavor is often a reflection of the scent. Thyme needs full sun and average, well-drained soil. Plant it out after the last frost date, following the directions for Mediterranean herbs on page 78.

Growing Tips
Water when the top ½ inch of soil is dry. Feed with compost tea every six to eight weeks.

Regional Advice and Care
Cut flower spikes as needed. Run your hand along the spike to pull the tiny flowers off. Cut pieces or use whole stems for cooking. The stems are a fragrant addition to a small bouquet. Dry or freeze the leaves for culinary use in winter. In spring, cut back any dead or broken branches.

Companion Planting and Design
Be sure to add thyme to your Mediterranean herb garden or the strawberry pot near the kitchen door. Put it in a lower "pocket" of the pot so it cascades downward. Thyme is a good container plant, making a lovely skirt for a small tree. Creeping thymes are ideal for placing between steppingstones. They can stand up to light foot traffic, which releases their scent. Thyme is a good edging plant for a border or raised bed where it can fall loosely, softening the edges.

Try These
There is confusion between English and French thyme—both *Thymus vulgaris*. English thymes (common seasoning in chowders, soups, and stuffing) have flat leaves, while French thyme (used in French cuisine and essential in a *fines herbes* mix) has leaf edges that curl under. 'Broad-leaf English' (mounding to 12 inches) has mauve flowers. 'Narrow-Leaf French' (to 16 inches) has small mauve blooms. Lemon-scented thyme (*T.* × *citriodorus*) is a rounded shrub with lemon-scented leaves and pale pinkish lavender flowers—also lightly lemony and superb for sorbet. Mother of thyme (wild thyme, *T. serphyllum*) is a beautiful mat-forming species with many cultivars.

ORNAMENTAL GRASSES

FOR THE PRAIRIE & PLAINS STATES

When most people think of the prairies and plains, they envision lots of tall grasses and some flowering plants such as black-eyed Susans, purple coneflowers, goldenrod, and sunflowers. In fact, a few robust native grasses and hundreds of wildflowers dominated the original prairies. The five most resilient and adaptable are big bluestem, Indiangrass, little bluestem, prairie dropseed, and switchgrass. Four of these are included here, as they are well suited to any home garden, while the fifth—Indiangrass—is larger and requires more space than most home gardeners have. Some of the other ornamental grasses I selected are annuals and some are perennials. Ornamental grasses form such a special group that I felt that they deserved their own space in this book.

In the Garden

Ornamental grasses started catching on as garden plants in the mid-1980s. More than anyone, the East Coast design team of Wolfgang Oehme and James Van Sweden

helped popularize them through their designs for public and private gardens as well as through their writing and speaking. The time was right for change in gardening ideas and design. The naturalistic garden became popular, and ornamental grasses were naturally a part of the movement.

There are many reasons to grow ornamental grasses. As a proponent of growing native plants, you need at least one original prairie grass. Ornamental grasses are generally tough plants—drought tolerant, heat resistant, and resilient to harsh winters—three qualities that make any plant stand out as a must-have for my Iowa garden. In addition, most grasses add winter

Ornamental grasses can add just the right touch to a landscape.

About the only maintenance for many ornamental grasses is to cut them back in late winter or early spring.

interest—some are evergreen—providing food and shelter for birds. And they'll even grow where many other plants won't—near black walnut trees (see page 12).

Planting and Care

I can't emphasize how important it is to choose the right site—the *first* time—for your ornamental grasses, especially the larger ones. Once established, you'd be hard-pressed to dig them out without a backhoe (I've tried and failed with zebra grass, porcupine grass, and other *Miscanthus* varieties). Determine its final size—height and spread. It may look like a lot of bare ground between plants when you first set them into the ground, but before you know it, you'll have a beautiful stand of ornamental grasses.

Most ornamental grasses come in pots. Before planting, place the pot in a bucket with several inches of transplant solution (diluted according to package directions). Dig a hole about the size and depth of the pot. Remove the plant from its pot, pour a cup of transplant solution in the hole, loosen the roots gently, and place the grass in the hole so that it's at the same depth it was previously. Gently press the plant down, adding soil around the edges, so there are no air holes. Water with an additional cup of transplant solution. Add several inches of organic mulch around the base of the plant to conserve moisture. Keep lightly watered to prevent the roots from drying out. Once established, grasses generally thrive on the water that Mother Nature provides. There's no need to feed, they do well on their own.

Ornamental grasses are very low maintenance. In early spring, unless otherwise specified in individual plant's "Regional Advice and Care" section, cut down the previous year's growth. For shorter plants (under 3 feet), cut to within 2 inches of the crown. For larger plants, I leave up to 6 inches to act as support for the new growth. Wear gloves and protective goggles as some grasses have sharp edges. Also, unless noted, there are no major pest or disease problems. That's about it!

No matter what size your garden, there is *at least* one ornamental grass for you— small or tall, rounded or upright, green, blue, or variegated. Believe me, you'll get years of enjoyment from these plants. Just sit back and enjoy watching the grasses grow, change color with the seasons, and sway with the breeze.

Big Bluestem

Andropogon gerardii

Botanical Pronunciation
an-dro-PO-gon jer-AR-dee-eye

Other Name Turkeyfoot

Bloom Period and Seasonal Colors
Late summer to early autumn, bronze to purplish red; fall into winter, reddish-bronze leaves

Mature Height × Spread 4 to 10 ft. × 2 to 3 ft.

Zones 4 to 8

How appropriate that the largest and most widespread grass of the North American prairie is the first listed. It formed prairie sod, which made settlers' sod houses. When I first saw it at a reclaimed prairie, I was overwhelmed—literally—as it towered above me. Walking through it, I was awed by the abundance of Nature before humans disturbed the land. I was fortunate to see big bluestem with its distinctive, purplish turkey feet—three-part seedheads—reaching for the sky. After a frost, the lush green leaves were turning into the magnificent reddish bronze with lavender highlights that last well into the winter. In spring, the new leaves are gray to blue-green; they slowly mature to red-tinged green in summer. Big bluestem is truly a four-season beauty.

When, Where, and How to Plant
Although you might find big bluestem locally, online and mail-order sources are the best sources. Big bluestem needs full sun, but it grows in most soils—even clay. Plant in mid- to late spring. See page 93 for planting information. Keep it lightly moist. Although you might expect it to rocket skyward, it takes its time growing an extensive root system that allows it to ward off drought after several years in the garden.

Growing Tips
Water weekly during the first year (when it does not rain) to encourage root growth. Fertilizing is not necessary.

Regional Advice and Care
Depending on your soil and moisture, big bluestem will vary in height. In rich soil with plenty of moisture, it can soar to 10 feet. In poorer soil, with less water, it will grow only 4 to 6 feet tall. In early spring, before new growth appears, cut the entire plant down to within 4 to 6 inches of the ground. Spring is also the ideal time to divide the plant. Dig up a clump, cut it into smaller pieces, and replant it or share with friends and neighbors.

Companion Planting and Design
Although big bluestem is tall, it is not thick with leaves. In fact, I would include it in the group of plants I call veil plants, such as Russian sage (*Perovskia atriplicifolia*) and tall vervain (*Verbena bonariensis*), with which it makes a striking late-summer trio. These plants are tall, but you can see through them. Big bluestem works equally well in the middle of a bed or border or in the back. It enhances the look of other prairie plants such as purple coneflower (*Echinacea purpurea*), prairie coneflower (*Ratibida pinnata*), Maximillian sunflower (*Helianthus maximilliani*), and the myriad asters (*Symphyotrichum* spp.). It is good for erosion control.

Try These
'Pawnee' (to 6 feet × 3 feet) has burgundy leaves in fall and purplish red flowers. 'Red October' (to 6 feet × 3 feet) has burgundy-tipped leaves that turn brilliant scarlet after frost, and red-purple flowers with orange anthers on red-bronze stems.

Blue Fescue

Festuca glauca

Botanical Pronunciation
fess-TOO-kah GLOK-ah

Bloom Period and Seasonal Colors
Late spring to early summer, blue-gray;
evergreen foliage

Mature Height × Spread
8 to 12 in. × 12 to 18 in.

Zones 4 to 8

Blue fescue is one of the most popular ornamental grasses—for good reasons. Relatively small, it can be incorporated in almost any type of garden—a rock garden, bed or border, contemporary garden, and even a formal garden. It makes a good edging plant. Unlike many other grasses, blue fescue has a neat habit and fine leaves. From a distance, it resembles a cushion. The blue appearance is from a thin, gray, glaucous coating on the leaves, which easily rubs off on your fingers. Often after a rough winter, blue fescue is green, but the glaucous coating returns. Its popularity in the garden is expressed by the number of cultivated varieties available (many only online or from mail-order sources), too many to mention here.

When, Where, and How to Plant
Container-grown plants are readily available locally in spring. Plant after all danger of frost has passed. See page 93 for planting information. It prefers average to rich, very well-drained soil. Mulch with pebbles or sand (not organic matter) to increase drainage. If you are daring, grow plants from seeds collected in summer. The resulting plants will have fun differences in color, size, or form.

Growing Tips
If there's no rain, water weekly until it is established. After that, blue fescue rarely needs watering. Do not fertilize.

Regional Advice and Care
Blue fescue is a short-lived perennial—about three years. If you don't like the look of the blue flower spikes, which turn brown as they mature to seed, cut them down. If the plant looks shabby or loses its compact habit, cut it back. In spring, prune to within 3 inches of the crown; it will come back refreshed. If it goes dormant in summer, cut it back to the crown; it will regrow when the weather cools. As the plant ages, the mound dies out in the center. Dig the plant up, cut it into sections, and replant. Increase or share your supply of blue fescue by taking small divisions from established plants in spring. It is relatively pest free.

Companion Planting and Design
With its neutral color, blue fescue works as a buffer between strong- and brightly colored flowers. Use it between two plants whose colors you would not necessarily mix, such as deep purple petunias (*Petunia* hybrids) and bright red zinnias (*Zinnia* hybrids). Blue fescue cools down hot colors, enlivens pastels, and intensifies whites. It's a plant that fits in anywhere.

Try These
'Boulder Blue' (to 12 inches high and wide) is the "bluest of the blues," and the heaviest bloomer, too. 'Elijah's Blue' (to 12 × 9 inches) is one of the palest blue fescue cultivars with a lovely silvery blue tone. 'Sea Urchin' ('Seeigel', to 12 × 18 inches) has a dense tuft of very fine, hairlike, blue-green leaves that sway at the slightest breeze like its underwater namesake.

Feather Reed Grass

Calamagrostis × *acutiflora* 'Stricta'

Botanical Pronunciation
kal-ah-mah-GROS-tiss ah-kew-tih-FLOOR-ah

Bloom Period and Seasonal Colors
Late spring to early summer, purplish brown; fall through winter, orange foliage

Mature Height × Spread 4 to 6 ft. × 20 to 24 in.

Zones 5 to 8

The dense, 2-foot-tall clumps of green grass with ¼- to ½-inch-wide leaves are lovely in spring but not very impressive. In late spring, it makes a remarkable exclamation point in the garden as the flowering stems rise militarily straight 3 to 4 feet above the leaves. In contrast to the foliage, the actual flower plumes are golden, open, and airy. In autumn, leaves turn a breathtaking golden orange and remain vibrant through the winter, adding much-needed bold color to what could be an otherwise dreary landscape. A clumping grass, it is slow to spread, so there is no worry of it taking over the garden. Long-lasting, it can grow for up to twenty-five years. It's effective as a specimen or in a mass planting.

When, Where, and How to Plant
Readily available locally as well as from online and mail-order sources. Plant feather reed grass in spring, after the danger of frost has passed (see page 93 for planting information). It grows best in humus-rich, moist, clayey soil, but it will tolerate almost any type of soil. It thrives in full sun but will grow in part sun, needing some afternoon shade in hot-summer areas.

Growing Tips
Keep the plant well watered until it is established. Fertilization is not necessary.

Regional Advice and Care
Feather reed grass is low maintenance and pest free. Allow the foliage and seedheads to remain for winter interest. Cut them back to within 4 inches of the ground in early spring. It's easy to propagate; if it gets too big or if you just want more plants, dig it up in spring and cut the sections in half or quarters. Replant each piece immediately or pot it up with garden soil and keep lightly moist and in the shade until you are ready to plant it.

Companion Planting and Design
Its stature and straight form make feather reed grass perfect for the back of a bed or border. It is striking enough to have a space of its own (a group of three plants) in the lawn as a specimen planting, much as you would a special tree. It combines with plants that have a looser more relaxed habit such as Joe-Pye weed (*Eutrochium maculatum* 'Gateway'), Fireworks goldenrod (*Solidago* 'Fireworks'), and Shasta daisy (*Leucanthemum* × *superbum*).

Try These
'Avalanche' (to 3 × 2 feet) is basically a variegated-leafed version of 'Karl Foerster' (green leaves with white centers). 'Karl Foerster' (to 3 × 2 feet), with narrow, stiff, rich green leaves that turn tan in winter, grows well in wet soil. Stalks topped with narrow plumes of purplish green flowers rise up to 6 feet in late spring (turn golden as seeds mature and then tan in winter). 'Overdam' (to 1 × 2 feet) has richly variegated green-and-white striped leaves and pinkish green flowers on stalks to 3 feet tall.

Golden Japanese Forest Grass

Hakonechloa macrantha 'Aureola'

Botanical Pronunciation
hah-ko-neh-KLO-ah MAK-rah

Other Name Golden hakone grass

Bloom Period and Seasonal Colors Midsummer to fall, pale green; fall to winter, pinkish red leaves

Mature Height × Spread 12 to 18 in. × 12 to 18 in.

Zones 5 to 8

Golden Japanese forest grass is one of my all-time favorite plants—and one of the few ornamental grasses for shade. A cliff-growing plant native to the island of Honshu, Japan, it spreads slowly by creeping stolons. Its 10-inch-long, lemony yellow leaves are lightly streaked with green. They grow from wiry stems, gracefully spilling over and hiding the stems in one direction, giving the illusion of a golden waterfall. Unlike many grasses, it is not a single mound, but as it expands, it becomes a series of cascades. In autumn, the leaf color slowly transforms to pink, starting at the tip and edges and working its way in until the entire plant has a warm pinkish red tone. This glorious color lasts well into winter.

When, Where, and How to Plant

Plants are available at some nurseries, garden centers, and home-improvement stores in spring. However, the selection of varieties is much greater (and less costly) from online and mail-order sources. Plant it after all danger of frost has passed, following the planting information on page 93. Golden Japanese forest grass grows best in part shade in rich, moist, well-drained soil amended with plenty of organic matter.

Growing Tips

Keep the soil lightly moist for the first growing season. After that, water deeply when there is little rain. In spring, spread a 1-inch layer of compost around the plant, and then mulch it with finely shredded hardwood bark, taking care to keep the mulch an inch away from the stems. No fertilization is needed.

Regional Advice and Care

This plant is very low maintenance. Simply cut back any old foliage when it looks ratty. Do *not* cut the entire plant back in spring. It may die back in coldest areas.

Companion Planting and Design

Golden Japanese forest grass can light up a partly shady area and add movement as no other plant can. In a Japanese-style garden or a rock garden, it makes a simple statement planted above a rock where it can flow onto the stone. It is perfect under a cutleaf Japanese maple (*Acer palmatum ornatum* 'Dissectum'), echoing its graceful leaves and semi-weeping form. For contrast, plant it with ferns with upright form such as cinnamon fern (*Osmunda cinnamomea*) or ostrich fern (*Matteuccia strutheopteris*). It makes a handsome edging to a bed of mixed hostas. Cut leaves and flowers to use in flower arrangements.

Try These

The species (*Hakonechloa macra*, to 18 × 24 inches) is less showy, with spilling, refreshing rich green leaves that turn rusty orange in autumn. 'All Gold' (to 14 × 18 inches) is more compact with bright golden-yellow foliage. 'Fubuki' (to 14 × 18 inches) translates to "snowstorm" in Japanese, appropriate for its green-and-white striped leaves that turn orange-bronze in autumn. Diminutive 'Stripe It Rich' (to 10 × 16 inches) is striking with its white-variegated golden leaves.

Japanese Grass Sedge

Carex morrowii 'Variegata'

Botanical Pronunciation
KARE-eks mor-OH-ee-eye

Bloom Period and Seasonal Colors
Late spring, green and brown; evergreen foliage

Mature Height × Spread
12 to 18 in. × 18 to 24 in.

Zones 5 to 8

U nlike the other ornamental grasses, with Japanese grass sedge, the grasslike foliage is the principal player; the flowers are the extras. The 12- to 16-inch-long leaves are beautiful and graceful—dark green outlined with white. They bring life to a shady area, especially when they sway in a wafting breeze. In late spring, the 15- to 18-inch-long flower stems rise up above the leaves, bearing spiky green and brown panicles of flowers. I often cut the spikes for an arrangement or just cut them back so I can appreciate the foliage even more. Although it is not listed as a plant for wildlife, I've seen baby bunnies and mice run for its protective cover when pursued by a predator.

When, Where, and How to Plant
Plants are readily available in spring locally and from online and mail-order sources. It grows best in fertile, moist, well-drained soil and performs equally well in any kind of shade. In cooler regions, it will tolerate sun. Wait to plant it until after the last frost date. Allow 2 feet between plants—center to center—for a beautiful edging. Give it more room if you are planting only a few plants among other perennials. (See page 93 for more on planting.)

Growing Tips
Japanese grass sedge needs regular watering; don't let it dry out. As its leaves are pendulous, drooping is not a sign of dryness. Keep soil uniformly lightly moist. Foliar feed once in early July with a half-strength solution of liquid kelp or fish emulsion.

Regional Advice and Care
Cut back the flowering stem—if you let it stay on the plant—when it finishes blooming. If the foliage looks weatherbeaten after winter, cut it back to the crown; however, if it still looks good, just remove any brown or dead leaves by combing through with your fingers.

Companion Planting and Design
Japanese grass sedge makes a handsome edge for a semi-shady border, shady path, or pond. One of the most innovative combinations I've seen was Japanese grass sedge planted among pink-flowered roses such as 'Simplicity', 'Carefree Beauty', or 'Gertrude Jekyll'. It's ideal in rain gardens or as a groundcover in a woodland setting.

Try These
'Aurea-variegata' (to 12 × 12 inches) is striking with its creamy white-and-green variegated foliage. 'Goldband' (to 12 × 24 inches) features whitish gold-and-green variegated leaves. 'Ice Dance' (to 12 × 24 inches) is hardier—to Zone 4—and evergreen in warmer regions. Its leaves are wider with more prominent creamy white margins. Unlike other sedges, gray sedge (*Carex grayi*, to 3 × 2 feet) seedheads are the showstoppers, although the green leaves are also attractive. Shaped like greenish yellow to brown spiked balls or medieval maces, the seedheads add unique interest in late spring and last throughout the gardening season.

Little Bluestem

Schizachyrium scoparium

Botanical Pronunciation
skiz-ah-KEER-ee-um sko-PAR-ee-um

Bloom Period and Seasonal Colors Summer, purplish bronze; fall through winter, orange leaves

Mature Height × Spread
2 to 5 ft. × 12 to 18 in.

Zones 4 to 8

Little bluestem's name is misleading. It usually ranges from 2 to 4 feet but can reach 5 feet tall. As for the blue, there's a touch near the base of the upright, slender green leaves. Name aside, it's a terrific addition to the garden—especially for its autumn color. The transformation from green to burnished orange is spectacular, echoed by the hues of many trees and shrubs. Purplish bronze flowers of summer become fluffy, silvery white seedheads lasting well into winter—sparkling with snow or a light coating of ice. The leaves maintain their autumn hue through winter, heating up the garden with their color. Use them in dried arrangements or twist onto wire forms for making wreaths. Its seeds attract sparrows and other small birds.

When, Where, and How to Plant
Little bluestem is readily available for purchase. It is a tough plant, thriving in most soils in full sun, flourishing in hot weather, high humidity, and drought. Plant it in spring after the last frost date (see page 93 for planting information). Or grow it from seed for a large area. After broadcasting the seed, use a water-filled roller to push the seeds down into the soil. Keep soil lightly moist until seed has sprouted and is established. Allow 5 to 6 inches between plants when growing it as a groundcover.

Growing Tips
Once established, little bluestem can survive on the water nature provides. Do not fertilize.

Regional Advice and Care
Seeds attract small birds, such as sparrows, and it looks beautiful in snow and ice, so let it remain throughout the winter. If you must cut it back in fall, use the leaves in bunches to add softness and color in dried arrangements. Cut back to within an inch of the crown in early spring. It usually does not self-sow. Pests are not a problem.

Companion Planting and Design
On a large scale, little bluestem is excellent for erosion control or as a groundcover for dry areas. It is a beautiful addition to a mixed border, perennial, or cottage gardens. Little bluestem is handsome with soft-textured perennials such as astilbe (*Astilbe* spp.), Russian sage (*Perovskia atriplicifolia*), and meadow rue (*Thalictrum delavayi*). Use it as a transitional plant between cultivated and naturalized areas of the garden. Include it in a meadow or prairie restoration.

Try These
'Blaze' (to 3 feet) is prized for its brilliant fall and winter color, turning deep red and then fading to pink over winter, and reddish brown flowers in summer. 'Carousel' (to 30 inches tall wide) has a rounder habit. Its blue-green leaves get pink highlights in midsummer and transition to a carousel of fall colors of copper, pink, and mahogany. 'The Blues' (to 4 feet) has gray-blue foliage held in erect clumps, which turn shades of orange, red, and purple in autumn.

Northern Sea Oats

Chasmanthium latifolium

Botanical Pronunciation
kaz-MAN-thee-um lat-ih-FOE-lee-um

Other Name
Inland sea oats

Bloom Period and Seasonal Colors
Summer, green; fall through winter, tan

Mature Height × Spread
1 to 3 ft. × 1 to 3 ft.

Northern sea oats are outstanding because they thrive in sun or shade. A clump-forming grass, they have broad, close-set leaves. Drooping clusters of green flowers appear in summer and quickly become seedheads, closely resembling oats. They are the main attraction for me. The little time I have to truly enjoy my garden is in the evening, which sets the tone for the northern sea oats. A breeze often arises and catches the leaves, making a swishing sound. The unique light rustling sound of the seedheads in fall and winter is music to my ears. Both the leaves and seedheads turn a lovely tan in fall, persisting through the winter. The seedheads are excellent cut for dried arrangements and can last a year with no preservatives.

When, Where, and How to Plant
Northern sea oats are readily available in spring locally and from online and mail-order sources. They grow best in rich, moist, well-drained soil in full sun, but also perform in part shade and poor or dry soil. Plant in spring after all danger of frost has passed. Space 24 to 30 inches apart if you are growing several plants, 2 feet apart for a mass planting. You can also grow northern sea oats from seed collected (or purchased) the previous fall. Sow seeds ½-inch deep and 6 inches apart. Keep the seedbed lightly moist. Once the plants are 4 to 6 inches tall, thin them to the proper spacing. To transplant the thinnings, dig each 6 inches deep and 4 inches wide. Dig a hole in the new location. Add 2 cups of transplant solution and place the transplant so that it is at the same height it was originally. Use your hands to gently firm the soil around the plant.

Growing Tips
Make sure the soil stays lightly moist for several weeks, keeping the plants well watered until they are established. You do not need to feed northern sea oats.

Regional Advice and Care
Cut the plant down to 3 to 4 inches in early spring. For drying or using in arrangements, cut seedheads in late summer. Northern sea oats readily self-sow.

Companion Planting and Design
Northern sea oats make a lovely border along a path, softening any hard edges. They are charming in a fall garden with Autumn Joy sedum (*Sedum* 'Autumn Joy'), Alma Potschke aster (*Symphyotrichum novae-angliae* 'Alma Potschke'), and Fireworks goldenrod (*Solidago* 'Fireworks'). Use them as specimen plants, include them in a meadow or native plant garden, or plant them along the edge of a water garden.

Try These
'River Mist' (to 30 inches tall and wide) is less hardy than the species (only to Zone 5), but it's worth growing it in colder zones as an annual. It makes a big splash with its bold white variegation that extends even into the seedheads.

Prairie Dropseed

Sporobolus heterolepis

Botanical Pronunciation
spoor-OB-oh-lus het-er-oh-LEP-siss

Other Name
Northern dropseed

Bloom Period and Seasonal Colors
Late summer to fall, pale pink; fall through winter, copper leaves

Mature Height × Spread
24 to 36 in. × 24 to 36 in.

If you have never grown ornamental grasses, start with prairie dropseed. It is small, elegant, has superb color, and is easy to grow. It forms a graceful mound of emerald-green, fine-textured leaves turning orange highlighted by gold in fall, fading to pale copper in winter. In late summer, airy panicles of small pink flowers rise 2 to 3 feet high. The flowers are lightly fragrant—an aroma that is diversely perceived and described by people as sweet, an unmistakable scent of cilantro, the unique smell of burnt buttered popcorn, pungent, or even odorless. Use fresh flowers in arrangements; it's fun to see how guests perceive the scent. Seeds drop in fall, attracting birds—hence the name. Native Americans made nutritious, delicious flour by grinding the seeds.

When, Where, and How to Plant
Purchase prairie dropseed from online or mail-order sources. It needs full sun and will grow in a range of soil types from sandy to loamy—even rocky soil. For good definition, space plants 18 to 24 inches apart; for a prairie effect or as a groundcover, allow 15 inches between plants. It may be shipped in containers or as bare-root plants (dormant). Follow planting information on page 93 for planting container plants. Soak bare-root plants in half-strength transplant solution overnight. Cut off any broken or overly long roots. Dig a hole the size of the root mass. Make a slight mound of soil at the bottom of the hole and place the plant so the crown is just below ground level. Fill with soil and firm gently. Water with 2 cups of diluted transplant solution. Keep the soil lightly moist until

there's a healthy mound of leaves. Alternatively, grow from seed sown directly on well-raked soil in fall or early spring. Water gently to avoid disturbing the seeds. Keep the soil lightly moist until seedlings are established. Thin to the proper distance.

Growing Tips
Keep the plant well watered until it is established. It is drought tolerant but does need some water. When the top 3 inches of soil is dry, give it a slow, deep watering. It does not require fertilizer.

Regional Advice and Care
Use a floating row cover to protect seeds while preventing the sun from drying out the soil. Have patience; prairie dropseed is slow to grow but worth the wait. Once established, it is very long-lived and trouble free.

Companion Planting and Design
Prairie dropseed is a distinctive and well-defined plant for inclusion in a perennial or mixed border. Combine it with butterfly weed (*Asclepias tuberosa*), New York aster (*Symphyotrichum novi-belgii*), and little bluestem (*Schizachyrium scoparium*). Planted *en masse*, it makes a handsome groundcover, which can be used effectively for erosion control on a slope.

Try These
'Tara' (to 24 inches tall) is less arching and more upright than the species. Green leaves turn a vibrant red-orange in fall.

Switchgrass

Panicum virgatum

Botanical Pronunciation
PAN-ih-kum ver-GAY-tum

Bloom Period and Seasonal Colors
Midsummer into winter, reddish purple through silvery white; fall through winter, colorful foliage

Mature Height × Spread
3 to 6 ft. × 2 to 3 ft.

Zones 5 to 8

Switchgrass is one of the five main grasses of the North American prairie, attesting to its toughness and reliability as a perennial, since it returns every year no matter how cold the winter or hot and dry the summer. Switchgrass forms attractive, narrow, green clumps that are flat, linear, and slender, growing upright to 24 inches. In midsummer, the real show begins as flower panicles emerge, opening reddish purple to silvery white, looking like clouds 12 to 16 inches above the leaves—beautiful in fresh or dried arrangements. In autumn, the foliage turns bright yellow, gold, or orange, lasting through the winter while the seedheads turn beige. Birds flock to the seeds in winter. It's excellent in perennial beds, mass plantings, or as a screen.

When, Where, and How to Plant
Switchgrass is readily available in spring. Versatile, it grows equally well in full to part sun in most soils—wet or dry, rich or poor. Plant it in spring after all danger of frost has passed, allowing 24 to 30 inches between plants. (See page 93 for information on planting.)

Growing Tips
Keep the soil lightly moist until the clumps are established. Switchgrass does not need fertilizer.

Regional Advice and Care
Keep switchgrass through winter to show off its beautiful coloration. It also serves as a winter cover for wildlife. Cut to within 3 to 4 inches of the ground in early spring. This vigorous plant benefits from dividing every three or four years. Dig up clumps and divide with a knife or shovel. Replant at the same soil level as they were growing. Water well with transplant solution. It may self-sow, but not reliably.

Companion Planting and Design
En masse, it makes a lovely vertical screen, useful for hiding unattractive views or for defining spaces in the garden. It is beautiful growing in a meadowlike setting (even a small 3 × 3 foot area in the garden) with beebalm (*Monarda didyma*), purple coneflower (*Echinacea purpurea*), and brown-eyed Susan (*Rudbeckia triloba*)—all plants that provide food for birds. Add a cutleaf staghorn sumac (*Rhus typhina* 'Dissecta') for a taller accent.

Try These
'Heavy Metal' (to 5 × 4 feet) has stunning, upright, metallic-blue leaves that amazingly transform to yellow in autumn. By winter, leaves bleach out to tan. 'Northwind' (to 6 × 2½ feet, a Perennial Plant Association Plant of the Year) has olive to bluish green foliage turning yellowish beige in fall. Panicles of yellow flowers in late summer turn beige as seeds mature. 'Prairie Fire' (to 5 × 2 feet) emerges blue-green; transformation is early, changing to shades of deep red in early summer, and then buttery yellow in late fall. 'Shenandoah' (to 3 × 6 feet) leaves are red-tipped in early summer; by fall the entire leaf is rich burgundy, made more attractive by pink plumes of flowers.

Tufted Hair Grass

Deschampsia caespitosa

Botanical Pronunciation
des-KAMP-see-ah sess-pih-TOE-sah

Other Name Tussock grass

Bloom Period and Seasonal Colors
Late spring through summer, silvery with purple tinge; fall through winter, golden tan

Mature Height × Spread 2 to 3 ft. × 1 to 2 ft.

Zones 4 to 8

A cool-season grass, tufted hair grass greens up early. It forms tussocks or mounds with attractive 24-inch long, narrow (⅕-inch), stiff green leaves. The real reason for growing it isn't the foliage—it merely sets the stage for the tall flowers that rise 18 to 48 inches above the leaves. The flowers are cloudlike; the airy panicles open a pale greenish yellow, quickly turning purple-tinged silver. In autumn, they turn a lovely golden-tan color. In the soft, warm light of early morning or late afternoon, especially when grown with deep green plants—such as evergreens that provide a dark backdrop—the flower plumes appear sun-kissed. Leaves are semi-evergreen, and the flower plumes remain for added winter interest. It's an excellent groundcover; seeds attract birds in autumn.

When, Where, and How to Plant
Plants of tufted hair grass are available at some garden centers, nurseries, and home-improvement stores as well as through online and mail-order sources. It grows best in rich, moist soil in part sun or part shade. Planting it in a low area, such as along a bog or lake, should provide ample moisture. It is also well suited for planting at the edge of a woodland. Space the plants 2 feet apart. Water well. (See page 93 for more on planting.)

Growing Tips
Tufted hair grass needs to be kept moist. Do not allow it to dry out. It needs no fertilization.

Regional Advice and Care
If winds make its flower panicles look ragged, cut them down. Otherwise, enjoy their beauty throughout winter. Cut the leaves all the way down to the crown in early spring. It seems extreme, but you'll quickly be rewarded with new healthy growth. If the plant gets too large or you want more, divide it in spring. Dig the plant up out of the ground—roots and all. Use a shovel or knife to cut into smaller portions; replant or share with friends. It occasionally self-sows and is relatively pest free. It's excellent as a cut flower, fresh or dried.

Companion Planting and Design
This plant makes a unique combination with lady's mantle (*Alchemilla mollis*). The light on dewdrops or raindrops on lady's mantle leaves echoes the sunlit blooms of tufted hair grass. It consorts well with colorful shade- and moisture-loving perennials including red cardinal flower (*Lobelia cardinalis*), pink turtlehead (*Chelone obliqua*), and yellow marsh marigold (*Caltha palustris*). It also adds early color to late-winter or early-spring woodland plantings with shrubs like witch hazel (*Hamamelis* spp.) and winterhazel (*Corylopsis spicata*).

Try These
'Northern Lights' (to 1 to 3 feet tall and wide) gray- and gold-streaked leaves turn pink-tipped gold in late summer. Panicles of tiny flowers in hues of purple, green, gold, and silver. 'Pixie Fountain' (to 24 × 20 inches), hardy to Zone 3, has silvery green foliage and silvery white flowers maturing to golden brown.

PERENNIALS

FOR THE PRAIRIE & PLAINS STATES

As people get into gardening, they often start off by adding annuals to whatever exists on their property—marigolds, petunias, begonias, and coleus are among the most popular. After a few years, they graduate to perennials, which, as their name implies, come back year after year.

The perennials included in this section are hardy (survive the winter) in all of the Prairie and Plains states and zones (see the USDA Hardiness Zone maps on page 16), unless I have mentioned specific zones, which means that plant is hardy *only* in that particular range. I chose plants that span the seasons, require the least maintenance, and perform well in our area. Many are natives, which means they thrive despite the great temperature fluctuations—extreme cold in the winter, hot and humid in the summer. These perennials range from tall prairie plants to more dainty cultivated varieties. Whether you are looking to create a woodland garden, grow a wildflower meadow, recreate a prairie, make a formal garden, or design a cottage garden, there are *many* choices available for you. Two of the biggest challenges I hear about from gardeners in our region are water (drought and water restrictions) and deer. So I've included as many drought-tolerant and deer-resistant plants as possible. Unless noted otherwise in the "Regional Care and Advice" section, there are no major pests or diseases.

Coral honeysuckle (*Lonicera sempervirens*) underplanted with black-eyed Susans.

Buying Perennials

Unfortunately, growers are now producing perennials that are in bloom when you purchase them—whether at a nursery, garden center, home-improvement store, or even supermarket parking lot "store." Moreover, people buy them because, as the adage goes, "What you see is what you get." This has been the practice used to market annuals for many years. And with annuals, even if you cut off the flowers and buds to encourage root growth (as you should), in a short time you'll be rewarded with more flowers. Most annuals rebloom and, in most cases, continue to flower throughout the growing season.

This is not true for perennials. Most have a limited flowering season and although a few will rebloom if you cut them back, the majority will not. That means when you buy perennials in mid-spring—in bloom—they'll look pretty in the garden for only a short while (most have bloom times ranging from two to six weeks and you have no idea how long they may already have been flowering when you bought them). Then, when summer comes (or whatever the plant's normal bloom time), it has already put on its show. You have to wait until the *next* year to see flowers. If possible, purchase perennials that *aren't* in bloom—unless it is their season. Even then, you'd be better off buying and planting them earlier to give them a chance to establish a strong root system. If the place where you regularly buy your perennials only offers plants in bloom, ask for ones that are in their proper season and not forced to bloom early. If enough people request this, growers—even for larger chains—will respond. Many small nurseries propagate and grow their own plant material; plants should be in their proper stage of growth for the season. Of course, if you shop online or through mail-order catalogs, you're almost guaranteed to get plants at the right time. I make a large note on the order form (or tell the operator if I'm doing it by phone) of the shipping date *I want*. Their shipping date is generally a week or so after the last frost date since nurseries in warmer zones than ours sometimes ship too early for me to plant. Find your last frost date at www.davesgarden.com/guides/freeze-frost-dates/#b.

Planting

Since a perennial will be in place for many years (I know of 100-year-old peonies), take the time to prepare the soil so that it is suitable for that particular plant. Dig a hole twice the size of the root mass, putting the soil from the hole on a tarp or

Once the bed is amended, position the plants in their containers to check spacing and to see if they complement one another.

Dig a planting hole two times as deep as the container, and twice as wide.

in a wheelbarrow. Amend the reserved soil as needed, depending on the plant's needs—pH, drainage, and/or benefits from additional organic matter. Fill the hole partway with the amended soil. Remove the plant from its container and gently loosen the roots. If it was shipped bareroot, soak it in room-temperature water for at least four hours or overnight. Form a cone of amended soil in the hole so that the crown of the plant is just below ground level and the roots spread out around the cone. Set the plant in the hole and water with 1 quart of transplant solution. Fill the hole with the remaining amended soil and use your hands to gently firm the soil. Water with an additional 2 quarts of transplant solution. Mulch with an organic mulch, unless the plant is a succulent or one that prefers dry soil—with the mulch 1 inch away from the stem(s). In that case, use sand, gravel, or pebbles (any material that doesn't retain moisture will keep the plant drier). Keep the soil lightly moist until the plant is established. Unless noted in the plant entry, winter mulch (on top of the plant's crown in late fall when the ground starts to freeze) is not necessary.

Containers Add Versatility

It is important to choose the right plant for the right place. Trying to grow garden heliotrope (*Valeriana officinalis*) that requires moist soil next to black-eyed Susan (*Rudbeckia fulgida* 'Goldsturm') that likes well-drained soil is a recipe for failure—if you try to grow them in the ground next to each other. However, you can get away with differing requirements by growing them in containers. There you can control the soil type, moisture level, and place the containers next to each other. If you have a plant that needs shade, place its container where it is shaded by the taller plants.

Some tall perennials may need staking.

It's fun to mix and match plants of different types in a container. One favorite from a recent garden was Autumn Joy sedum (*Sedum* 'Autumn Joy'), Pink Chaos coleus (*Plectranthus scutellarioides* 'Pink Chaos'), and Fireworks goldenrod (*Solidago* 'Fireworks') with a dozen silk forsythia stems early in the season to add interest until the other plants grew up. Silk flowers aren't as delicate as their name implies; the stems I use are eighteen years old and have even overwintered outdoors for several years. The fact that this combo was in a large 3-foot pot made it even more eye-catching.

Varying the heights in the garden adds a great deal of interest because you look up, down, and around to take it all in; this is easily accomplished by using containers of different sizes. Outside, the green metal plant stands used indoors are even more versatile, raising a container towards eye level while the green stand blends into the garden. A small blue and white ceramic container with red flowers is easily overlooked on the ground, but it grabs your attention when it is up on a plant stand—even more so if that stand is repainted cobalt blue.

Remember to remove perennials from the container and plant them in the ground several weeks before the first frost date. You could sink the container in the ground or move it into a cool, dark place for winter where it can go into dormancy (about 40 degrees Fahrenheit—not down to freezing).

In addition to the trees and shrubs you put in your garden, perennials will provide many years of beauty and delight for you. One advantage these smaller plants have is that for the most part you can readily move them if you want. Even better, in time many grow and spread, so you can divide them and have more plants to beautify your property—or share with others. Enjoy!

Other Choice Perennials

There are so many to choose from, but the choice was limited as to which perennials to feature in this book. Here are some other excellent ones to consider adding to your garden:

Blanket flower	*Gaillardia* × *grandiflora*
Bleeding heart	*Lamprocapnos spectabilis*
Blue false indigo	*Baptisia australis*
Chrysanthemum	*Dendranthema* spp.
Columbine meadow rue	*Thalictrum aquilegifolium*
Dame's rocket	*Hesperis matronalis*
Fringed loosestrife	*Lysimachia ciliata* 'Fire Cracker'
Gayfeather	*Liatris spicata*
Globe thistle	*Echinops ritro*
Great white trillium	*Trillium grandiflorum*
Heartleaf bergenia	*Bergenia cordifolia*
Heartleaf foamflower	*Tiarella cordifolia*
Jack-in-the-pulpit	*Arisaema triphyllum*
Japanese iris	*Iris ensata*
Jupiter's beard	*Centranthus ruber*
Mayapple	*Podophyllum peltatum*
Meadowsweet	*Filipendula vulgaris* 'Plena'
Speedwell	*Veronica spicata*
Sundrops	*Oenothera fruticosa*
True forget-me-not	*Myosotis scorpioides*

Beebalm

Monarda didyma

Botanical Pronunciation
moe-NAR-dah DID-ih-mah

Other Name Oswego tea

Bloom Period and Seasonal Colors
Mid- to late summer, red, pink, purplish

Mature Height × Spread 2 to 4 ft. × 2 to 3 ft.

Zones 4 to 8

I find beebalm's history fascinating. New York's Oswego Indians introduced beebalm to the Colonists, teaching them to make tea from its leaves and flowers. This proved very useful after the Boston Tea Party. Beebalm has a slightly spicy mint flavor; its edible flowers are sweeter than the leaves. I admire its unusual flower form—1½-inch whorls of red florets with prominent stamens and red-tinged bracts. Often one flower grows above another after the lower one finishes blooming. Square stems identify beebalm as a mint family member. Pick individual florets for eating or cooking—it makes delicious ice cream, pound cake, and an interesting sauce with fish or chicken. Both butterflies and hummingbirds flock to the plant for its nectar, while bees go after the pollen.

When, Where, and How to Plant

Beebalm plants—the species and some cultivars— are available locally, but you'll find a wider choice of varieties through online and mail-order sources. Beebalm grows best in rich, moist, well-drained soil in full to part sun. It tolerates clay and wet soils and a range of pH. To help prevent powdery mildew, allow ample space around the plant. Plant in spring after all danger of frost has passed, following the directions on page 105. Water well.

Growing Tips

Do not let the plant dry out. When watering, water the soil, not the leaves. If you use an overhead sprinkler, water early in the day so leaves can dry. Foliar feed monthly with a solution of kelp or fish emulsion.

Regional Advice and Care

Beebalm is susceptible to powdery mildew; allow ample room between plants for good air circulation. At the first sign, remove the infected leaves. Spray the plant every seven to ten days with baking soda solution (see page 175 for directions). Be sure to spray both tops and bottoms of the leaves. Thin in spring to allow air circulation. Deadhead to extend bloom time. Divide clumps in spring when necessary.

Companion Planting and Design

Beebalm makes a bright combination with sunny yellow tickseed (*Coreopsis* spp.) and blue Russian sage (*Perovskia atriplicifolia*). Keep it away from other plants prone to mildew like garden phlox (*Phlox paniculata*) and black-eyed Susan (*Rudbeckia* spp.). Include beebalm in an herb garden, meadow, cutting garden, perennial border, rain garden, or alongside a water feature. It attracts bees, making it a good pollinator plant.

Try These

Always taste any cultivar before using it in cooking, as some are reminiscent of mothballs. Next to the species, 'Cambridge Scarlet' (36 to 42 inches tall) and 'Jacob Cline' (48 to 60 inches and mildew resistant) with their bright red, 2-inch blooms have the best flavor. 'Croftway Pink' (30 to 36 inches) has a soft rose color. Reddish purple-flowered 'Scorpion' (36 to 48 inches) and shaggy purple-flowered 'Purple Rooster' (36 to 40 inches) are most mildew resistant.

Black-Eyed Susan

Rudbeckia fulgida var. *sullivantii* 'Goldsturm'

Botanical Pronunciation
rud-BEK-ee-ah FULL-jih-dah sul-ih-VAN-tee-eye

Other Name
Orange coneflower

Bloom Period and Seasonal Colors
Midsummer to fall, yellow with brown centers

Mature Height × Spread
22 to 26 in. × 15 to 18 in.

Black-eyed Susan is one of the original native prairie plants, a rhizomatous perennial that readily self-seeds. The cultivated variety 'Goldsturm' has become *the* gold standard for its large flowerheads. It is a well-branched plant, producing an abundance of flowers—enough for enjoying outside and cutting to bring inside for arrangements and bouquets. Easy to grow, it brightens the garden from midsummer to fall with its 3½- to 5-inch flowers comprised of golden ray florets (petals) surrounding the conical brown disk florets (center). It is wondrous to watch the bees and butterflies that flock to it while it is in bloom. As summer wanes, avoid cutting down the spent flowerstalks because birds, especially colorful finches, will come to the garden and feed on its seedheads.

When, Where, and How to Plant
'Goldsturm' black-eyed Susan plants are readily available in spring at nurseries, garden centers, and home-improvement stores as well as through mail-order sources, and online. It grows best in average, lightly moist, well-drained garden soil in full sun. Plant it after the last frost date in spring or in late summer. Follow the planting instructions on page 105. Water-in well with transplant solution.

Growing Tips
Keep the plant lightly moist until it is established. Do not let it dry out. To avoid powdery mildew, water at soil level or early in the day. If the soil is poor, topdress with 1 to 2 inches of compost around the base of the plant in spring. Do not fertilize regularly, as that will result in soft, floppy growth, making it more susceptible to powdery mildew.

Regional Advice and Care
Deadhead the first flush of flowers to encourage reblooming. Leave the later flowers on the plants to mature so that the birds can eat the seeds in fall and winter. When plants get too large, dig up and divide in spring or late summer. To defend against powdery mildew, do not plant black-eyed Susan near beebalm, zinnias, lilacs, or other susceptible plants; give it room for air to circulate. See beebalm on page 108 for tips on dealing with powdery mildew.

Companion Planting and Design
Black-eyed Susan is handsome with Shasta daisies (*Leucanthemum* × *superbum*) and annual melampodium (*Melampodium paludosum*). It is lovely in a meadow planting, perennial border, mixed flowerbeds, or even in a cutting garden.

Try These
'Little Goldstar' (12 to 16 inches tall) is a dwarf hybrid that grows in tidy clumps with golden yellow flowers. *Rudbeckia hirta* (a native, also known as black-eyed Susan or Gloriosa daisy) resembles 'Goldsturm'. Cultivars include 'Green Eyes' ('Irish Eyes', 24 to 30 inches), which has a pale green center surrounded by bright yellow petals. 'Cherry Brandy' (20 to 24 inches) is a standout with cherry red petals surrounding a black eye. 'Toto' ('Toto Gold' 12 to 16 inches) is a delightful dwarf variety.

Butterfly Weed

Asclepias tuberosa

Botanical Pronunciation
ah-SKLEE-pee-us too-ber-OH-sah

Other Name
Butterfly milkweed

Bloom Period and Seasonal Colors
Late spring through summer, orange and yellow

Mature Height × Spread
2 to 3 ft. × 8 to 12 in.

Butterfly weed has been a must-have plant for me since childhood. I remember seeing it—growing in the wild—with butterflies fluttering all around it. This handsome, summer-blooming perennial attracts butterflies (especially monarchs), bees, and other pollinators to the nectar-rich, 1½- to 2-inch clusters of vivid orange or yellow flowers. Growing 2 to 3 feet tall, it has hairy, thick, unbranched stems with 4- to 5½-inch, lance-shaped leaves that spiral up the stem. The flowers are borne in the leaf axils and at the ends of the stems. A native plant of dry fields and roadsides, it naturalizes over time without becoming invasive. Besides its beauty, butterfly weed is an easy-to-grow, low-maintenance, drought-tolerant addition to my garden. Seedpods are attractive additions to dried-flower arrangements.

When, Where, and How to Plant
Butterfly weed is readily available locally in spring. It's often are included in "butterfly plant" collections since monarch butterflies flock to its nectar. Seed-grown plants can take up to three years to bloom, so unless you're a patient, avid gardener with an indoor heated seed-growing area complete with grow lights, purchase container-grown plants. Butterfly weed needs full sun and well-drained soil. The soil can be average or rich, dry or lightly moist—as long as it *drains well*. Take care when planting as butterfly weed has a long, brittle taproot. Follow basic planting instructions on page 105. Gently remove it from its pot, disturbing the soil as little as possible, and place in the planting hole (loosen the soil several inches deeper than the pot). Water-in well with transplant solution. Mulch with

pebbles or grit. You can often find plants on sale at the end of summer; they're a good bargain. That's also a fine time for planting.

Growing Tips
Keep lightly moist until plants establish. After that, water when the top inch of soil is dry. Fertilization is not necessary.

Regional Advice and Care
Because of its long taproot, butterfly weed does not transplant well. It is slow to emerge in spring, so mark its spot to prevent accidentally disturbing it or overplanting with something else. Butterfly weed is self-seeding. If aphids are a problem, a blast of water can often get rid of them. If that doesn't work, spray with insecticidal soap.

Companion Planting and Design
Butterfly weed is an excellent plant in a meadow-type, perennial, or naturalistic garden as well as a mixed border. It grows well with other drought-tolerant plants, such as fountain grass (*Pennisetum alopecuroides* 'Hameln' or 'Little Bunny'), black-eyed Susan (*Rudbeckia fulgida* 'Goldsturm'), and wild bergamot (*Monarda fistulosa*). Grow some milkweed (*Asclepias syriaca*) as well. Both provide the leaves monarch caterpillars eat. And after they pupate, the butterflies drink the nectar.

Try This One
'Gay Butterflies' (2 to 3 feet tall), with its red, orange, and yellow flowers, also makes a good cut flower.

Cardinal Flower

Lobelia cardinalis

Botanical Pronunciation
lo-BEE-lee-ah kar-din-AL-iss

Bloom Period and Seasonal Colors
Midsummer to fall, brilliant red

Mature Height × Spread
2 to 4 ft. × 12 to 18 in.

Cardinal flower's brilliant red color is magnificent, especially when backlit by early morning or late afternoon sun. Look closely at an individual flower and you can see how it got its name; it looks like its namesake bird taking flight. Cardinal flower is one of my favorite perennials because it is so versatile. Masses of ruby red flowers adorn slender, purplish, 24- to 30-inch spikes from late summer through early autumn. This native can grow in that low damp spot at the edge of the mixed border or it can even grow in a water garden. Thriving in light shade, it is gorgeous highlighting the edge of a woodland, blooming with the brilliance of a stained glass window with the sun radiating through the blooms.

When, Where, and How to Plant

Plants are available in spring locally and from online and mail-order sources. It needs wet soil; thriving in wet, boggy soils—even up to 4 inches of water. Give it deep, rich soil in full sun to part shade. Allow 12 to 18 inches between plants. Grow in groups of three, five, or more for the most drama. When growing it in water, pot the plant in a ½-quart or 1-gallon container in heavy, acidic soil. Add peat moss to increase acidity and to retain water. Place 1 inch of fine pebbles on the soil to keep it from leaching into the pond. Place the pot so the top is 1 to 4 inches below water level. Alternatively, if you have a clay-bottomed pond, plant it at the appropriate depth without a pot.

Growing Tips

Keep the plant moist. Do not let the soil dry out. Foliar feed garden plants every six weeks with a solution of kelp or fish emulsion. Use special aquatic plant food tablets for potted plants in the water; follow package instructions.

Regional Advice and Care

Cardinal flower is a short-lived perennial that self-seeds freely. On the flower stalk, the lower, spent flowers may have ripe seed while the upper flowers have yet to bloom. It needs dividing every two to three years. Lift the clumps in early fall, remove the new rosettes of leaves, and replant immediately in amended soil. When the ground freezes, add 4 to 6 inches of organic mulch; remove in spring when the temperature is moderate. Cardinal flower is pest free.

Companion Planting and Design

Cardinal flower is ideal as a waterside planting, in a low-lying wet area, or in a boggy spot where not much else will grow. It consorts well with daylilies (*Hemerocallis* spp.), Japanese iris (*Iris ensata*), leopard plant (*Ligularia dentata*), marsh marigold (*Caltha palustris*), and Siberian iris (*Iris siberica*).

Try These

'Fried Green Tomatoes' (to 35 inches) is long-lived; spring leaves are maroon aging to bronze and olive green. 'Queen Victoria' (to 48 inches) sports dark reddish purple stems and leaves.

Compass Plant

Silphium laciniatum

Botanical Pronunciation
SILL-fee-um lah-sin-ee-AY-tum

Other Name
Pilot plant

Bloom Period and Seasonal Colors
Late summer to early fall, yellow

Mature Height × Spread
5 to 9 ft. × 18 to 36 in.

This eye-catching, clump-former is native to fields and open woodlands. Compass plant makes a bold exclamation at the back of any garden. From a large, deep underground root, its hairy stems shoot up to 9 feet topped with narrow clusters of 5-inch, nodding yellow sunflowerlike blossoms in summer. Its deeply cut leaves point north and south (their flat sides face east and west). It inspired Longfellow to write, "Its leaves are turned to the north as true as the magnet: This is the compass flower." Sandpapery leaves and stems are sticky with a resin that smells like turpentine. Native Americans used the dried tacky resin as a mouth-cleansing chewing gum. In late fall and early winter, goldfinches and other birds feast on the small seeds.

When, Where, and How to Plant
Find compass plant locally and from online or mail-order sources. It grows best in full sun in moderately fertile heavy or clay soils with an alkaline or neutral pH. When setting out nursery-grown plants, take care not to disturb the roots. Plant at same depth it was growing in the pot, and water deeply, not frequently, to encourage wide-ranging and deep root development. Once you have plants growing, you can multiply what you have. As soon as the seeds ripen in the fall, sow them in containers using seed-starting mix. They'll overwinter happily outside; then plant them the following spring. Or, divide mature plants in spring. Be sure to use a good strong shovel—the taproot is really deep, even in very heavy soils.

Growing Tips
Foliar feed twice in the spring and water during long dry spells.

Regional Advice and Care
Compass plant has no major insect and disease problems, which is good because sprays would harm the many butterflies, other insects, and birds that feed on both pollen and seeds.

Companion Planting and Design
Use compass plant towards the back of a perennial border or mixed planting, partly because its flowers tower above other plants, and partly to hide its leaves, which may not be very attractive during wet seasons. Its distinctive height and welcome color provide a dramatic flair to prairie plantings, glades, wetlands, or rain gardens. Compass plant is also excellent for naturalizing in fields and a wild or woodland garden where it can catch and sway in breezes, especially when loaded with butterflies.

Try These
Another great, tall *Silphium* is cup plant (*S. perfoliatum*, 4 to 7 feet tall), which is a robust, strongly upright perennial with remarkable square stems. The leaves, which grow in pairs on the stem, are joined at their bases to form cups that hold water, attracting butterflies, songbirds, and hummingbirds to stop by for a drink. An abundance of yellow, daisylike blossoms open in mid- to late summer, attracting large numbers of butterflies. 'The Holy Grail' is outstanding for its bold chartreuse foliage.

Cranesbill

Geranium spp.

Botanical Pronunciation
jer-AY-nee-um

Other Name Geranium

Bloom Period and Seasonal Colors
Late spring to summer or autumn, white, red, rose, pink, purple, blue

Mature Height × Spread
4 to 24 in. × 1 ft. to indefinite

Zone 4

Not to be confused with the typical red-flowered container-grown geranium (botanically *Pelargonium*), cranesbill includes dozens of species and hundreds of cultivars. Cherished by gardeners for the range of size from 4-inch-tall bloody cranesbill to the stout 24 × 36-inch 'Wargrave Pink', other admirable cranesbill features are the wide choice and variety of colors, its long bloom time, and the ability to grow in most soil types. The leaves are exceptionally beautiful. Some are even evergreen, adding year-round interest to any garden. Most geraniums naturalize readily—by rhizomes and/or self-seeding, so one plant can easily become an investment for the future of the garden. Every garden should have several.

When, Where, and How to Plant

Although you can find cranesbill locally, to discover its true variety and range, go to online and mail-order sources. Plant in spring after all danger of frost has passed. The larger, clump-forming cranesbills and most hybrids thrive in fertile soil in full sun to part shade. They are tolerant of most soil types providing they are well drained. Mulch with 3 inches of organic matter. Smaller varieties need humus-rich, very well-drained soil in full sun. To improve soil drainage, mulch with 2 inches of sand, grit, pebbles, or gravel. See page 105 for more planting information.

Growing Tips

Keep well watered during the growing season. Foliar feed in spring and early summer with kelp or fish emulsion.

Regional Advice and Care

In areas with hot summers, provide afternoon shade. Remove spent flower stems and cut off old leaves to encourage new growth. Some varieties may stop blooming in the heat of summer and rebloom in fall. Divide in spring (share with friends and neighbors). Cranesbills have no pest problems. It is rabbit resistant.

Companion Planting and Design

In shady areas, cranesbills consort with bleeding heart (*Lamprocapnos spectabilis*) and wake robin (*Trillium* spp.). In the garden, mix with foxglove (*Digitalis* spp.) and Jacob's ladder (*Polemonium* 'Lambrook Mauve'). Geraniums are versatile—equally at home in a cottage garden, woodland walk, formal bed or border, rock garden, as a groundcover, or in a collector's garden.

Try These

'Rozanne' (20 × 24 inches), a patented hybrid, blooms nonstop with 2½-inch, white-centered, veined, violet-blue flowers. Clump-forming bloody cranesbill (*Geranium sanguineum*, 3 to 18 inches × 6 to 16 inches) has deeply cut—almost fernlike—leaves. 'Alpenglow' bears red blooms in spring and summer. Bigroot cranesbill (*G. macrorrhizum*, to 20 × 24 inches) has strongly scented leaves. 'Album' has pink stamens in white flowers in early through midsummer. *G. incanum* is a mounded evergreen with aromatic leaves. 'Johnson's Blue' (12 to 18 inches × 20 to 24 inches) an all-time favorite, forms a dense mat of lobed leaves with 2-inch, pink-centered, lavender-blue flowers.

Daylily

Hemerocallis spp.

Botanical Pronunciation
hem-er-oh-KAL-iss

Bloom Period and Seasonal Colors
Spring through summer, rainbow hues (except blue), single, bicolors, tricolors

Mature Height and Spread
6 to 48 in. × 1 to 4 ft.

There are thousands of daylilies from which to choose. They're easy to grow and beautiful in single and double flowers of varying shapes— triangular, circular, star, spider, and ruffled—in rainbow hues (single and bi- and tricolored). The American Hemerocallis Society touts them as tough—growing in water, drought, and salty soil, even planted in winter. Californians and others use them for firescaping to surround property to protect it from wildfires; they don't burn easily. Every part of the plant is edible. Add 6-inch-long new shoots in spring to salads or stir-fries, sauté or steam buds, and use flower petals in salads and hors d'oeuvres. In autumn, substitute rhizomes of *Hemerocallis fulva* for water chestnuts. Warning: once you start growing daylilies, you may become addicted.

When, Where, and How to Plant
Daylilies are readily available locally from spring through summer. Explore online and mail-order sources to see the true range of these carefree perennials. Although they thrive in full sun and fertile, moist, well-drained soil, they'll grow and flower in nearly any soil. Plant pale-colored daylilies in full sun; dark-colored varieties benefit from part shade to keep from fading. Plant anytime. Go to page 105 for detailed planting information.

Growing Tips
From spring until buds form, water freely. If you're looking for spectacular blooms, foliar feed every two to three weeks; or just let the plants grow on their own.

Regional Advice and Care
Deadhead and remove flower stalks to encourage rebloom. Pick day-bloomers in midafternoon for cooking that evening (remove pistils and stamens). Daylilies are excellent cut flowers, as each scape will open a new flower each day. To maintain vigor, divide in spring every three to five years. Daylilies have no pest problems.

Companion Planting and Design
Daylilies are lovely with many varieties planted *en masse* and are an excellent addition to a cottage garden, naturalistic landscape, mixed border, or a rain garden. Depending on their height, daylilies are superb paired with short plants like pansies and chamomile or with taller ones like foxgloves and beebalm. I plant daylilies among late spring-blooming bulbs to hide the ripening foliage.

Try These
Hemerocallis fulva (to 3 × 4 feet) is the ordinary 2½- to 4-inch, orange daylily (known as ditch lily). Simple, elegant, and delicious, it's traditionally used in Chinese cuisine. 'Flore-Pleno' is double flowered. *H. lilio-asphodelus* (formerly *H. flava*, to 3 tall and wide), is the first daylily to flower in spring, bearing night-blooming, fragrant, sweet-tasting, 3½-inch, star-shaped yellow blooms. Ever-popular 'Stella de Oro' (to 12 × 18 inches) blooms early and, if kept picked, reblooms until frost. Stuff its lovely 2-inch, bright yellow flowers with a flavorful dip as an hors d'oeuvre. *H. citrina* (to 48 × 30 inches) is night-blooming, citrus-scented and -flavored with star-shaped, pale yellow 3½- to 5-inch blooms. Have fun exploring the wide world of hybrid daylilies!

False Sunflower

Heliopsis helianthoides

Botanical Pronunciation
hee-lee-OP-sis hee-lee-an-THOY-deez

Other Name
Smooth oxeye

Bloom Period and Seasonal Colors
Summer to fall, golden yellow

Mature Height × Spread
36 to 60 in. × 24 to 42 in.

False sunflower, also known as sunflower heliopsis, is one of the brightest rays of sunshine in the garden. It is hard to miss—growing 3 to 5 feet tall. A bushy, well-branched plant with 2- to 3-inch, daisylike flowers with golden yellow petals and brownish yellow centers, it's the earliest bloomer in the daisy family, flowering from late spring through midsummer. Its leaves are unusual—triangular in shape. A native prairie plant, it is tough enough to put up with harsh winters, floods, drought, heat, and humidity—and still look great. Enjoy it indoors as a long-lasting cut flower. It is a versatile plant that looks as good in a perennial border as it does in a naturalistic meadow or restored prairie.

When, Where, and How to Plant

You can find false sunflower locally and from online and mail-order sources in spring. Heliopsis (derived from the Latin *helios*, meaning "sun") grows best in full sun, but tolerates part sun. It prefers fertile, moist, well-drained soil. A prairie native, it tolerates drier soil but will have fewer blooms. Plant, following the instructions on page 105, after all danger of frost has passed. Taller species may require staking; place supports when planting. Leave ample room around the plant for good air circulation. Mulch with 2 to 3 inches of organic matter; renew in spring.

Growing Tips

Water when the top 2 inches of soil are dry or if the plant shows any signs of wilting. Fertilization is not necessary, but you can add a 2-inch layer of compost around the plant in spring before renewing the mulch.

Regional Advice and Care

False sunflower grown in rich soil needs to be divided every two to three years; in poorer soil, divide it only as necessary to rejuvenate the plant or to keep it within bounds. It has no pest or disease problems, although aphids can invade, they really don't cause problems. It naturalizes well.

Companion Planting and Design

False sunflower consorts well with other prairie plants including gayfeather (*Liatris spicata*), tickseed (*Coreopsis* spp.), and goldenrod (*Solidago* spp.). It is beautiful in a cottage garden, adds brightness to a long bed or border, perennial garden, or mixed border, and fits in perfectly in a naturalistic meadow. It attracts pollinators so it is good to have near vegetables and fruits that rely on bees and wasps for fruiting.

Try These

Subspecies *scabra* (to 3 × 3 feet) is less floriferous than the species and has coarse, hairy leaves. 'Golden Plume' ('Goldefeider', to 4½ feet tall) bears double flowers with golden ray flowers around green disk florets. Purple-stemmed 'Prairie Sunset' (to 4 feet) has purple-veined foliage and maroon-centered, yellow flowers. 'Summer Sun' ('Sommersonne', to 3 feet) produces masses of single or double flowers with deep yellow ray flowers—occasionally with an orangish yellow flush—and brownish yellow disk florets.

Garden Heliotrope

Valeriana officinalis

Botanical Pronunciation
vah-lair-ee-AY-nuh oh-fi-shi-NAH-lis

Other Name Common valerian

Bloom Period and Seasonal Colors
Late spring to midsummer, white to pale pink

Mature Height × Spread
3 to 6 ft. × 2 to 4 ft.

Zones 4 to 8

Garden heliotrope, used since Hippocrates' time as a mild sedative, is found today in herbal teas. (However, for legal reasons, I avoid giving advice about medicinal use of plants.) In Latin *valere* means, "to be strong and healthy," referring to its health virtues. Garden heliotrope has divided leaves with many pairs of lance-shaped leaflets; its hollow stems are topped with dense heads of intensely fragrant white or pale pink flowers that attract bees. It makes an excellent cut flower. Seeds have fluffy crowns that help them spread by wind. The fresh root looks like a mop—a mass of long, white, and relatively unbranched rootlets. Fresh valerian root has a much more pleasant aroma than the dried; it has even been used in perfumery.

When, Where, and How to Plant
Plants are available locally as well as from online and mail-order sources. Garden heliotrope, native to sunny western European marshes and streams, prefers wetter conditions than many other herbs. It prefers rich, moist loam but will grow in average soil. Follow directions on page 105 for planting. Seeds are slow to germinate. Sow them in spring under glass or plastic and plant out in summer in a sunny, well-prepared, moist bed.

Growing Tips
Keep soil moist, not wet, until it is established. Garden heliotrope needs to be kept a bit damp, especially if grown in full sun. Add a 4- to 6-inch layer of organic mulch to maintain soil moisture and keep soil cool.

Regional Advice and Care
Garden heliotrope may require staking if the soil is very fertile. Cut down spent flowers to avoid reseeding; garden heliotrope can become invasive. (Save some seed if you want to increase your plantings.) Divide mature plants in spring or autumn, but don't disturb them when in bloom. It has few pests but may suffer from leaf diseases during an unusually rainy season.

Companion Planting and Design
Don't confuse this tall herb with the common red valerian (Jupiter's beard, *Centranthus ruber*) often seen in cottage gardens, but they do look handsome together. Use garden heliotrope as a specimen or accent beside an arbor or towards the back of an herb garden. Include it in a cottage or cutting garden. A tall plant in a narrow bed looks awkward unless planted near a pole, statue, wall, or similar feature; limit the height of tall plants to half the diameter of the garden, or trim to a lower size. Naturalize garden heliotrope on creek banks or ditches in moist, well-drained soil. Grow it in a container, or interplant with other moisture-loving plants like willow blue star (*Amsonia tabernae-montana*) and canna (*Canna × generalis*).

Try These
Valeriana 'Aurea' is a clump-forming, spreading perennial with soft yellow leaves in the spring that turn to lime or medium green by summer. In early summer, branching stems bear rounded clusters of small white flowers.

Garden Phlox

Phlox paniculata

Botanical Pronunciation
FLOKS pah-nik-yew-LAY-tah

Other Name Summer phlox

Bloom Period and Seasonal Colors
Summer to mid-fall, white, pink, lavender, rose, magenta to dark lilac (some with a contrasting colored center

Mature Height × Spread 2 to 5 ft. × 18 to 36 in.

Zones 4 to 8

I remember the sweet scent of garden phlox from childhood visits to my grandmother. The varieties were limited then; much breeding has been done since, especially for mildew resistance. The flowers were just at nose-height for me. I'd walk through them in the early evening inhaling their perfume, comparing one to another, fascinated with what Nana called the "eye" (the darker center of some). Fragrant in the daytime, they were more so at night. I'll never forget the evening she made me sit still, promising me magic. Fireflies were out, but they weren't the show. I heard a soft whirring sound I thought were dozens of hummingbirds, our common day visitors. There were sphinx moths (pupated from tomato hornworms—garden enemies nevermore) flocking to the phlox!

When, Where, and How to Plant

Many varieties of garden phlox are available locally, but online and mail-order sources have the best selection. This native plant prefers rich, lightly moist soil in full sun to part shade. In my experience, there is less chance of powdery mildew when grown in full sun. Follow planting directions on page 105. For good measure, stake tall varieties at planting time. Allow 12 to 18 inches between plants for good air circulation—another mildew preventative.

Growing Tips

Keep soil lightly moist; don't let it dry out. Water at ground level, using soaker hoses to avoid wetting the leaves. If you must water overhead, do so in early morning on a sunny day. Water with compost tea in spring.

Regional Advice and Care

To encourage larger flowers, remove weaker shoots in spring when the growth is small. Regularly deadhead the clusters of flowers to encourage rebloom. Because they are prone to powdery mildew, keep them away from similarly prone plants. Use baking soda spray (see page 175) as a preventative every seven to ten days, but do not spray when the temperature is over 80 degrees Fahrenheit. When it is finished blooming, cut the plant down to the ground.

Companion Planting and Design

Garden phlox is an essential cottage garden plant and is also lovely in beds, borders, and cutting gardens. Grow with any shorter varieties of dianthus (*Dianthus* spp.). It pairs well with Japanese iris (*Iris ensata*) and variegated Dalmatian iris (*Iris pallida* 'Variegata').

Try These

Mildew-resistant varieties include crimson-eyed pink 'Bright Eyes' (30 to 36 inches × 12 to 18 inches), white 'David' (3 to 5 feet × 3 to 4 feet), lavender-pink 'Jeana' (2 to 4 feet × 3 feet), pink-and-white striped 'Peppermint Twist' (12 to 18 inches tall and wide), and white-eyed, lavender-pink 'Shockwave' (12 to 18 inches × 12 inches) with showy variegated yellow-edged leaves. Other charmers, not necessarily mildew resistant, include white 'Mt. Fuji' (2 to 4 feet × 2 to 3 feet), which doesn't need staking, and salmon-orange 'Orange Perfection' (2 to 3 feet × 2 feet).

Goldenrod

Solidago spp.

Botanical Pronunciation
sol-ih-DAY-go

Bloom Period and Seasonal Colors
Midsummer through fall, yellow

Mature Height × Spread
2 to 72 in. × 6 to 36 in.

Zones 4 to 8

First, let me clear up two misconceptions. Goldenrod is *not* a weed—unless it's growing where you don't want it. There are more than 80 indigenous species and many hybrids. Most important, it does *not* cause hay fever; in the wild it often grows with tiny, inconspicuous-flowered, allergenic ragweed. Goldenrod is a beautiful, blazing yellow-flowered plant with elongated flowerheads comprised of numerous florets from summer to fall. Many goldenrods are sweet smelling, attracting bees and butterflies. Native Americans make a delicious tea from the flowers and flour from the pollen. In the wild, it grows in poor soil—wastelands, ditches, near beaches—and can be invasive. Goldenrod thrives in any cultivated garden, and hybrids are well behaved. It is excellent cut fresh or dried.

When, Where, and How to Plant
You can find a few goldenrods locally, but online and mail-order sources have a complete array of these underutilized native plants. Goldenrod grows best in sandy, poor to moderately fertile, well-drained soil in full sun, but tolerates less sun and clay soil. Plant in spring after danger of frost has passed according to instructions on page 105. Mulch with sand or gravel.

Growing Tips
Goldenrod is quite drought tolerant. Water when the top 2 to 3 inches of soil are dry. Fertilization is not necessary.

Regional Advice and Care
This is an easy-care plant. Divide in early spring or mid-fall if necessary or if you simply want more

plants. It may get a fungal problem. Treatment is not necessary but you could use baking soda spray if desired (see page 175).

Companion Planting and Design
A striking combination is brilliant-hued Fireworks goldenrod, pictured above (to 30 × 18 inches) with spiky, outward-radiating racemes and Purple Dome aster (*Symphyotrichum novae-angliae* 'Purple Dome'), pictured above. Grow goldenrod in a wildflower or meadow garden. Include it in a cottage garden (mixed with asters) or use tall varieties in the middle or back of a mixed border. Diminutive goldenrods are perfect in rock gardens or the front of herb gardens.

Try These
'Crown of Rays' (to 24 × 18 inches) has 10-inch-long flattened, radiating panicles of flowers in mid- to late summer. Upright 'Early Bird' (2 to 3 feet tall and wide) blooms in early summer. 'Goldenmosa' (to 30 × 18 inches) is compact, bushy, vigorous, and has an upright flower habit with unusual wrinkled leaves; it has a tendency to be invasive. Clump-forming 'Little Lemon' ('Dansolitlem' to 14 × 18 inches) has upright, tiny, light yellow flowers in mid- to late summer; cut back for a second flush of bloom. *Solidago sphacelata* 'Golden Fleece' (to 18 × 24 inches) is one of the latest-flowering goldenrods. Mound-forming *S. virgaurea* subsp. *minuta* (2 to 8 inches × 6 to 8 inches) has leathery, lance-shaped leaves and 1¼-inch-long, spiky racemes of deep yellow florets; perfect for rock gardens but needs more moisture than most goldenrods.

Joe-Pye Weed

Eutrochium maculatum

Botanical Pronunciation
yew-TRO-kee-um mak-yew-LAY-tum

Other Name Purple boneset

Bloom Period and Seasonal Colors
Midsummer to early autumn, pinkish purple

Mature Height × Spread
4 to 7 ft. × 3 to 4 ft.

Zones 4 to 8

Named in honor of the Native American medicine man who utilized it, Joe-Pye weed (formerly *Eupatorium maculatum*) is impressive for its massive size—growing 4 to 7 feet tall topped with large clusters of purplish pink flowers. I first saw it growing at the back of a 6-foot-deep mixed border. What I didn't realize until I saw steps at the end of the long border was that it cleverly disguised a steep bank. Atop the bank, Joe-Pye weed was enormously tall. It has a light vanilla fragrance, and you will often see bees and butterflies at the flowers, taking in the pollen and nectar. Unfortunately, it usually blooms too late for hummingbirds. It is a fabulous, long-lasting cut flower for a striking arrangement.

When, Where, and How to Plant
Joe-Pye weed is generally available locally and from online and mail-order sources. It grows best in average to rich, moist soil in full or part sun. Plant in spring after all danger of frost has passed. Follow planting instructions on page 105. Mulch with 3 to 4 inches of organic matter, taking care to keep the mulch at least 1 inch away from the stems.

Growing Tips
Keep the soil moist; do not allow it to dry out. Fertilization is not necessary.

Regional Advice and Care
Joe-Pye weed may be big, but it is an easy-care plant. It often takes two years to reach its full size. Once established, it spreads outward to form a dense, good-sized, bushy clump. If the clump gets too large, divide it in spring or fall. You'll need a knife or heavy-duty shears to cut through the tough crown. Cut the plant down to the ground after it has finished blooming in fall to prevent reseeding. Joe-Pye weed is free of pests.

Companion Planting and Design
Since Joe-Pye weed likes moist soil, it thrives near a pond or stream or in a boggy area. It is equally at home in a cottage garden setting as part of a woodland area, a naturalized bog, or rain garden. Other moisture-loving plants that work well with Joe-Pye weed include spring bloomers that add interest while it is growing such as Jack-in-the-pulpit (*Arisaema triphyllum*), marsh marigold (*Caltha palustris*), and trout lily (*Erythronium americanum*). Summer bloomers include rose mallow (*Hibiscus moscheutos*), blue flag *(Iris versicolor)*, and cardinal flower (*Lobelia cardinalis*). Summer to fall bloomers include turtlehead (*Chelone obliqua*), New England aster (*Symphyotrichum novae-angliae*), sneezeweed (*Helenium autumnale*), gayfeather (*Liatris spicata*), and bugbane (*Actaea racemosa*).

Try These
Compact 'Little Red' (to 4 × 3 feet) has 4- to 6-inch clusters of tiny pink-purple blooms; seedheads may last into winter. 'Phantom' (to 4 × 2 feet) bears long-lasting, dome-shaped clusters of tiny, wine-red flowers. *Eutrochium purpureum* subsp. *maculatum* 'Gateway' (to 5 × 2 feet) has rosy purple, lightly scented, domed flowerheads.

New England Aster

Symphyotrichum nova-angliae 'Purple Dome'

Botanical Pronunciation
sim-fie-yo-TRIKE-um NO-vee ANG-glee-ay

Bloom Period and Seasonal Colors
Late summer to fall, deep purple

Mature Height × Spread
18 to 24 in. × 24 to 36 in.

Zones 5 to 8

'Purple Dome' is the most impressive of the New England aster hybrids (formerly *Aster nova-angliae*) as evidenced by its continuing popularity. Magnificent sprays of 2-inch daisylike flowers comprised of royal purple, double petals surround a small yellow center, attracting bees and butterflies alike. It is eye-catching and long-lasting, beginning blooming in midsummer and often lasting (with deadheading) until frost. From a distance, this compact plant looks like a bold purple hemisphere. The flowers are so profuse you barely see the hairy stems or lance-shaped leaves. For most of the growing season, it blends into the background—until it blooms. Many folks treat it as an annual, purchasing the plant in midsummer just before it flowers, but it readily comes back year after year.

When, Where, and How to Plant
Purple Dome aster is readily locally. Although sometimes seen in spring, like chrysanthemums, it is more often available in summer as smallish plants or full-grown container plantings. It grows best in deep, fertile, moist soil in full sun. Plant as soon as it you get it, following the instructions on page 105. 'Purple Dome' makes a good container plant. If you purchase it already growing in a 6-inch or larger container, upsize it to a container at least 2 inches wider. If you grow it in a container, look for a potting mix that has moisture-holding crystals. You can also mix in finely shredded peat moss to the potting mix. Lightly wet the mix before putting it in the pot to ensure even moisture. Mulch with fine bark to maintain moisture.

Growing Tips
Keep plants well watered. Do not let them dry out. Foliar feed every three weeks in season with a kelp or fish emulsion solution, following the package instructions.

Regional Advice and Care
Keep plants well watered; do not let them dry out. Foliar feed every three weeks with a kelp or fish emulsion solution, following package instructions. Attention to deadheading rewards you with a multitude of continuous blooms. If you get the plant in spring, pinch the stems back to the next lower set of leaves every three weeks until mid-July to create a bushy plant.

Companion Planting and Design
'Purple Dome' is majestic in a cottage garden, eye-catching at the edge of a woodland, and lovely in a meadow or butterfly garden. Grow it with brilliant yellow Fireworks goldenrod (*Solidago* 'Fireworks') for a show-stopping combo. Plant it with other asters in varying hues. It also mixes well with chrysanthemums (*Dendranthema* spp.).

Try These
'Alma Potschke' ('Andenken an Alma Pötschke', to 42 × 36 inches) has 2-inch, yellow-centered cerise blooms. 'Harrington's Pink' (to 5 × 3 feet) requires staking for its late-blooming, salmon-pink flowers. 'Honeysong Pink' (to 42 × 30 inches) has showy 1½-inch-wide, yellow-centered pink flowers. Dainty 'Purple Pixie' (12 to 18 inches tall and wide) bears 1½-inch, royal purple blooms with yellow centers.

Oriental Poppy

Papaver orientale

Botanical Pronunciation
pah-PAH-ver or-ee-en-TAL-ee

Bloom Period and Seasonal Colors
Late spring to early summer, orange

Mature Height × Spread
18 to 24 in. × 2 to 3 ft.

Zones 3 to 7

A planting of Oriental poppies is absolutely eye-popping, especially with the low rays of the early morning or late afternoon sun illuminating the crepe-paperlike, brilliant orange petals. Look closely at the 4- to 6-inch, cup-shaped flowers. The base of the petals is usually black, surrounding a prominent central ring of black stamens. You will often hear buzzing before you get close to the flowers, which attract a bevy of buzzing bees. The blossoms are borne singly on hairy stems rising above hairy, gray-green leaves. After the flower blooms, an attractive 1-inch seedpod forms, which you can let ripen or cut for flower arrangements. The plant goes dormant in summer, disappearing altogether. It is very drought tolerant with a deep taproot that makes it difficult to transplant.

When, Where, and How to Plant
You can buy young potted plants locally in spring. For a wide choice of varieties, buy seed from online or mail-order sources. Oriental poppies need deep, fertile, well-drained soil and full sun. Because of its brittle taproot, take care when planting. Allow 15 to 18 inches between plants. Dig a hole the size of the potted poppy, but 4 inches deeper. Add 4 inches of builder's sand to the hole to ensure that the root will not become waterlogged when the plant is dormant. Dipping the potted poppy in transplant solution for a minute helps keep the soil mass intact. Carefully remove the plant from the pot, and insert the entire soil mass into the hole. Add extra soil if necessary, and firm gently with your hands. Water-in with transplant solution.

Growing Tips
Oriental poppies are very drought resistant; normal rainfall should suffice. In case of drought and the top 3 to 4 inches of soil are dry, water the plants. Fertilization is not necessary.

Regional Advice and Care
Oriental poppies will probably not bloom their first year, but they will leaf out. By midsummer, the leaves die back and the plants go dormant. At that time, add several inches of organic mulch to keep the soil temperature cool. By spring, the mulch will have broken down and will feed the plant. It may take two or three years for the plant to bloom, but it is well worth the wait. If you want to use Oriental poppies in flower arrangements, cut the flower and immediate sear the cut end with a match. After several minutes, put it in water. Oriental poppies are pest free.

Companion Planting and Design
Oriental poppies are beautiful with blue- and purple-flowered plants such as blue false indigo (*Baptisia australis*), speedwell (*Veronica spicata*, and bellflowers (*Campanula* spp.).

Try These
'Allegro' (to 18 inches tall) has bold black basal markings on bright orange petals. 'Beauty of Livermere' ('Beauty of Livermore', to 40 inches) bears crimson-scarlet flowers with prominent black stamens. 'Perry's White' (to 36 inches) sports white blooms.

Peony

Paeonia lactiflora

Botanical Pronunciation
pay-OH-nee-ah lak-tih-FLOOR-ah

Other Name
Common garden peony

Bloom Period and Seasonal Colors
Late spring to early summer, white, pink, and red, single and bicolors

Mature Height × Spread
18 to 36 in. × 24 to 36 in.

Peonies are the very essence of late spring with blousy 3- to 6-inch-wide, rounded, single or double flowers that rise above handsome, shiny lobed leaves. For me, their sweet perfume is the precursor to roses that will soon bloom. Peonies are among the longest-lived perennials. I used to live at the end of a long drive, 100 feet of which was lined on both sides with more than 20 different peonies—planted in 1906. They're still blooming in profusion with little attention: sadly, most of their names were lost over time. All too often, a heavy rain or unseasonably early heat shortens the season, but they are worth it. Pick the flowers to keep the plant blooming. Both leaves and flowers are superb in arrangements.

When, Where, and How to Plant
Container-grown peonies are available locally in spring. Online and mail-order sources ship bare-root plants. Peonies grow best in deep, fertile, moist, well-drained soil in full to part sun. Choose your location well as they don't like to be disturbed. Dig a hole 1½ times the size of the container. Mix plenty of organic matter (compost, well-rotted manure, leaf mold, or humus) to the soil from the hole. Add amended soil to the hole; place the plant so the eyes (buds) are 2 inches below the soil surface. Fill with remaining soil and tamp down with your hands. Allow at least 3 feet between plants. Be patient, it may be several years before the plant blooms. For bare-root plants, follow planting instructions on page 105.

Growing Tips
Do not let soil dry out; keep it lightly moist. In spring, add 2 inches of compost around the plant to feed the soil during the growing season.

Regional Advice and Care
Use peony hoops to support double-flowered varieties. Cut the leaves down as they die off in fall. Add a 4-inch layer of organic mulch after the first freeze to keep the plant from heaving during winter thaws. Remove mulch in spring. Peonies are relatively pest free; ants on buds are not a problem.

Companion Planting and Design
Peonies are iconic with foxgloves (*Digitalis* spp.) and larkspur (*Consolida ajacis*) against a picket fence in a cottage garden. A backdrop of lilacs (*Syringa* spp.) in a mixed border heralds their bloom. The emerging foliage of peonies nicely hides yellowing leaves of early bulbs like crocus (*Crocus* spp.) and grape hyacinths (*Muscari armeniacum*).

Try These
'Buttercup' is a single white with yellow stamens. 'Do Tell' has pale shell-pink petals with showy dark rose-pink stamens. Double-flowered 'Duchesse de Nemours' bears pure white blooms. Heirloom 'Festiva Maxima' has double, red-flecked white blossoms. 'Karl Rosenfeld' bears double, dark crimson blooms; 'Sarah Bernhardt' has double, rose-pink flowers. Fernleaf peony (*Paeonia tenuifolia*, 12 to 18 inches) has ferny foliage and 2½- to 3-inch-wide ruby-red blossoms; 'Rubra Plena' has magnificent double blooms.

Purple Coneflower

Echinacea purpurea

Botanical Pronunciation
eh-kih-NAY-shah per-per-EE-ah

Bloom Period and Seasonal Colors
Summer to early fall, rose-pink, white, red, magenta; fall into winter, brown seedheads

Mature Height × Spread
2 to 5 ft. × 15 to 18 in.

Purple coneflower is one of the quintessential native prairie plants. The numerous varieties attest to its popularity among gardeners throughout America. It is a versatile, handsome plant that is at home in any type of garden—prairie restoration, wildflower meadow, cottage garden, or even a cutting garden. In summer, butterflies, bees, and the occasional hummingbird visit the flowers. The plant is well branched and shrubby, usually growing 2 to 4 feet tall. The stems bear dozens of flowerheads comprised of purplish pink ray flowers and a central brown cone of disk flowers from summer to fall. I love purple coneflower as a "lazy gardener's plant." In fall, just leave the flower stems and birds will come eat the seeds well into winter.

When, Where, and How to Plant
Purple coneflower is readily available locally in spring, but many of the more diverse cultivated varieties are only available through online and mail-order sources. It grows best in full sun in rich, loamy, well-drained soil. Plant in spring after the last frost date. Allow at least 18 inches between plants for good air circulation. Follow planting instructions on page 105. Mulch with 3 inches of organic material; keep it at least 1 inch from the stems.

Growing Tips
Keep the soil lightly moist until the plant is established. Purple coneflower is susceptible to powdery mildew, so water at ground level or early in the morning. Once established, its long taproot make the plant quite drought tolerant. Fertilization is not necessary.

Regional Advice and Care
At the first sign of powdery mildew, spray the leaves with baking soda solution (see page 175 for complete directions). Continue spraying every seven to ten days. Otherwise, purple coneflower is carefree. Division is not recommended (or needed), as plants that have been divided are bushier but far less floriferous. Cut flowers for fresh or dried arrangements—and encourage rebloom.

Companion Planting and Design
Due to its susceptibility to powdery mildew, do *not* grow it with other susceptible plants including beebalm (*Monarda didyma*), garden phlox (*Phlox paniculata*), black-eyed Susan (*Rudbeckia* spp.) or zinnias (*Zinnia elegans*). It is lovely in a cottage setting with chrysanthemums (*Dendranthema* spp.), Jupiter's beard (*Centranthus ruber*), and threadleaf coreopsis (*Coreopsis verticillata* 'Moonbeam'). It is handsome with ornamental grasses like blue fescue (*Festuca glauca*) and little bluestem (*Schizachyrium scoparium*).

Try These
'Bright Star' ('Leuchtstern', to 48 × 18 inches) has bright rosy to lavender-pink petals, maroon centers. 'Pink Double Delight' (to 24 × 18 inches) bears 3-inch, pink, pom-pom-like double flowers. 'Prairie Splendor' (to 24 inches tall and wide) has downward-arching, 4- to 5-inch-wide, rose-magenta flowers. 'Red Knee High' (to 18 inches tall and wide) is a long bloomer with magenta-red petals. 'White Swan' (to 36 × 24 inches) is an early bloomer with drooping white petals, coppery orange center.

Queen of the Prairie

Filipendula rubra

Botanical Pronunciation
fil-ih-PEND-yew-lah ROO-bruh

Other Name
Meadowsweet

Bloom Period and Seasonal Colors
Early to midsummer, pale pink

Mature Height × Spread
6 to 8 ft. × 3 to 4 ft.

With its majestic size and shape, queen of the prairie is a well-deserved name. Its foliage is bold with 8-inch-wide, three-lobed, toothed leaves. In early to midsummer, branching red stems bear 6-inch, feathery clusters of closely packed, pale pink florets. Considering that it is one of the native plants of the tall prairies, I continue to be in awe of our forefathers (including some of my forebears) traveling on foot or in wagons, going through these plants that are larger than life. Queen of the prairie is a water-loving plant that is perfect for a boggy area or rain garden. Both leaves and flowers are delightfully lightly fragrant, adding to its charms. And I have to admire anything that stands tall and strong without staking.

When, Where, and How to Plant
Queen of the prairie can be found locally in spring, with greater choices available through online and mail-order sources. Queen of the prairie grows best in moderately rich, consistently moist soil in full sun to part shade. It thrives in the soil along lakes, ponds, streams, or by your own water garden. Plant after the last frost date in spring (see page 105 for planting instructions). Allow at least 3 feet between plants. Mulch with 3 inches of organic material, taking care to keep it at least 1 inch away from the stems.

Growing Tips
Keep the soil evenly moist; do not let it dry out. Fertilizing is not necessary.

Regional Advice and Care
Clumps can spread rapidly by creeping stolons. Lift and divide clumps in fall if they have overstepped their bounds or if they are getting too large. If the clump is old, you'll need a sharp knife or heavy-duty shears to separate it. Replant the divisions 3 feet apart. To encourage the plant to rebloom, cut back any spent flowerheads. Once the blooms are finished for the season, you can either cut them down or let them be and enjoy their beauty as they catch the breeze. It attracts bees and other pollinators.

Companion Planting and Design
Thriving in wet or boggy soil, queen of the prairie mixes well with astilbe (*Astilbe* cvs.), bergenia (*Bergenia* spp.), Japanese iris (*Iris ensata*), Siberian iris (*Iris siberica*), true forget-me-not (*Myosotis scorpioides*), primroses (*Primula* spp.), cardinal flower (*Lobelia cardinalis*), meadow rue (*Thalictrum* spp.), and great blue lobelia (*Lobelia syphilitica*). It is striking *en masse*, at the back of a border or cottage garden, or in a meadow or rain garden.

Try These
'Albicans' ('Magnificum Album', to 6 × 3 feet) blooms white. 'Venusta' ('Magnifica', to 8 × 4 feet) has deep rose pink flowers fading to soft pink as they age. *Filipendula vulgaris* 'Plena' (meadowsweet, to 2 × 2 feet) has fully double white flowers. *F. palmata* (Siberian meadowsweet, to 4 × 2 feet) bears 4- to 5-inch open clusters of pink florets.

Russian Sage

Perovskia atriplicifolia

Botanical Pronunciation
per-OV-skee-ah at-trih-pliss-ih-FOE-lee-ah

Bloom Period and Seasonal Colors
Summer, violet-blue; fall, gray seedheads

Mature Height × Spread
3 to 5 ft. × 2 to 3 ft.

Zones
5 to 8

Russian sage is a lightly fragrant shrubby plant with a delicate air about it—one of those wonderful plants I call a veil plant. Although tall, growing 3 to 5 feet high, it is slender. You see through it as if you were wearing a blue-gray veil. Plantings behind it take on a more interesting appearance as you view them through the willowy silvery stems and long slender panicles of small, tubular, violet-blue flowers. For that reason, it works equally well in the front, middle, or back of a garden bed. Russian sage goes through three seasonal stages: soft grayish green shoots in springtime, followed by tiny violet-blue flowers in summer, and finishing the growing season with silky gray seedheads in fall.

When, Where, and How to Plant
Russian sage is readily available locally. Look for the named varieties from online and mail-order sources. It requires full sun and grows best in poor to average, well-drained soil. Plant after all danger of frost has passed, following instructions on page 105. Allow at least 3 feet between plants if you want to maintain a light veil effect. If you choose a shrubbier, thicker look, plant them 2 feet apart and there will be plenty of overlapping among plants. Mulch with 2 inches of grit, gravel, sand, or pebbles. Keep the mulch at least 1 inch away from the stems.

Growing Tips
Water lightly until the plant is established. Silver or gray foliage is a good indicator that a plant is drought tolerant. Water when the top 2 inches of soil are dry. Fertilizing is not necessary.

Regional Advice and Care
Russian sage is low maintenance and rarely needs dividing. Its hardiness rating has been underrated, listed as Zone 6 in many books. Although it will die back to the ground, have no fear; it will resprout in spring in Zone 5 (sometimes in Zone 4). The only chore is to cut the stems down to 1 inch in spring (or after a hard freeze in winter if you want a tidy garden). It is resistant to rabbits and attracts bees and other pollinators.

Companion Planting and Design
With its silvery foliage, use Russian sage to cool down hot-colored plants like zinnias (*Zinnia* spp.) and red-orange Mexican sunflower (*Tithonia rotundifolia*), or to separate blatant colors, such as magenta winecups (*Callirhoe involucrata*) and Europa rose (*Rosa* 'Europa'), which has dark burgundy-green stems and velvety red flowers. It's always pretty with pink flowers like garden phlox (*Phlox paniculata)* and magic lily (*Lycoris squamagera*).

Try These
'Lacey Blue' ('Lisslett', to 24 inches tall and wide) bears lavender-blue blooms. 'Little Spire' (18 to 24 inches tall and wide) has violet-blue flowers lasting until frost. Peek-a-Blue® ('WALPPB', 24 to 30 × 18 to 30 inches), a patented variety (illegal to propagate), has very lacy silvery green foliage, and lavender-blue flowers.

Sedum

Sedum 'Autumn Joy'

Botanical Pronunciation SEE-dum

Other Name Stonecrop

Bloom Period and Seasonal Colors
Summer through fall, pink to coppery red; winter, coppery brown

Mature Height × Spread
18 to 24 in. × 18 to 24 in.

Formerly *Hylotelephium*, 'Autumn Joy' ('Herbstfreude') is a joy to behold—in all four seasons. A bushy, succulent-leafed perennial, it has slightly glaucous, green stems and 3- to 5-inch-long, fleshy, glaucous green, oval leaves with slightly serrated edges. The flower clusters begin to form in summer, looking like light green heads of broccoli. As the season turns, so do the 8-inch wide clusters of tiny, ½-inch, star-shaped florets, gradually turning deep pink and attracting bees and butterflies. As autumn progresses, they become pinkish bronze and then coppery red. By winter, they fade to coppery brown, lasting through all but the toughest winters. The leaves slowly disappear. Then suddenly in spring, small rosettes of leaves appear at ground level and this beautiful sedum begins its four-season metamorphosis once more.

When, Where, and How to Plant
'Autumn Joy' is likely the most popular sedum, readily available locally—even at grocery and hardware stores that sell plants in spring. It prefers average to rich, well-drained soil but will grow in nearly any well-drained soil in full sun. Wait until several weeks after the last frost date to plant. Follow planting instructions on page 105; allow 2 feet between plants. Mulch with 3 inches of gravel, sand, grit, or pebbles. Keep the mulch at least 1 inch away from the stems.

Growing Tips
Water lightly until the plant is established. 'Autumn Joy' is drought tolerant. Water when the top 3 inches of soil are dry. Fertilizing is not necessary.

Regional Advice and Care
It's a relatively carefree plant, virtually pest and disease free. Butterflies and bees flock to it in late summer and fall. In spring, cut any broken stems. It may need dividing after several years—you will know this if the center opens and splays out. Divide and replant divisions, discarding the dead centers. Cut flowers to use fresh or dried in arrangements.

Companion Planting and Design
This succulent is quite versatile—lovely clustered in a cottage garden, handsome in a mixed bed or border, perfect in a rock garden, and even elegant enough to edge a formal garden. It mixes well with other fall-blooming plants such as New England aster (*Symphyotrichum novae-angliae*), New York aster (*S. novi-belgii*), goldenrod (*Solidago* spp.), and berried shrubs like Japanese barberry (*Berberis thunbergii* 'Atropurpurea'), rockspray (*Cotoneaster horizontalis*), and bearberry (*Arctostaphylos uva-ursi*).

Try These
'Autumn Delight' (to 3 feet tall and wide), is striking with slightly serrated, dark green-edged, lime green leaves that set off deep pink heads of tiny florets. 'Neon' (to 24 inches high and wide) has light gray-green leaves, bright neon pink flower clusters. 'Ruby Glow' (to 10 × 18 inches) has red stems with deep blue-green leaves and clusters of small, star-shaped, rosy-red flowers. *Sedum telephium* 'Matrona' (to 30 × 24 inches) has purplish red stems bearing bronze-tinged, gray-green leaves set off flat heads of pink florets.

Threadleaf Coreopsis

Coreopsis verticillata 'Moonbeam'

Botanical Pronunciation
kor-ee-OP-sis ver-tiss-ill-LAY-tah

Other Name Tickseed

Bloom Period and Seasonal Colors
Early summer into fall, creamy yellow

Mature Height × Spread
18 to 30 in. × 18 in. to spreading

Coreopsis is usually thought of as a basketball-sized clump of leaves with many tall, wire-stemmed, daisylike cut flowers of golden yellow that reseeds freely. But threadleaf coreopsis is a lower-growing, thin-leaf perennial plant, native to the prairies, that spreads steadily by rhizomes into a mass of needlelike dark green leaves with taller stems of smaller, dainty daisylike flowers. Cheerful, buttery yellow 'Moonbeam' was named a Perennial Plant Association Plant of the Year. A must-have for its beautiful spreading form and continuous stream of 1- to 2-inch-wide flowers from early summer to fall. It is easy to grow, drought tolerant, naturalizes readily, attracts bees and butterflies to the blooms, and to top it off, makes an excellent cut flower. Make room for this sun-loving gem.

When, Where, and How to Plant
Threadleaf coreopsis is readily available locally in spring as well as from online and mail-order sources. It needs full sun and prefers dry (even rocky), well-drained soil, although it will grow in slightly moist soil as long as it is very well-drained. Add some builder's sand to the soil to enhance drainage. Follow directions on page 105 for planting. Water only to prevent wilting, and fertilize lightly to get plants started.

Growing Tips
Water deeply but infrequently, and fertilize lightly in spring and early summer.

Regional Advice and Care
Threadleaf coreopsis needs very little care, other than regular deadheading to remove seedpods, which produces more flowers. Shear back by one-third to reinvigorate a plant if it seems tired (or after too much rain). Divide mature clumps every three or four years to maintain vigor. There are no major insect or disease problems, except fungal diseases caused by overwatering or rainy spells. No control is needed, as new buds will appear quickly during drier, hotter weather.

Companion Planting and Design
Threadleaf coreopsis grows well as a specimen beside steps, and in wildflower plantings. Combine with other plants in a cottage garden, perennial bed, or flower border, especially with veronicas (*Veronica* spp.) and daylilies (*Hemerocallis* spp.). It is tidy enough to include in rock gardens and drought- and heat-tolerant enough to cascade from containers on hot decks in the summer sun. Because it grows new foliage in spring and blooms in summer, it is perfect planted over spring-blooming bulbs, such as crocus (*Crocus* spp.) and daffodils (*Narcissus* spp.), which are dormant in summer.

Try These
'Golden Gain' (12 to 18 inches tall and wide) with golden yellow petals that surround darker centers of 1- to 2-inch-wide blooms, self-sows. 'Grandiflora' (2 to 3 feet tall and wide) has bright yellow petals with a darker yellow center. 'Zagreb' (to 18 inches tall and wide) bears deep golden-yellow, 1- to 2-inch-wide flowers. *Coreopsis rosea* looks like threadleaf coreopsis but has mauve-pink flowers from summer to early fall and naturalizes well on dry slopes.

Willow Blue Star

Amsonia tabernaemontana

Botanical Pronunciation
am-SO-nee-ah tab-er-nay-mon-TAN-ah

Other Name
Blue star

Bloom Period and Seasonal Colors
Mid- to late spring, blue; fall, yellow foliage

Mature Height × Spread
2 to 3 ft. × 2 to 3 ft.

This refined milkweed relative resembles a miniature, blue, spring-flowering garden phlox (*Phlox paniculata*) in growth habit and flower shape. Willow blue star grows naturally in some of the most miserable places, such as clay-based ditches, and spots that are wet all winter and spring but cracked and dry in summer. Its many unbranched stems have narrow, willow-like leaves, and each stem is topped with loose but showy clusters of small, star-shaped, pale or sky blue flowers. Although the seedpods are narrow and not showy, the clear yellow autumn leaf color is an added bonus. Flower clusters are on long stems, making them easy to cut and use in flower arrangements; wear gloves when stripping off the narrow leaves—some people are allergic to the sap.

When, Where, and How to Plant
Willow blue star plants are rarely available locally, but are available through online and mail-order sources. It loves sunlight and thrives in average, well-drained, moist, loamy soil, but will grow well in part shade and in heavy (clay) soils. The easiest way to get started is to find someone who is growing it and will share his or her plant. Divide the plant—root and stems—in early spring. If the plant is in full bloom or it's summertime, simply cut back the stems before digging off a nice-sized chunk of the roots. Plant the division at the same level as it was growing originally. If you buy plants, follow the planting directions on page 105.

Growing Tips
Water only during extended periods of drought, and fertilize sparingly.

Regional Advice and Care
Willow blue star grows under great duress, needing no care at all, other than perhaps cutting down the faded foliage after a hard freeze or snowstorm. Rust may cause some discoloration on some of the foliage, but it doesn't harm the plant.

Companion Planting and Design
Plant blue star in a rain garden or in low wet areas, near the bottoms of ditch banks, alongside a pond or water garden, or any other place that stays wet in the winter and spring, even if it dries out in midsummer. Companions that complement willow blue star and tolerate wet or heavy soils include ornamental grasses such as *Miscanthus* spp. or northern sea oats (*Chasmanthium latifolium*), cardinal flower (*Lobelia cardinalis*), canna (*Canna × generalis*), and elderberry (*Sambucus canadensis*). Its fall colors also set off chrysanthemums (*Dendranthema* spp.) when they come into bloom.

Try These
'Montana' (to 18 × 12 inches) is more compact than the species, has slightly wider leaves, and deeper blue flowers, which bloom up to two weeks earlier than the species. 'Short Stack' (to 12 × 18 inches) has sky blue flowers in early spring. Willow-leaf amsonia (willow-leaf blue star, *Amsonia hubrectii*, 2 to 3 feet tall and wide) has very soft, fine, needle-shaped leaves and powdery blue flowers.

Yucca

Yucca filamentosa

Botanical Pronunciation
YUCK-ah fill-uh-men-TOE-sah

Other Name Adam's needle

Bloom Period and Seasonal Color
Early to midsummer, white; evergreen foliage

Mature Height × Spread
2 to 4 ft. × 3 to 5 ft.

Zones 5 to 8

Yucca has a bad reputation, partly because everyone gets warned not to poke an eye out on one. Actually, soft-tipped native kinds are not dangerous, and since their bold evergreen forms and striking flowers are such useful accents for architectural or tropical effects, they are nearly overused. Spreading rosettes of slender, swordlike leaves up to 2 or more feet long with sharply pointed but soft tips grow in whorls from a short trunk. Each mounding clump has several crowns of these rosettes; leaf edges are fringed with small filaments, like threads from a brand-new shirt. In the summer, nearly every crown sprouts a 4- to 6-foot-tall spire with dozens of 2- to 3-inch-wide fragrant, white with pink tinge, perfectly edible (when cooked), bell-shaped flowers.

When, Where, and How to Plant

Yucca plants are available at nurseries, garden centers, and home-improvement stores as well as from online and mail-order sources. Yucca thrives in any sunny, well-drained, dry soil with moderate to low fertility. See page 105 for planting instructions. Mulch with several inches of sand, gravel, or grit.

Growing Tips

Tolerant of prolonged dry spells, yucca is fine with normal rainfall. These deer- and rabbit-resistant xeriscape plants can thrive without water. No fertilizing is needed.

Regional Advice and Care

Young plants grow slowly at first; they fill in and usually become quite solid. Divide clumps in the spring by removing suckers or "pups" from the base of plants. Root in moist potting soil, or bury root sections of stems in sandy soil in fall. Remove faded flower stems, leaving a few long enough for birds to perch on. Occasionally, foliage will be mottled from a heavy infestation of spider mites or scale insects; control with a dormant oil application in late winter.

Companion Planting and Design

Yucca grows well in tight, dry, sloped spots or small areas next to pavement with reflected heat where not much else can survive. Grown for its bold, linear leaves, its coarse clump-forming habit, and its strikingly tall flower stem, yucca can be used effectively either as a single specimen, in showy groups, or as a fabulous contrast with more traditional garden plants such as coneflowers (*Rudbeckia* spp. and *Echinacea purpurea*), daylilies (*Hemerocallis* spp.), and ornamental grasses in beds and borders. Its winter form can help define a bed. Though the commonly grown plain green yucca can be very effective, several stunning cultivars add "oomph" to the landscape.

Try These

'Color Guard' (2 to 3 feet tall and wide) has 4-inch-wide gold-centered green leaves, a 5- to 6-foot flower stalk in late spring. 'Variegata' (18 to 24 inches tall and wide) has blue-green leaves with creamy white margins that turn pinkish in winter and a 5- to 6-foot-tall flower spike in summer.

ROSES

FOR THE PRAIRIE & PLAINS STATES

Roses are among the most ancient flowers; fossil evidence dates them back more than 40 million years. The Chinese were the first in recorded history to cultivate roses about 2737 B.C. In the western world, the ancient Romans took rose cultivation seriously. They were attracted to roses not just for their fragrance and beauty, but for their medicinal and culinary properties too. The ancient Greek poet Sappho gave roses the appellation "Queen of Flowers" more than 2,500 years ago. No wonder they are so beloved. Today, millennia later, when asked what they want to have in their garden, most people say roses.

A white Iceberg rose contrasts beautifully with garden lobelia (*Lobelia erinus*).

The Four Key Points to Growing Roses

Roses have the stigma of being hard to grow. Follow these four guidelines for rose-growing success:

1. Choose a spot that gets at least six hours of sun, has good air circulation, and is away from trees and shrubs that cast shadows and compete for soil nutrients.
2. Select a rose with at least three healthy canes, ideally grown on its own rootstock and hardy for your area.
3. Provide good, rich soil with good drainage.
4. Give plenty of TLC (tender loving care), including proper mulching, feeding, watering, pruning, preparing for winter dormancy, and controlling pests and diseases.

Selecting a Rose

Before setting out to buy a rose, do some research. Walk around your neighborhood, visit local public and botanical gardens, and see what people are growing. If something catches your eye, ask about it. Get the name, type of rose, hardiness (how well it survives the winter—with or without protection), how long it has been growing (to determine long-term performance), and any pest and disease problems. Contact your local Cooperative Extension Service for information on roses suited for your area.

Container-grown roses are found locally throughout the growing season. The choices are limited compared to bare-root plants. However, they are available later in the season—even in bloom—so you can judge a plant's vigor. Roses shipped to you are dormant, bare-root roses. Some cardboard-boxed roses in stores are simply bare roots wrapped with wood shavings or newspaper. You can judge by the heft whether it's bare root or containerized. Check the canes (stems) to be sure they are healthy with green or reddish color and are firm to the touch. Avoid ones that appear dry, broken, or have a lot of new growth.

Test your soil to make sure the pH is between 6.0 and 6.5 before planting roses.

Planting

Roses are heavy feeders and need good, rich, well-drained, slightly acidic soil with a pH between 6.0 to 6.5. Consider site spacing before you plant. Allow 12 inches between miniature roses, 24 inches between hybrid teas, 30 inches between grandifloras, 36 inches between floribundas, and 7 feet between climbers.

Container-grown roses are easy to plant. Dig a hole a few inches deeper and wider than the container. Amend the soil with 1 cup superphosphate and 2 cups (or more) of compost. Add about 6 inches of amended soil to the hole. Pour in 1 quart transplant solution; let it soak in. Remove rose from its container (even "plantable" boxes). If it is grafted (look for the knoblike bud union, where rootstock and main plant were joined), plant the bud union 2 to 3 inches *below* ground level. Add soil, filling the hole halfway, and gently firm. Pour in 1 quart transplant solution. Add remaining soil; water with 2 quarts transplant solution. Add 2 to 3 inches of organic mulch (keeping 1 inch away from the stem) around the plant.

Bare-root roses are worth the effort. As soon as you get one, unwrap and soak in water for at least eight hours. If you cannot plant within twenty-four hours, wrap in wet newspaper and store at 40 degrees Fahrenheit in the dark for up to a week. Dig a hole at least 12 to 18 inches deep and 12 inches wide. Amend soil as described. Fill the hole with transplant solution and let it soak in. Prune to three or four healthy canes. Cut back damaged roots or disproportionately long ones. Form a cone of soil to support the roots, high enough so the bud union is 2 to 3 inches *below* soil level. Position the plant, spreading its roots over the cone. Add amended soil, filling two-thirds of the hole. Add 2 quarts transplant solution; let it soak in. Fill the hole; firm soil gently with your hands. Add 2 quarts transplant solution; let it soak in. Cover two-thirds of the plant with moistened soil to protect it from wind and weather, while providing extra moisture. Check weekly. When new growth is 1 to 2 inches long, gently remove the extra soil, smoothing to soil level. Mulch well.

Feeding Your Roses

Roses are *heavy* feeders. But do not feed newly planted roses for at least at month. Feed species, shrub roses, ramblers, and climbers only once, in early spring before they leaf out. Feed hybrid teas, floribundas, and grandifloras three times—in early spring before they leaf out, when flowering begins, and in early August.

If using all-purpose rose fertilizer, avoid ones with weed and pest killers. Always follow package instructions. Or, use a granular, general-purpose (5-10-5) fertilizer. Spread a handful or cupful around the base of each plant (several inches away from canes) and water well. For the third feeding, use a formulation without nitrogen like 0-10-10.

I prefer an organic approach. In early spring, apply 2 to 3 cups compost, ½ cup bone meal, and ½ cup bloodmeal. Water in with 1 gallon of water (2 tablespoons Epsom salts added). Top with 4 to 6 inches of organic mulch. Foliar feed monthly with a solution of fish emulsion or kelp, spraying leaves top and bottom but not when the temperature is above 80 degrees Fahrenheit.

Watering

Roses need the equivalent of at least 1 inch of rain a week. The best way to measure is with an inexpensive rain gauge. Several factors influence the amount of water needed.

In hot, humid weather, roses need less water than when it is hot and dry. Factor in summer "breezes," which increase evaporation.

The best way to tell if a rose needs water is to stick a finger into the soil. If it feels dry more than 1 inch down, water. Water at ground level to avoid wetting the leaves and some of the fungal problems of roses. One of the easiest ways is with a soaker hose attached to a timer.

Pruning

Why prune? To remove diseased or deadwood, encourage new growth, and train the plant to grow with an open crown, allowing for optimal air circulation. When you cut a rose for a bouquet or cut one back that has faded, that is also pruning.

Major pruning is done in early spring. Hybrid teas, grandifloras, and floribundas can be cut back to 6 inches. Be sure to cut out all dead wood (rub stem gently with your thumbnail; if you see green, it is alive). Look for bud eyes—small nubs on the stems. Make a 45-degree cut ¼ to ½ inch above an outward-facing bud eye to encourage outward growth. When the plant is in full leaf, cut just above the lowest five- or seven-leaflet leaf. That gives a nice long stem for flower arranging, and a new stem will grow where you cut. Do not prune after the end of August to mid-September—deadhead only.

Getting Ready for Winter

Hybrid teas and grandifloras need the most attention. Check the hardiness of your floribundas and other roses. After the first *light* frost, mound 4 to 6 inches of light soil around established roses. After a *hard* frost, when that layer has frozen, add another few inches of soil, allowing each layer to freeze before adding another until it is about 12 inches high. You'll have a broad cone of soil with rose canes sticking up from that. In Zones 4 and lower (and for hybrid teas), cover the frozen mound with leaves. Cover any new plant *completely* or the extreme cold will kill tender canes. Do not use the Styrofoam™ covers to protect roses as the temperature inside can heat up on warm winter days, making the rose break dormancy too early.

It's Spring!

Spring is fickle; don't be in a rush to remove winter protection. Even light frosts can kill tender growth. Peek under the mulch to see if any growth has begun. When danger of frost has passed, *gently* remove mulch, taking care not to injure tender growth. Keep some hay on hand in case of a late freeze. A light covering can prevent a late winterkill.

Another benefit to roses, assuming that you grow them organically, is that the petals of many varieties are delicious. Remove the bitter base of the petal before using. Their edibility dates back to Roman times. The hips (fruit) are higher in Vitamin C than oranges. Roses also attract bees and other pollinators to the garden.

Now that you know what to do, here are some choice roses to get your garden going.

Alchymist Rose

Rosa 'Alchymist'

Botanical Pronunciation
ROE-zuh

Bloom Period and Seasonal Colors
Early summer, apricot blend

Mature Height × Spread
8 to 12 ft. × 4 to 8 ft.

Zones 4 to 8

'Alchymist' is classified in several different rose categories—large-flowered climber, modern shrub, and shrub. It was bred by Kordes in Germany (known for breeding cold-hardy roses) and introduced in 1956. It is a stunning rose, growing 8 to 12 feet high. It can be trained on an arbor, fence, or pillar. It blooms early in the season with outstanding 3½- to 4-inch double blooms (sometimes quartered—like old-fashioned roses) in shades of apricot from the deepest part of the center, fading at the outer petals. Strongly perfumed, if its size and color don't draw you to it, the fragrance will. The petals (remove bitter bases) have a pure rose flavor. Not only can it handle our cold winters, it thrives in the heat of the summer.

When, Where, and How to Plant

'Alchymist' is available as a container-grown or bare-root plant. If you buy it bare root, look for an "own-root" plant, which means the entire plant is all 'Alchymist', not grafted onto hardier rootstock. Plant bare-root 'Alchymist' when the soil can be worked in spring. Container-grown plants available later in spring should be hardened off and can take the chill, even before the last frost date. See complete planting instructions on page 131.

Growing Tips

Keep the plant well watered until it is established. Mulch well to keep the soil moist. Foliar feed once a month.

Regional Advice and Care

'Alchymist' may be prone to blackspot, a fungal disease that manifests as small black spots on the leaves. At the first sign, remove and destroy any affected leaves. Check stems for spotting; if they are affected, cut them off and destroy them. Dip pruners in alcohol between cuts to avoid spreading the disease. Clean up around the plant, removing any leaves on the ground. Blackspot starts on the lowest branches and spreads by spores when you water from above and by rain. When a water droplet hits mature spores, they are hurled to leaves above. Removing the mulch around the plant and replacing with fresh mulch helps as spores lodge in mulch. At the first sign, or if it has been a problem in the past, spray with baking soda solution (see page 175) as soon as the plant leafs out. Re-spray the entire plant, including tops and bottoms of leaves and canes, every seven to ten days. Do not spray if the temperature is over 80 degrees Fahrenheit. Since this rose does not rebloom, take advantage and cut plenty of flowers to enjoy indoors. For detailed rose care information, see page 132.

Companion Planting and Design

'Alchymist' is beautiful sharing a trellis with 'Goldflame' honeysuckle (*Lonicera* × *heckrottii*). Go bold and paint the trellis cobalt blue; be subtle with dark green.

Try These

'Buff Beauty' (to 6 feet tall) is a hybrid musk shrub rose with slightly paler blooms in midseason.

Bonica® Rose

Rosa Bonica®

Botanical Pronunciation
ROE-zuh

Bloom Period and Seasonal Colors
Summer, medium pink

Mature Height × Spread
3 to 5 ft. × 2 to 4 ft.

Zones 4 to 8

Bonica® is a shrub rose developed by the famous house of Meilland in France in 1982. In 1987, it became the first shrub rose named an All-America Rose Selection; a decade later, it was named World's Favorite Rose. It is a carefree rose, being very disease resistant. The 1- to 2-inch-wide, double flowers (with more than forty petals) are in rosette form, borne in clusters. Blooms are medium pink, fading to a lighter pink at the slightly frilled edges. The canes are strongly arched, and flowers are produced along their length throughout much of the summer. It is a good repeat bloomer. The glossy leaves are handsome—an unusually coppery light green color. It's perfect for small gardens, but note that it has no fragrance.

When, Where, and How to Plant
Bonica is readily available locally as an own-root, container-grown plant. You can also purchase bare-root plants through online and mail-order sources. Follow detailed planting directions on page 131. This tough plant can be put in the ground before the last frost date as long as the ground is workable, the soil is not too wet, and the plant is dormant. If it has already leafed out, keep it in a cool, bright place until danger of frost has passed. Otherwise, the tender leaves and buds could freeze. Whether it's container-grown or bare root, be sure to water at planting with transplant solution.

Growing Tips
Keep the soil lightly moist until the plant is established. A thick layer of mulch helps retain moisture and prevents weeds. Unless it is very hot and dry, weekly watering will suffice. Foliar feed monthly.

Regional Advice and Care
This rose is very carefree since it is not bothered by pests or diseases. Cut the faded blooms to encourage rebloom. Always cut at a 45-degree angle just above an outward-facing leaflet that has five to seven leaves. This makes the new growth develop outward from the shrub, rather than crowding the center. After August 15, do not cut back the faded flowers. Let them develop into the bright orange fruit (rose hips) that will attract birds and other creatures. You can cut the hips and use them in fresh or dried in flower arrangements. For more rose care information, see page 132. Bonica® is patented, which means it is illegal to propagate it.

Companion Planting and Design
'Bonica' is beautiful paired with the airy blue spikes of Russian sage (*Perovskia atriplicifolia*). Planted in front of tall ornamental grasses, it adds color and softens their strongly vertical lines.

Try These
'Cecile Brunner' (to 4 feet tall) is the "sweetheart rose," an excellent shrub rose, although hardy only hardy to Zone 5. Unlike Bonica, its flowers are lightly fragrant, and are a paler pink. It is disease resistant. There's a climbing 'Cecile Brunner' that grows 10+ feet tall.

Carefree Beauty Rose

Rosa 'Carefree Beauty'

Botanical Pronunciation
ROE-zuh

Bloom Period and Seasonal Colors
Late spring to fall, shades of pink

Mature Height × Spread
2 to 6 ft. × 3 to 4 ft.

Zones 4 to 8

'Carefree Beauty' is one of the most popular Buck roses, with long, pointed buds that open to slightly cupped, medium pink flowers averaging 5 inches across with a pleasant fragrance. Edible spherical orange hips follow the flowers, which are borne is small clusters. The vigorous plant is bushy, well clothed with large, leathery, dark green foliage. No book that includes roses for the Prairie and Plains states could be complete without highlighting the super-hardy landscape roses developed by Iowa State University rose hybridizer Dr. Griffith Buck. From over eighty of his best constant-blooming shrubs, dozens of "own root" (not grafted) cultivars have proven themselves to be solid performers, year in and year out, and are becoming more popular with northern gardeners with every season that passes.

When, Where, and How to Plant
'Carefree Beauty' is readily available locally as well as from online and mail-order sources. Buck roses prefer full sun and well-drained soil. Plant in a wide hole slightly amended with organic matter (just enough to get roots started). Follow detailed directions on page 131. Fertilize lightly at planting time. Unlike other roses, encourage important deep root growth by watering deeply only every two or three weeks.

Growing Tips
Foliar feed in spring and midsummer, and water deeply as needed to keep plants from drying out in the sun and wind. Overwatering can lead to problems. It is best to water in the morning, or late enough in the afternoon for foliage to dry by dusk.

Care and Maintenance
'Carefree Beauty' rarely gets blackspot or powdery mildew (the two most common rose diseases). Prune ever-blooming Buck roses only if they get too large, by shearing the previous year's growth by about one-third. Water deeply right before the winter's first hard freeze, and mulch to reduce the freeze/thaw cycle that can damage roots when there is little snow cover. Otherwise, they need no winter protection. Flower petals are delicious—*if* grown organically—in fruit salads or sorbet.

Companion Planting and Design
Shrub roses can be used wherever a small ever-blooming shrub is required, including perennial borders, small hedges, or even mass-planted as a bedding plant.

Try These
Great Buck roses include 'Applejack' (to 6 × 5 feet, or 9 feet as a climber) bearing 3½-inch, single, bright deep pink blossoms with a strong apple and clove scent. 'Pearlie Mae' (to 4 × 4 feet) bears 5-inch, double blooms Dr. Buck described as "a blend of empire yellow and lemon yellow." 'Prairie Harvest' (to 4 × 3 feet) has 5-inch, double, light yellow flowers. 'Prairie Sunset' (to 5 × 5 feet) has very fragrant, unique double blooms—deep pink petals with yellow undersides. 'Winter Sunset' ('Fuzzy Navel', to 5 × 3 feet) has bright golden-yellow, 4-inch, double blooms with a fruity fragrance.

Flower Carpet® Red Rose

Rosa Flower Carpet® Red

Botanical Pronunciation
ROE-zuh

Bloom Period and Seasonal Colors
Summer to frost, deep red

Mature Height and Spread
18 to 24 in. × 4 to 6 ft.

Zones 5 to 8

I was given five Flower Carpet® Red roses (the first in the series) to test in my garden a year before it came on the market in 1990. It was a revolutionary new type of rose, a landscape/groundcover rose. I planted it in full sun, part sun, clay soil, sandy soil, and good garden soil. It performed beautifully *everywhere*. From a plant 6- to 8-inches across, it grew almost like an octopus—sprawling in one area at least 8 feet. A profusion of 3-inch, single, velvety, deep red flowers adorned shiny green leaves right up until frost. Best of all, I discovered it tasted delicious. Many years later (and now living in Iowa), I still grow it—and some newer roses in the series too.

When, Where, and How to Plant

Flower Carpet® roses are *only* available at nurseries, garden centers, and home-improvement stores. They grow best in full sun and well-drained soil with added organic matter, but thrive—with only a slight reduction of blooms—in part sun and most any soil type. Dig a hole slightly larger than the pot, amend the soil with organic matter, plant the rose at the same level it was in the pot, and water-in with transplant solution. Mulching is optional; plants grow thick enough to keep weeds from sprouting.

Growing Tips

Keep lightly watered until it is established. After that, watering every seven to ten days is usually ample. Slow-release fertilizer is already mixed in the soil in which the rose is growing, so no further feeding is necessary the first year.

Regional Advice and Care

Flower Carpet® Red is a self-cleaning rose. When the flowers finish blooming, the petals drop by themselves. Prune it, if necessary, to keep it within bounds. If you're in Zone 5, mulch in winter. Remove the mulch in spring. In Zone 8, it is evergreen. In early spring, prune it back to one-third its size. Feed in early spring and when it begins to bloom. For rose care information, see page 132. Flower Carpet® roses are patented; it is illegal to propagate them.

Companion Planting and Design

Flower Carpet® Red is ideal for patio pots, borders, and walkways where a blast of color brightens the landscape. It is beautiful as a groundcover under a tree and can protect a tree by keeping pets and children away. To grow as a groundcover, allow two plants per square yard; otherwise, space individual plants 4 feet apart.

Try These

Other Flower Carpet® roses are Amber (to 30 × 36 inches), which has fragrant, soft orange-yellow blooms, aging to peach-blushed, soft pink. Pink Supreme (to 32 × 40 inches) has lipstick pink blooms. Scarlet (to 36 × 36 inches) has scarlet-red flowers. White (to 36 × 36 inches) bears masses of fragrant, snowy blooms; it's evergreen in Zone 8. Yellow (to 36 × 24 inches) has bright yellow blossoms.

Harison's Yellow Rose

Rosa × harisonii

Botanical Pronunciation
ROE-zuh har-iss-OHN-ee-eye

Other Name The Yellow Rose of Texas

Bloom Period and Seasonal Color
Late spring, bright yellow

Mature Height × Spread 5 to 7 ft. × 3 to 5 ft.

Zones 4 to 8

Harison's Yellow rose was thought to be from Texas, as Texans claim it as "The Yellow Rose of Texas." Research by Stephen Scaniello discovered that it was first found—and named—growing on George F. Harison's farm in *Manhattan* in the 1830s. It was such a tough rose (hardy from Zones 2 through 9), that settlers took it with them as they moved west. It can still be found growing on abandoned homesteads. The infatuation with this rose is not for its looks—it is rather gangly. Its charm lies in the fact that it's the first rose to bloom—often in spring at the same time as lilacs or peonies—and it's *very* fragrant. Brilliant yellow, double flowers are a portent of summer.

When, Where, and How to Plant

Harison's Yellow rose is most often found through online or mail-order sources. It has several distinguishing characteristics that make it appealing. It will grow in sandy soil, rocky soil, clayey soil, and even good garden soil. An added bonus is that it will grow in full sun or partial shade—a rare characteristic for a rose. It's no surprise settlers in the mid-1800s brought it west with them; some roses are still growing today where they were planted. Plant it as soon as you get it, as long as the ground can be worked. See complete planting instructions on page 131. It is such an early bloomer that it may not flower until the next year, as it may have already bloomed before you obtained it. Water it well. Mulch with 3 to 4 inches of wood chips.

Growing Tips

This is a tough plant and quite drought tolerant. However, in the heat of summer, when there is no rain, water once every ten to fourteen days. As an alternative to monthly foliar feeding, lay an inch of compost around the base of the plant in spring. It will decompose and slowly feed the soil, which in turn feeds the plant.

Regional Advice and Care

Its bloom season is early and short. Take advantage by cutting some of its deep yellow, 2- to 2½-inch blooms to perfume the indoors. Be careful, as it is quite a thorny plant. Petals are sweet and delicious (eat *only* if grown organically) as a garnish, made into syrup (think baklava), or jelly. It has no pest or disease problems.

Companion Planting and Design

'Harison's Yellow' has an arching shape, good for the back of a border. After flowering, the thorny, dark mahogany brown canes add interest when espaliered against a light-colored wall. Emphasize its tenacity with long-blooming, edible pansies (*Viola × wittrockiana*). Follow the yellow theme with the shrubby Japanese rose (*Kerria japonica*).

Try These

'Golden Showers' (to 10 feet tall) is a slightly later blooming, lovely, bright yellow, honey-scented, large-flowered climbing rose.

Redleaf Rose

Rosa glauca

Botanical Pronunciation
ROE-zuh GLAW-kuh

Bloom Period and Seasonal Colors
Early summer, pink; fall, reddish orange hips,
violet leaves; fall through winter, violet canes

Mature Height × Spread
6 to 8 ft. × 4 to 6 ft.

Redleaf rose (formerly *R. rubrifolia*) is unique among roses. All its names refer to the foliage—waxy reddish-bluish-purple leaves. This is one of the few roses not grown for its flowers, although the clusters of flat, 1½-inch, bright pink flowers in early summer on long, arching, purplish canes are a delight. However, they are fragile and fleeting, with the petals easily blown off during a rainstorm or high winds. Let the plant do its own thing, and by late summer to early fall, you will be rewarded with a plethora of spherical reddish orange hips (fruit) that stand out against the intensifying color of the leaves and canes (becoming almost violet). Come winter, the canes alone garner attention. And there's its hardiness—to Zone 2.

When, Where, and How to Plant

You might find redleaf rose as a container-grown plant at a local nursery, garden center, or home-improvement store. Otherwise, look to online and mail-order sources for bare-root plants. Choosing the right place for this rose is critical. It is *not* like your typical hybrid tea or floribunda rose. Treat it like a specimen plant, giving it a special place to be viewed and admired from all sides. Its size—with branches arching to 8 feet—would look out of place in a typical rose garden of 4- or 5-foot plants. Give it room to expand. Unless you are trying to make a hedge, one redleaf rose (or two in a mixed bed or border) is ample. Plant it as soon as you get it. See complete planting instructions on page 131.

Growing Tips

Keep redleaf rose well watered until it is established. Unless the weather is very hot and dry, water once a week. Although I foliar feed most plants, redleaf rose's leaves are one of its highlights, so I do not want to risk discoloring them. Instead, I water and feed every three weeks with compost tea.

Regional Advice and Care

This is one of the most carefree roses I have ever grown. The only reason I prune is to keep the shape balanced, which it usually does by itself. You can prune it partway back to encourage a more bushy form; however, its canes were not meant to stand upright. So, unless you can enjoy a lush, lax rose with interesting, colored leaves and stems, stick with regular garden roses. It is virtually pest and disease free.

Companion Planting and Design

Redleaf rose is lovely with dainty early-spring bulbs such as snow crocus (*Crocus tommasinianus, C. chrysanthus*), Dutch crocus (*C. vernus*), snowdrops (*Galanthus nivalis*), and glory-of-the-snow (*Chionodoxa luciliae*). In fall, autumn crocus (*Colchicum autumnale*) adds a colorful accent at ground level. All of these recommended bulbs highlight the color of the canes and leaves.

Try These

There is no comparable rose. Redleaf rose is one of a kind.

Rugosa Rose

Rosa rugosa

Botanical Pronunciation
ROE-zuh roo-GO-sah

Other Name Japanese rose

Bloom Period and Seasonal Colors
Early summer and fall, rose-pink, white; fall, orange-red hips

Mature Height × Spread 3 to 6 ft. × 3 to 6 ft.

Zones 3 to 7

Rugosa rose is lovely and versatile. I grew up on Long Island, New York, where it grew wild on many of the beaches, so I assumed it was native. However, it came from Japan. First and foremost, it is the best-tasting of roses, excellent for ice cream, sauces, jellies, or just munching as you work in the garden (if grown organically). The flowers of the species are single; some hybrids are double. All are delightfully fragrant. Left on the plant, they will become terrific, large orange-red rose hips in fall, packed with Vitamin C. If you do not pick them for jelly making, the hips attract wildlife. The botanical name refers to the winsome wrinkled leaves. The thorny canes act as a good barrier hedge.

When, Where, and How to Plant
Rugosa roses—species and hybrids—are readily available locally, usually as container-grown "own-root" plants, and bare root through online and mail-order sources. Tough and easy to grow, it is tolerant of most soil types, although it thrives in rich, lightly moist, well-drained soil and full sun. Plant as soon as the soil can be worked in spring. See complete planting instructions on page 131.

Growing Tips
After transplanting, water deeply every seven to ten days. Once, in the heat of summer, one of my rugosas slowly turned brown, appearing dead. I watered and foliar fed it, and cut down one-third of the branches. Within two weeks, there was new growth; soon it was full of blossoms. Because I eat the flowers, I normally do not foliar feed. Instead, in early spring, I put a 2-inch layer of compost around the plant, water, and cover it with 3 inches of organic mulch.

Regional Advice and Care
Pruning is only necessary to maintain shape or height. Prune in early spring just as the buds appear. For more rose care information, see page 132. It is virtually pest and disease free.

Companion Planting and Design
Rugosa rose is lovely with blue flowers like willow blue star (*Amsonia tabernaemontana*), Russian sage (*Perovskia atriplicifolia*), and bluebeard (*Caryopteris × clandonensis* 'Blue Mist'). With its extremely thorny canes, rugosa rose makes a great barrier and hedge that few animals (or children) can get through.

Try These
All the rugosa roses are about the same size. *Rosa rugosa* var. *alba* (pictured above) is one of the best-tasting roses with 3½-inch, fragrant white flowers; var. *rosea* has rose-pink blooms; and var. *rubra* bears purplish red blossoms. 'Basye's Purple' is striking with single, wine-red flowers, purple stamens, and dark purple canes. 'Blanc Double de Coubert' sports double, fruity-scented, white flowers. 'F. J. Grootendorst' (or 'Grootendorst') bears ruffled, deep red, double blooms. 'Hansa' has reddish purple flowers with an intensely spicy scent. 'Sarah Van Fleet' has semi-double pink blossoms. 'Thérèse Bugnet' has double, rose-red blooms that fade to pink. 'Topaz Jewel' bears semi-double, light yellow flowers.

William Baffin Rose

Rosa 'William Baffin'

Botanical Pronunciation
ROE-zuh

Bloom Period and Seasonal Colors
Summer to frost, deep strawberry pink

Mature Height × Spread
5 to 9 ft. × 4 to 6 ft.

'William Baffin' is the best known of the Canadian Explorer series, which were developed to withstand cold Canadian winters, thrive in warm, humid summers with continuous bloom, and are virtually disease free. It is a vigorous rose that can be treated either as a climber or a sprawling shrub. Clusters of up to thirty deep strawberry pink blooms cascade down the plant—a very impressive sight. Each semi-double flower is about 2½ inches wide with twenty petals. It is a midseason bloomer with excellent repeat bloom, so the more you cut the flowers to bring indoors for arrangements or bouquets, the more flowers will be produced—right up until frost. Glossy green leaves are a gorgeous contrast to the flowers. Unfortunately, it has little fragrance.

When, Where, and How to Plant
'William Baffin' may be found in some nurseries or garden centers that specialize in older, hardy, and well-proven varieties of roses. Otherwise, find it through online and mail-order sources. It grows in full or part sun. It should be "own-stock," not grafted. Plant as soon as you get it, whether container-grown or bare root. If bare root, there should not be any rounded bud union on the stem. Plant so the bottom 2 or 3 inches of the stem is below ground level. For detailed planting instructions, see page 131.

Growing Tips
Keep the soil lightly moist until it is established and is sending out new growth, buds, and leaves. If there's no rain, a slow, deep, weekly watering should be adequate. Its height can be daunting for foliar

feeding; use a diluter spray attachment for the hose set for the proper dilution ratio. Spray the entire plant monthly as you would when using a watering nozzle.

Regional Advice and Care
For the northernmost gardeners in our region, this may be the only repeat-blooming climber available. In its first two years, the plant is focused on foliage growth. Prune only to thin out weak or crossed canes. After that it will be covered with blossoms. Like other Explorer roses, it is disease and pest resistant.

Companion Planting and Design
'William Baffin' can quickly cover an arbor, trellis, or pillar and thrive year after year with a minimum of fuss. Provide support to best show it off. Grow a purple Jackman clematis (*Clematis* × *jackmanii*) with it for color contrast. Or paint the arbor cobalt blue.

Try These
Other Canadian Explorer roses include 'Jens Monk' (to 4½ × 4½ feet), sporting clusters of 3-inch, fragrant, candy pink, semi-double flowers. 'J.P. Connell' (to 5 × 7 feet) bears 3½-inch fragrant, lemony yellow flowers that fade to cream. 'Martin Frobisher' (to 6 × 4 feet), the original Explorer rose introduced in 1968, has lightly fragrant, light pink, double flowers. 'Simon Fraser' (to 2 × 2 feet) makes an excellent groundcover with lightly fragrant, medium pink, semi-double blossoms.

SHRUBS

FOR THE PRAIRIE & PLAINS STATES

Many people often confuse a tree with a shrub. One of the easiest ways to tell the difference is that many—but not all—shrubs have multiple stems at their base, while a tree has a single trunk. Another differentiation is size. A shrub is generally less than 20 feet tall, while a tree is greater than 20 feet. Again, this can be challenging, as many dwarf varieties of trees are quite low—some even are designated as groundcovers. And of course, there is the English yew, which branches down to the ground and that you keep pruned at a height of 5 feet, even though it wants to grow to 40 feet. No matter, it is still a tree, just artificially constrained to shrub size.

As with trees, there are evergreen and deciduous shrubs. To me, variety is the spice of life, which adds life to the garden, so include both types. When choosing a deciduous shrub, it is a bonus if it has an interesting or unique architectural form that will draw the eye in winter when there is less to see in a garden or landscape. One of my favorite plants, Harry Lauder's walking stick (*Corylus avellana* 'Contorta') has such marvelous twisted branches that it looks better in winter than in summer when the interesting branches are hidden by leaves.

You'll probably shop for shrubs at a garden center. Look at each carefully to determine if it's healthy.

Choosing Your Shrubs

It's all a matter of the right plant for the right place. One of the main uses of shrubs is as a foundation plant, grown around the house—especially the front—to hide the foundation and make the house look more inviting. Find out what the mature height of the plant is (spread as well, although that's not as important), especially for shrubs in front of windows. You don't want something that is going to grow 18 feet in front of a picture or bay window, unless for some reason you are trying to obscure the view. First and foremost, that's a lot of work for you. I prefer a landscape I can plant and enjoy, other than the routine maintenance of feeding, watering, or pruning dead or broken limbs. Second, such a plant would need constant pruning to keep it in bounds.

Another important consideration for foundation plantings is soil pH. Why should that be more important for a foundation planting than any other garden area? Because the foundations of most houses are concrete, over time some of the lime from the concrete leaches out into the soil, making it alkaline. A serious consideration in much of our region is that the soil is already alkaline. It is essential to have to soil near a home's foundation tested for pH. You can get a soil sample and take it to your local Cooperative Extension Service or local nursery where, usually for a small fee, they can test the pH. Alternatively, you can buy an inexpensive pH test kit. You can even use old-fashioned litmus paper (remember that from high school chemistry? It turns red or pink in the presence of acid and blue when the soil is basic or alkaline.) You can find litmus paper that is more specific—within several points of 7.0, which is neutral pH for plants. Check out pool supply stores; they often stock it.

If your soil is already alkaline, the leaching of lime can take it over the limit, putting the pH higher than 9, and making the choice of plants limited, if not nearly impossible. You can add organic matter mixed with fine peat moss to lower the pH, making it less alkaline. Between a pH range of 7 to 8.5, there is a good choice of foundation plants. However, it certainly doesn't make sense to try to grow a plant, such as a rhododendron or azalea, that thrives in acidic soil with a pH closer to 5. You would have to constantly monitor and amend the soil.

Once you get past the foundation, as with any other plants, the choices of shrubs to include in your landscape are almost limitless—except for the hardiness limitations. Walk around your neighborhood, drive around your town, and you will spot plants that appeal to you. Don't hesitate to ring the bell and ask the homeowner what a plant is, or if you are shy, leave a note in the mailbox. Visit a local public garden, arboretum, or botanical garden to see some great shrubs that are right for your area. If they have been growing well for a while, they probably overwinter well. One of the best sources of information is your local Cooperative Extension Service. They often have printed lists or booklets of the best shrubs for our region. Take their advice; they have plenty of knowledge backing them up. Most of the shrubs in this chapter are available at garden centers, nurseries, and home-improvement stores. Unless otherwise noted, there are no major pests or diseases.

After taking the plant out of the pot, loosen the roots. For trees and shrubs, dig a planting hole as deep as the rootball and twice as wide. Once it is planted, topdress with mulch to conserve moisture.

Planting

Planting a shrub is very similar to planting a tree (as described in the trees chapter), except the overall size of the planting hole is relatively smaller as shrubs are generally smaller. Turn to page 159 in the tree chapter introduction for complete directions on planting bare-root, container-grown, and balled-and-burlapped plants. (Balled-and-burlapped types are rare in shrubs, but are still found with some larger ones.)

Shrubs for Difficult Sites

The length of this book limits the number of shrubs—or any of the plants, for that matter—that can be included. People often run into challenging sites on their property, so here are some additional plants to consider. They should be available at local nurseries, garden centers and home-improvement stores; in addition, there are always online and mail-order plant sources.

Dry Areas

- Dwarf fothergilla (*Fothergilla gardenii*, Zones 5 to 8) has lovely bottlebrush-like white flowers in late spring.
- Fragrant sumac (*Rhus aromatica*, Zones 3 to 8) is a tough plant that will grow in many difficult places. It has great fall color and long-lasting large clusters of small, reddish brown fruit.
- Shrubby cinquefoil (*Potentilla fruticosa*, Zones 3 to 7) is a low-growing shrub with a long bloom time of yellow flowers from late spring through summer.

Shade Areas

- Dwarf fothergilla—see Dry Areas.
- Oakleaf hydrangea (*Hydrangea quercifolia*, Zones 5 to 8) is exceptional with long-lasting, white flowers, outstanding fall colors of red to purple, and leaves resembling oak leaves.
- Mapleleaf viburnum (*Viburnum acerifolium*, Zones 3 to 8) is a good woodland plant for year-round interest with white flowers, black fruit, and rosy fall foliage.

- Harry Lauder's walking stick (*Corylus avellana* 'Contorta', Zones 4 to 8) almost looks best in fall and winter when its twisted, spiraling branches show off; it has yellowish brown male catkins in spring.
- Nanking cherry (*Prunus tomentosa*, Zones 3 to 7) has fragrant white flowers in spring, edible red cherries, and handsome shiny bark.
- Shadbush (*Amelanchier canadensis*, Zones 4 to 8) has white blooms in spring, edible fruit, reddish fall foliage, and grows well in moist soil.
- Siberian pea tree (*Caragana arborescens*, Zones 3 to 7) has showy yellow blooms and is good for hedges or windbreaks.
- Spicebush *(Lindera benzoin*, Zone 4 to 8) is dioecious with small yellow blooms in early spring, red fruit on female plants, fragrant leaves, and yellow fall foliage.
- Sweet pepperbush (*Clethra alnifolia*, Zones 3 to 8) has fragrant white blooms from mid- to late summer and yellow fall foliage.

For me, shrubs are the icing on the cake that is the garden. They can accentuate and highlight the other plantings, especially perennials and trees. Usually larger than perennials but smaller than trees; shrubs are the unifying force. They tie the garden together.

Oakleaf hydrangea (*Hydrangea quercifolia*) is a great option for a shady site. Its summer blooms turn russet in fall.

Bridalwreath Spirea

Spiraea × *vanhouttei*

Botanical Pronunciation
spy-REE-uh van-HOW-tee-eye

Other Name Vanhoutte spirea

Bloom Period and Seasonal Colors
Mid-spring, white

Mature Height × Spread
5 to 8 ft. × 7 to 10 ft.

Spirea smells "dusty" to me—not a bad dusty—it reminds me of old houses and gardens, which is good. Vanhoutte spirea, the latest blooming bridalwreath (*Spiraea prunifolia* is also called bridalwreath), has long been recognized as one of the toughest shrubs. An 1888 garden catalog proclaimed it "the most showy of all the spiraeas, and one of the very best shrubs in cultivation." It was also inexpensive. A 1930s mail-order company offered a dozen 18- to 24-inch Vanhoutte spireas for 45 cents. The long fingernail-like foliage is a distinctive blue-green, and the white flowers are borne in mid-spring, in wide, flat-topped clusters that line stems so thickly the entire shrub appears arched toward the earth. It makes an excellent cut flower—or bridal bouquet.

When, Where, and How to Plant

Bridalwreath spirea is available at nurseries, garden centers, and home-improvement stores in spring. Check out online and mail-order sources for specific varieties. Like all spireas, bridalwreath is tough, and will grow in full to part sun in nearly any soil, as long as it does not stand in water or go months without moisture. Dig a wide hole, loosen potbound roots of nursery-grown shrubs, then water enough during the first summer to get the plant established. See page 159 for detailed planting information. No fertilizer is needed the first year.

Growing Tips

Water during prolonged drought. Fertilize lightly every two to three years.

Regional Advice and Care

Established plants rarely need any care (spireas often survive for decades in cemeteries); however, watering deeply during prolonged hot spells can prevent leaf burn. Because heavy snow may break branches and older plants can get leggy, every year or two prune up to one-third of old stems close to the ground after they finish flowering. This will stimulate new arching branches. Iron chlorosis and rabbits can be problems, as can foliage diseases in very wet seasons. Cuttings taken in summer root quite easily and can be planted the same fall or the next spring.

Companion Planting and Design

Bridalwreath spirea tolerates de-icing salts, grows rapidly, and is often used as a hedge or screen. It is bold enough to stand alone as a specimen in the lawn and can blend in well along the foundation of an older home. Use it to provide a backdrop to spring and summer bulbs including tulips (*Tulipa* spp.) and lilies (*Lilium* spp.), perennials, and smaller shrubs like Annabelle hydrangea (*Hydrangea arborescens* 'Annabelle') in a mixed border.

Try These

'Gold Fountain' (golden Vanhoutte spirea, to 8 × 12 feet) has eye-catching, delicate golden leaves. 'Pink Ice' (to 5 × 5 feet) is stunning with pink-flushed new growth and young stems and white-variegated green leaves. 'Renaissance' (to 5 × 6 feet) is an improved selection with more resistance to foliage diseases; unlike the species, it has colorful orange-red fall foliage.

Burkwood Viburnum

Viburnum × burkwoodii

Botanical Pronunciation
vy-BURN-um burk-WOOD-ee-eye

Bloom Period and Seasonal Colors
Midspring, white; fall, orange-red foliage

Mature Height × Spread
8 to 10 ft. × 5 to 7 ft.

Zones 4 to 8

When a Burkwood viburnum is added to a landscape, everyone will notice. Its rounded form, tough foliage, fragrant flowers, bird-attracting berries, and intense fall colors turn heads in every season. This medium-sized shrub has glossy, dark green leaves with white, fuzzy undersides. The foliage turns orange-red in autumn before shedding to reveal birds' nests left over from the summer. The 4-inch wide, domed clusters of pink florets slowly open into eye-catching white, tubular flowers, each with five petals and showy yellow stamens attracting bees and butterflies. Burkwood fragrance is often described as gardenia-like—a welcome spring event. Flattened, red summer berries gradually ripen into blue-black fruit valued by birds. Plant guru and author Michael Dirr sums it up, saying this shrub "asks little, gives much."

When, Where, and How to Plant

Burkwood viburnum is readily available at most nurseries, garden centers, and home-improvement stores. Look for the recommended varieties at online and mail-order sources. This tough shrub grows best in moderately fertile, slightly acidic soil in full sun, although part shade is preferred in areas with long, hot summers. Dig a wide hole and add peat moss to acidify the backfill soil. Plant, and then water deeply. For more information on planting, go to page 159. Fruit production is heaviest if two different cultivars are planted near each other for cross-pollination.

Growing Tips

Keep soil lightly moist until established. Overwatering can invite root rot. Fresh organic mulch each spring provides ample fertilization.

Regional Advice and Care

Mulch plants to keep roots cool and moist. Burkwood viburnum is evergreen in Zones 7 and 8. There are no major pest problems under normal growing conditions, although powdery mildew, leaf spots, and a little twig die-back may appear some years. It is also susceptible to aphids, scale, and Japanese beetles.

Companion Planting and Design

This upright, fully branched shrub can be used as an accent plant, hedge, screen, or in a mixed shrub border or woodland garden. Wherever you plant it, be assured it will attract all sorts of good wildlife. Birds often nest in it in the summer, close to its ripening berries. It is tall enough to be used for good effect against an arbor where its long twigs make it look almost like a climber. Tie, prune, or train it as an espalier against a sunny wall or on a trellis.

Try These

'Conoy' (to 5 × 8 feet) foliage is finer textured and it bears abundant glossy red fruit that persists for six to eight weeks in autumn. 'Mohawk' (to 8 feet tall) is more of a show-off with long-lasting dark red buds that open to stronger and spicier-scented white flowers. In fall, the foliage turns eye-catching orange-red to burgundy. It is also resistant to some of the leaf spot diseases that sometimes plague viburnums.

Butterfly Bush

Buddleja davidii (formerly Buddleia)

Botanical Pronunciation
BUD-lee-ah dah-VID-ee-eye

Other Name Summer lilac

Bloom Period and Seasonal Colors
Summer to fall, purple, white, magenta, pink

Mature Height × Spread
6 to 10 ft. × 6 to 10 ft.

Zones 5 to 8

With the booming interest in wildlife and butterfly gardens, there has been a jump in sales and introductions of new cultivars of this fragrant, old-time favorite shrub. It is a vigorous plant with slightly arching stems that end in long foxtail clusters of orange-eyed florets. The lance-shaped leaves are dark green above, soft and white below. The most common flower color is dark purple, but there are many colors, including hues of white, pink, magenta—all with the distinctive orange eye at the center of each floret. The flowers are fragrant, enhancing the garden from summer to frost. Above all, they attract butterflies by the dozens—bees and hummingbirds too. There is nothing more enjoyable than watching nature in action on a butterfly bush.

When, Where, and How to Plant

With the increasing number of cultivars, you can find butterfly bushes available locally. However, the greatest choice is through online and mail-order sources. Butterfly bush grows best in rich, but not heavy, well-drained soil in full sun. Although tolerant of most soils, it *does not* like wet feet. It is best in a spot protected from wind. For detailed planting instructions, see page 159.

Growing Tips

Plants are fairly drought tolerant once they're established; water when the top inch of soil is dry or when leaves droop. Fertilize with a low-nitrogen, high-phosphate fertilizer, such as 5-10-5, two or three times during the growing season.

Regional Advice and Care

This is a plant that, unless it is pruned yearly, will be short-lived. Prune back the previous year's wood in late winter to early spring; cut it down almost to the ground and it will regrow—more vigorous and flowerful. Cut faded flowers to encourage new bloom. There are no major pests or diseases. If you have children or friends who are severely allergic to bees, keep them a safe distance, as the plant attracts many insects with its nectar. Butterfly bush makes very attractive cut flowers.

Companion Planting and Design

A butterfly bush makes an *excellent* specimen plant. Site it where you can enjoy its full benefits. It is also a good in a mixed border along with asters (*Symphyotrichum* spp.) and goldenrod (*Solidago* spp.) for fall interest. Its long branches make it an excellent candidate to espalier against a wall or trellis or to grow on an arbor or pergola.

Try These

There is a host of cultivars including 'Black Knight' (to 8 feet tall), which has very dark purple flowers; the orange eye really stands out. 'Evil Ways' (to 5 feet) is show-stopping with bright yellow leaves and dark purple flowers. 'Nanho Purple' (to 5 feet) is compact—even more so if pruned back in late winter—with lavender-purple flowers. Lo and Behold® series (to 2 feet) is patented (illegal to propagate) and includes 'Blue Chip' with intense blue flowers—ideal for containers.

Elderberry

Sambucus canadensis

Botanical Pronunciation
sam-BOO-kus kan-ah-DEN-sis

Other Name
American elder

Bloom Period and Seasonal Colors
Late spring to early summer, creamy white

Mature Height × Spread
5 to 12 ft. × 5 to 8 ft.

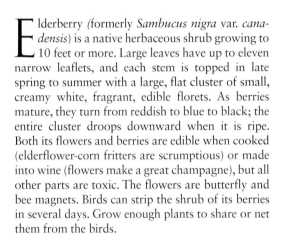

Elderberry (formerly *Sambucus nigra* var. *canadensis*) is a native herbaceous shrub growing to 10 feet or more. Large leaves have up to eleven narrow leaflets, and each stem is topped in late spring to summer with a large, flat cluster of small, creamy white, fragrant, edible florets. As berries mature, they turn from reddish to blue to black; the entire cluster droops downward when it is ripe. Both its flowers and berries are edible when cooked (elderflower-corn fritters are scrumptious) or made into wine (flowers make a great champagne), but all other parts are toxic. The flowers are butterfly and bee magnets. Birds can strip the shrub of its berries in several days. Grow enough plants to share or net them from the birds.

When, Where, and How to Plant
Elderberry is readily available locally. However, for named varieties, go to online and mail-order sources. It grows and produces best in moist garden soil and full sun but tolerates part sun. When planting nursery-grown cultivars, spread the roots out, and water the fast-growing plant through its first full season. Go to page 159 for detailed planting information.

Growing Tips
Water only during very long dry spells. Fertilization is not necessary.

Regional Advice and Care
Keep plants vigorous and within bounds by pruning 2- or 3-year-old stems at ground level. New canes will quickly replace them. Flowers appear on new growth, so pruning in winter is acceptable. Berry ripening is affected by long summer drought, so for flavorful berries be prepared to water. Fruit is traditionally use to make jelly, jam, pies, preserves, and wine. Add ripe elderberries to an apple pie recipe, in a 40/60 elder-to-apple mix. For an early summer treat, pick a blooming elderberry flowerhead, remove the florets, and add them into thin pancake batter; sprinkle with powdered sugar and cinnamon.

Companion Planting and Design
Elderberry is most easily used as a specimen along a woodland edge or backed up against a wall where its form and flowers can be enjoyed. But it makes a lovely hedge. Include elderberry in a wildlife garden as well as in an edible landscape. Or use it as an accent in a meadow or large wildflower garden. It is quite a versatile shrub. It is especially handsome with the purple-domed flowerheads of angelica (*Angelica gigas*).

Try These
'Aurea' (to 12 feet tall) has yellow to chartreuse foliage. 'Laciniata' ('Acutiloba', to 8 feet) has lacy, deeply cut, green leaves. Closely related black elder (*Sambucus nigra*, a European native) has some outstanding patented varieties (it is illegal to propagate them). Its fruit is not as flavorful as elderberry. Black Beauty® ('Gerda', to 10 feet) has dark purple leaves and pink blooms. Black Lace® ('Eva', to 8 feet) features deeply cut, dark purple leaves and pink flowers.

Forsythia

Forsythia × intermedia

Botanical Pronunciation
for-SITH-ee-ah in-ter-MEE-dee-ah

Other Name Golden bells

Bloom Period and Seasonal Colors
Early spring, yellow; fall, burgundy foliage

Mature Height × Spread
6 to 10 ft. × 5 to 9 ft.

Zones 5 to 8

Perhaps the most common early spring show-stopper around old homeplaces is golden bells—an aptly descriptive common name for this old-fashioned flowering shrub. Commonly escaped from older gardens to the point where it is considered weedy by some, forsythia can survive where an old homestead has long disappeared. This fountain-shaped deciduous shrub has long, stiff, arching branches arising from a fairly narrow basal clump, with pointed, slender oval leaves up to 4 inches long produced in pairs. Flowers are inch-long trumpets of lemon- to golden-yellow, produced in clusters at leaf joints along the entire length of the stem. When in bloom, the whole shrub is an eruption of yellow fireworks. If that's not enough, this nearly indestructible shrub has lovely burgundy fall foliage.

When, Where, and How to Plant
Forsythia is readily available locally. It grows in sun, in any kind of soil, and in most any place, including abandoned gardens and into the woods. Plant in a wide, loose hole, water two or three times to get new plants established, and move on to other chores. See page 159 for more detailed information on planting. Divide a crowded clump in fall or winter, or take root cuttings in late spring or summer.

Growing Tips
Water infrequently, if at all, once plants are established. Fertilize only sparingly.

Regional Advice and Care
Few gardeners expect this shrub to get as large as it will. Luckily, forsythia can be pruned by thinning old canes close to the ground or cutting the entire shrub to a few inches tall to force strong, arching, new growth to shoot up over summer and fall. To rejuvenate an overgrown or unsightly forsythia while achieving the fullest fountain effect, prune one-third of the old stems to the ground every year for three years; your patience will be rewarded. Avoid tight pruning or lollipop shapes; allow it to spread into in its natural arching form.

Companion Planting and Design
Forsythia is an excellent specimen plant. It fits in well with conifers and spring-flowering shrubs, including spirea (*Spiraea* spp.), weigela (*Weigela florida*), and lilac (*Syringa vulgaris*). It makes a good backdrop to a flower border. Forsythia is awesome when massed and makes a great hedge. In midwinter, cut a few long stems that are in bud and place in a tall container of water to force them into early bloom inside. Alternatively, wait until it blooms for dramatic indoor flower arrangements.

Try These
'Beatrix Farrand' (to 8 feet tall) bears 2-inch golden yellow flowers. 'Gold Leaf' (to 5 feet) has light yellow flowers; lime-green leaves mature to golden yellow. 'Kolgold' ('Magical Gold', to 8 feet) has very large, bright yellow blooms. 'Lynwood Variety' (to 9 feet) has large yellow flowers; foliage turns yellow in fall. 'Variegata' (to 10 feet) bears cream-and-green variegated leaves.

Lilac

Syringa vulgaris

Botanical Pronunciation
sih-RIN-guh vul-GAR-is

Other Name Common lilac

Bloom Period and Seasonal Colors
Mid- to late spring, hues of white, purple,
pink, lavender

Mature Height × Spread 12 to 16 ft. × 8 to 12 ft.

Zones 3 to 7

Of the plants cold-climate gardeners who move to the West Coast or South yearn for most, lilacs top the list. Imagine the first spring day when the sweet lilac fragrance wafts your way—your spirits soar. Talk about aromatherapy! The old lilac shrub from grandmother's garden is still alive, though its big leaves are a bit raggedy and there are dead stems in need of pruning out. But the dense, conical clusters of single or double flowers—purple, lavender, pink, or white—still fill the air with a perfume so intense you have to go out and cut some blooms to bring inside and enjoy as long as you can. Its flowers (when grown organically) are edible; some have a perfumed flavor that's great on vanilla ice cream.

When, Where, and How to Plant

Many different lilac varieties are readily available at locally. However, the greatest choice can be found from online and mail-order sources. Lilacs flower best in full sun, but will grow in part sun. Well-drained neutral or alkaline soil is a must, or root rot will set in. Work in enough compost or other organic matter in a wide hole to get roots started off well. Cover the soil with organic mulch to conserve moisture while shading roots. For detailed planting instructions, go to page 159. Cut off faded flower stalks the first season to help young plants put their energy into root growth.

Growing Tips

Water during prolonged drought, and fertilize lightly once every spring.

Regional Advice and Care

Most people don't know the cultivar name of their lilacs. If a friend has one you like, consider taking a cutting. Hard pruning will rejuvenate old shrubs, by getting rid of old, partly dead trunks and branches, and stimulating strong, healthy new shoots, which quickly get back up to flowering size. Do any pruning *immediately* after the shrub finishes blooming. There are many minor pests, but powdery mildew is a real headache to some gardeners. Try baking soda spray (see page 175) to slow the spread to non-infected leaves.

Companion Planting and Design

Lilacs are commonly used as specimen plants or as hedges along property lines. They consort well with forsythia (*Forsythia* spp.), roses (*Rosa* spp.), and other flowering shrubs, and provide a deep green backdrop to perennial borders. Consider a hedge of all different varieties of lilacs fronted by an equal number of different peonies (*Paeonia lactiflora*) for spectacular visual and fragrant impact.

Try These

'Avalanche' (to 9 feet tall) bears clusters of fragrant single white flowers. 'Beauty of Moscow' ('Krasa-vitska Moskovy', to 12 feet) has pale pink buds that open to double white florets with a pink blush that gives a two-tone effect. 'Charles Joly' (to 15 feet) bears fragrant, deep reddish purple, double florets. 'Scentsation' (to 15 feet) has deep purple florets edged in white, great aroma, and a sweet flavor.

Red Japanese Barberry

Berberis thunbergii f. *atropurpurea*

Botanical Pronunciation
BER-ber-iss thun-BER-jee-eye at-roe-pur-PUR-ee-uh

Bloom Period and Seasonal Colors
Spring, yellow; fall, orange foliage

Mature Height × Spread 2 to 3 ft. × 3 to 6 ft.

Zones 4 to 8

This is not about plain old Japanese barberry, the rounded, 4- or 5-foot tall and wider-than-that bush full of bright green leaves that turn a brilliant orange in the fall. It isn't about the very fine thorns that keep us on the straight and narrow. Sure, there are several interesting cultivars, including 'Aurea' with bright yellow young foliage, tiny yellow barberry-typical flowers, and showy red fruit in the fall and winter that attracts birds. What catches my imagination and designer's eye is the intense development of delightful dwarf cultivars, starting with 'Rose Glow' that go way beyond the commonly planted 'Crimson Pygmy' that appears in front of every fast-food joint. This is about trying a new twist on a familiar, favorite, but overused plant.

When, Where, and How to Plant
Red Japanese barberry is available at some nurseries, garden centers, and home-improvement stores, but online and mail-order sources are best for finding more unusual varieties. Any well-drained soil in full or part sun will do nicely for these deciduous shrubs. Dig wide holes and lightly amend the soil with organic matter (compost, humus, or leaf mold). Loosen the roots of the plants as they are often rootbound. See page 159 for more planting information. Water deeply to get plants established, but do not keep soil soggy wet or risk root rot. Buy nursery-grown plants. Many are patented, so growing from cuttings is a no-no.

Growing Tips
Water when the soil is dry. Feed very lightly once in the spring.

Regional Advice and Care
Older growth makes the best fall colors, so the less pruning done, the better. However, barberry can be selectively thinned. Don't worry about the thorns, which point up and won't snag you like a rose. Put on a good pair of gloves and just snip out a few wayward branches, leaving most untouched, and you will end up with a more relaxed, energetic look than when clipped into a tight box or gumdrop. Tiny yellow spring flowers attract bees.

Companion Planting and Design
Widely used as specimen shrubs, masses of color, or accents in flower gardens, red Japanese barberries have become a mainstay of the garden design world. In addition, their needlelike spines are just stiff enough to help keep people—including those interested in checking out your windows after hours—and neighbor's pets where they belong.

Try These
'Atropurpurea Nana' (to 2 feet tall) is a charming, mounding dwarf. 'Bagatelle' (to 1½ feet) has lovely coppery red foliage. 'Concorde' (to 2½ feet) has deep red-burgundy foliage that turns bright crimson in autumn; yellow blooms in spring are more prominent on this variety. 'Golden Ring' (to 4 feet) bears narrowly golden-yellow-edged, nearly purple leaves. 'Harlequin' (to 4 feet) has reddish purple leaves variegated cream and pink. 'Rose Glow' (to 5 feet) is burgundy in spring, but soon turns rose-pink splotched purplish red.

Redtwig Dogwood

Cornus alba

Botanical Pronunciation KOR-nus AL-bah

Other Name Tatarian dogwood

Bloom Period and Seasonal Colors
Late spring, white; winter, red stems

Mature Height × Spread 5 to 10 ft. × 5 to 10 ft.

Zones 3 to 7

Blood red twigs poking up out of the snow can be a little off-putting to folks raised with gumdrop- and meatball-shaped shrubs scattered in front of the house. But if ever a plant were to get people excited, redtwig dogwood is it. The shrub is a four-season delight—a vigorous little thicket of upright stems and long, pointy-oval dark green leaves. Flat heads of small, fragrant, creamy white flowers are a joy in late spring, especially growing behind perennials. The variegated-leaved cultivars are not as vigorous as those with all-green leaves. Come summer there are white berrylike fruits, sometimes tinged mysteriously in blue. For good measure, throw in some red or orange fall color. However, its those winter twigs that make this a must-have plant.

When, Where, and How to Plant
Redtwig dogwood may be available locally, but for the best selection, go to online and mail-order sources. It has best stem color in full sun, but tolerates even thin, wet soils. Because of its thicket-forming nature, give redtwig dogwood ample room to grow. Loosen the soil in a wide circle to encourage wide roots. For more detailed planting information, go to page 159. Mulch with 3 inches of organic matter to keep roots cool in summer (remember, the plant is native to Siberia). Feed very lightly the first summer.

Growing Tips
Little care is needed for this Siberian native. Little water, little fertilizer.

Regional Advice and Care
This plant has few needs, and pests are not serious. Thin wayward branches in winter when you can see them better. For a really good show in winter, cut *everything* back to within a few inches of the ground in spring after it flowers (blooms attract butterflies, bees, and other pollinators). Lots of sturdy new growth will come up for a more colorful effect the next winter. Birds flock to its fruit.

Companion Planting and Design
This plant is best used as a strong winter focal point in a prominent location. Groups scattered across a nearby hillside or along a sunny drive can be stunning. Mulch with a dark mulch or plant evergreen groundcover such as wintercreeper (*Euonymus fortunei*) underneath to complement its stark winter stems. Consider adding redtwig dogwood to a rain garden.

Try These
'Elegantissima' ('Argenteomarginata', to 10 feet) has gray-green leaves with irregular white margins and bright red twigs in winter. Ivory Halo® ('Bailhalo', to 6 feet) bears medium green leaves edged with white and bright red winter twigs; it is patented, so it's illegal to propagate. 'Kesselringii' (to 6 feet) has green leaves that turn a beautiful reddish purple in fall; winter twigs are dark purple. 'Prairie Fire' (to 8 feet) has golden-yellow leaves that turn bright red in fall; it has bright red winter twigs. 'Sibirica' (to 7 feet) has reddish purple autumn leaves and brilliant red winter shoots.

Rose of Sharon

Hibiscus syriacus

Botanical Pronunciation
hy-BIS-kus seer-ee-AY-kus

Other Name Althea

Bloom Period and Seasonal Colors
Mid- to late summer, white, pink, red, lavender, mauve; winter, brown seed capsules

Mature Height × Spread 8 to 12 ft. × 4 to 8 ft.

Zones 5 to 8

This old-garden shrub, which gets both its common and Latin names from the Syrian Plains of Sharon, graces many older neighborhoods out of sheer persistence. Interesting varieties abound which, once set into the garden, quickly become long-lived focal points from summer to fall for their prolific edible flowers and winter branches tipped with light brown seed capsules, which can be used in flower arrangements. The vase-shaped shrub grows to 10 feet or more with medium-sized dark green lobed leaves that often turn golden in autumn. Typical rose of Sharon flowers are single or double, bell-like and up to 4 inches across, in white, pink, red, lavender, pale blue, sometimes with a contrasting "eye" or flower streaks. Its flowers are great bee and butterfly attractors.

When, Where, and How to Plant

Rose of Sharon is readily available at local nurseries, garden centers, and home-improvement stores. For the full range of varieties, go to online and mail-order sources. It flowers best in full sun but will do well in part shade. Rose of Sharon prefers moist, rich, well-drained soil, but is tolerant of poor soil and some drought. Plant container-grown specimens whenever you get them. For detailed planting information, go to page 159. Water and lightly feed new plants to get them established, then gradually withhold water to toughen them up.

Growing Tips

Little or no supplemental watering is needed, and only light feedings.

Regional Advice and Care

In general, unless you are training the shrub into a single stem specimen, or espaliering against a wall, prune only to thin unwanted clutter, wayward branches, or to remove seed capsules to prevent the production of many unwanted seedlings. Rejuvenate old, overgrown plants by cutting them back severely in late winter or early spring; flowers will appear on new growth. Sticky black "sooty mold" is sometimes a problem on altheas infested with aphids. A strong blast of water from the hose is often enough to get rid of aphids; otherwise use insecticidal soap. It makes a dynamic cut flower in an arrangements.

Companion Planting and Design

Rose of Sharon does well as a medium-sized accent shrub, singly or in groups, especially where summer color may be lacking in part shade. It also works well as a hedge. Underplant it with daffodils (*Narcissus* spp.), iris (*Iris* spp.), daylilies (*Hemerocallis* spp.), and other perennials that tolerate part shade. Include it as a focal point in a cottage garden or mixed border.

Try These

'Aphrodite' (to 8 feet tall) has large (to 4 inches) ruffled, pink flowers with a dark red eye. 'Blue Bird' (to 8 feet tall) has pale violet-blue flowers (which may appear a bit lavender in hot summers) with a deep maroon eye. 'Diana' (to 10 feet) is pure white and unlike other varieties, the flowers remain open at night. 'Lucy' (to 8 feet) bears double red-pink blooms.

Smooth Hydrangea

Hydrangea arborescens 'Annabelle'

Botanical Pronunciation
hy-DRAIN-jah ar-bor-RES-senz

Other Name
Wild hydrangea

Bloom Period and Seasonal Colors
Early summer to fall, white

Mature Height × Spread
3 to 5 ft. × 4 to 5 ft.

Annabelle hydrangea, named after the town of Anna, Illinois, where it was discovered, is one of the most stunning showstoppers in the early-summer garden. These small shrubs have large, deep green leaves that serve as platters for foot-wide piles of mashed potato-white flowers so overloaded they often bend over under their weight, and may need staking. 'Annabelle' accepts almost any soil type, even moderately alkaline, and makes a spectacular show after very cold winters because it blooms on new growth even if cut to the ground; in fact, pruning close to the ground in winter increases the flower size. Flowerheads dry beautifully on the plant and they can be used in cut or dried flower arrangements. Try spray-painting them for a fun holiday effect.

When, Where, and How to Plant

'Annabelle' is available locally as well as from online and mail-order sources. Whether planted in part sun or part shade, get this hydrangea started right with well-prepared bed—blend the native soil with organic matter in the planting hole. It tolerates dry, wet, or rocky soil. For more planting information, go to page 159. Water newly set out plants deeply, as needed, just often enough to keep young plants from staying wilted. Feed lightly at planting time to get them started.

Growing Tips

Light fertilization and occasional deep soakings are all that the shrubs will need later.

Regional Advice and Care

Add a 3- to 5-inch layer of organic mulch around the plant to keep roots cool and moist. Keep mulch at least an inch away from stems. Stake flowering stems if they flop. Insect pests are unheard of. Although leafspot may be a problem during exceptionally wet springs and summer, no control is recommended. This shrub is rabbit resistant and can grow near black walnut trees.

Companion Planting and Design

Grow 'Annabelle' as a low hedge or in a mixed flower border to bridge the season between spring- and summer-flowering shrubs. Astilbe (*Astilbe* spp.), columbine (*Aquilegia canadensis*), and other fine-textured, late-spring and early-summer perennials are livened up with the bold flowers and coarse foliage of this small but flower-packed shrub. Underplant with daffodils (*Narcissus* spp.) for spring interest, as long as the bed they share does not get so much water in summer that the dormant bulbs rot.

Try These

'Grandiflora' (to 6 feet tall) has white flowerheads up to 8 inches across. Endless Summer Bella Anna® ('Piiha-I', to 3 feet) is patented (it's illegal to propagate) and produces magenta-pink mophead type, 5- × 3-inch flowerheads. Incrediball® ('Abetwo', to 5 feet), also patented, has flowerheads to 12 inches across and thicker stems that support the flowers without flopping. Invincibelle® Spirit (to 4 feet), another patented variety, bears hot pink flowerheads from summer to frost.

Staghorn Sumac

Rhus typhina 'Dissecta'

Botanical Pronunciation
RUS ty-FEE-nah

Bloom Period and Seasonal Color
Summer, greenish yellow; fall, orange foliage;
winter, burgundy-red berries

Mature Height × Spread
9 to 15 ft. × 12 to 15 ft.

Cherished in European landscapes, this outstanding native forms small colonies of fast-growing, sparsely branched small trees with furry red new stems, reminiscent of the velvet on stag's horns. 'Dissecta' is fernier and less aggressive than the species, yet still has gorgeous orange fall colors. Its greenish yellow summer flowers, produced in pointy clusters above the foliage, are an outstanding nectar source for bees, butterflies, and hummingbirds. Plants are either male or female; only female flowers form the fuzzy burgundy-red berries held in tight, triangular clusters above branches, which are very showy well into winter. When seeds first begin to from in summer, their sticky fuzz tastes lemony, and can be steeped in water with sugar to make tea. The dried berries are an African spice.

When, Where, and How to Plant
Staghorn sumac may be available at some garden centers, nurseries, and home-improvement stores. But for best availability of cultivars, check out online and mail-order sources. Although it will grow in most well-drained soil in full sun to part shade, the best fall color comes from plants growing in full sun and relatively poor, very well-drained soil. Seeds are available online for the species, but it is best to purchase container-grown plants. Follow planting instructions on page 159. Staghorn sumac is an excellent choice for a large container or raised bed, as long as the soil is not too rich.

Growing Tips
Only minimal watering should be done to get plants established. No fertilizer is needed.

Regional Advice and Care
The major problems for staghorn sumac are gardeners who water and fertilize too much, causing it to lose its fantastic fall colors. No major insect or disease problems affect this plant. Staghorn sumac can grow near black walnut trees (*Juglans nigra*) with no ill effects. Rabbits don't bother staghorn sumac, but deer do like to munch it, preferring the female plants with their tasty flowers and fruit.

Companion Planting and Design
Because of its round-topped colony-forming habit, staghorn sumac is best used as an accent, or planted along a hot, dry fence row. Grow it on a steep bank where it can spread with abandon with native wildflowers for company. Underplant it with yucca (*Yucca filamentosa*) for year-round naturalistic effect. It's also very good for large containers, especially paired with colorful coleus (*Plectranthus scutellarioides*). Plant Tiger Eyes® as a specimen plant.

Try These
'Laciniata' is a naturally occurring staghorn variety with finely divided, almost ferny leaflets and distinct orange fall color; it's less vigorous than the species. Patented Tiger Eyes® ('Bailtiger', to 6 feet tall and wide) has caught gardeners' eyes with its deeply dissected, fernlike leaves that open chartreuse in spring and then turn bright yellow. Come fall, the leaves take on striking hues of scarlet and orange. It is illegal to propagate this shrub.

Weigela

Weigela florida

Botanical Pronunciation
wy-JEE-lah FLOOR-ih-dah

Bloom Period and Seasonal Colors
Spring, repeat bloom mid- to late summer, rose pink

Mature Height × Spread
4 to 6 ft. × 4 to 6 ft.

Zones 4 to 8

Some old-fashioned deciduous shrubs just won't fade away, including weigela, whose late-spring flowers knock my slippers off. This outstanding hummingbird magnet has arching branches that give it a fountainlike effect up to 6 feet tall and wide. Long oval leaves are dark green or variegated (in some varieties). In late spring (and a small reprise in mid- to late summer) loose clusters of rose-pink, 1½-inch, narrow trumpet flowers appear, weighing branches downward as if to show off the flowers. The *florida* in its Latin name simply means, "producing abundant flowers." The plant I got in 1997 as a 3-inch cutting has been abused, yet is thriving in my front yard despite being moved on a 102-degree August day. Talk about a tough plant!

When, Where, and How to Plant
Weigela is available at nurseries, garden centers, and home-improvement stores as well as from online and mail-order sources. Any well-drained soil will do, but for best foliage and flower color, weigela prefers a good loamy soil with moderate fertility, and full sun. For detailed planting information, go to page 159. Add several inches of organic mulch around the base of the plant to keep the roots cool, taking care to keep the mulch at least 1 inch away from any stems. Maintain lightly moist soil until the plant is established.

Growing Tips
Water only when it's desperately needed. Fertilize lightly every spring.

Regional Advice and Care
Preserve weigela's natural shape by pruning after flowering—if at all. Other than cutting it back by half when moving (twice), my 'Wine and Roses' (pictured) has been left alone and is gorgeous with a second burst of bloom in summer lasting well into fall. If you do prune, selectively thin older canes in late spring and early summer, and leave others to fill in. It has no major pests. Hummingbirds are welcome guests visiting throughout the flowering season.

Companion Planting and Design
Weigela provides an excellent color bridge after lilacs (*Syringa vulgaris*) and before summer perennials kick in. Use it as a specimen. Plant shrubs intermittently down a long fence to add interest and color. Used in groups on a hillside or other broad area, the flowers and form can be a stunning focal point. Utilize it as a small screen; weigela tolerates reflected heat well enough to use around parking areas.

Try These
'Dropmore Pink' (to 6 feet) has rose-pink flowers and deep green leaves. Patented Eyecatcher® ('Walweigeye', to 3 feet) is a show-stopper (it's illegal to propagate) with variegated foliage— bright yellow with irregular green centers— and dark rose-red blooms. My Monet® ('Verweig', to 18 inches), has tricolor leaves (green center with creamy white and pink) and small, soft pink blossoms. Patented Wine and Roses® ('Alexandra' to 5 feet), pictured, sports purple leaves that turn very dark purple in fall and hot rose-pink flowers.

TREES

FOR THE PRAIRIE & PLAINS STATES

Trees are the dominant plants in the landscape for their mere size alone. Their uses are many and varied. Trees can define the border of the property, line a driveway, shade the house in summer, protect the house from cold winter winds, provide privacy from the road or neighbors, hide an unsightly outbuilding or neighboring property, and muffle road noise. Even a single tree can perform some of those functions. In addition, the choice of trees can set the tone for the entire landscape. Depending on how they are sited, the effect on the home and surrounding property can vary tremendously.

A single tree—set apart (usually in the lawn away from other plants)—is called a specimen. This may be a tree with a unique form or shape—pendulous, columnar, sinuous, dwarf, or angular—that provides year-round interest. Or it may be one with appealing color (foliage, flowers, fruit). Evergreens are good specimen plants, providing year-round interest. Depending on the size of your property, you can have more than one specimen tree. However, on a typical suburban lot, two or more specimens lose their uniqueness and impact, as they tend to blend into the surrounding landscape.

Evergreen and Deciduous Types

An evergreen tree keeps its leaves throughout the entire year, while a deciduous tree sheds its leaves, usually in autumn. We often think of evergreens as conifers—cone-bearing, needled trees such as pines, firs, hemlocks, or spruces. However, there is another group of evergreens—broadleaved evergreens, which include hollies and some magnolias.

When planning your garden, remember that it's more interesting to have a combination of different types of trees. Of course, evergreens provide winter interest with their color, but look for variegated evergreens for additional appeal. Many deciduous trees are great accents in winter for their form or unusual bark.

Choosing a Tree

When you buy a tree, it may come one of three ways—bare root, container grown, or balled and burlapped (B&B). Bare-root trees are most likely to come from online and mail-order sources, while container-grown and balled-and-burlapped are available locally.

When purchasing a tree, your budget may be limited. However, unless you have the patience or you are buying a fast-growing tree, it is best to invest in the largest

tree you can afford, especially when buying bare-root trees as they are usually smaller, and younger. When buying locally, check out several nurseries, garden centers, and home-improvement stores. You'll find a difference in price and quality. It's best to buy a deciduous tree in spring before it leafs out, cutting the danger of transplant shock. The ideal planting time is spring; second best is early fall. Inspect the tree to make sure that there is no damage to major limbs, that the bark is intact, and that there are no holes that might indicate insect damage or infestation.

Planting

When you receive a bare-root tree, unpack it immediately and soak the roots and about 12 inches of the trunk in muddy water with 1 tablespoon undiluted transplant solution overnight. If you cannot plant the tree the next day, heel it in—dig a trench and lay the tree at an angle so the roots are completely buried. Kept well watered, a tree can remain heeled in up to a month.

To plant a tree, dig a hole about one-and-one-half times the width and depth of the root system and loosen the soil removed from the hole. Add back about one-third of the loosened soil to the hole. If you are planting a **bare-root tree**, make a cone of soil of a proper height and width so that the roots can spread down around the cone with the base of the trunk at ground level. Place the tree on the cone and make any adjustments necessary. Fill in the hole with remaining soil. Gently tamp the soil down with your hands. Make a 3-inch high ring of soil—creating a water basin—around the planting hole. Water with several gallons of transplant solution (following

Dig a hole 1½ times as deep and wide as the root system. Do *not* amend soil. Remove all burlap from the plant, and position in the hole. Adjust the height so the tree is setting slightly above where it was in its container or the nursery (if **B&B**). Shovel in the remaining soil, tamping lightly as you go.

package directions for diluting it). Mulch with 3 inches of wood chips (plain, not colored); keep the mulch several inches from the trunk. Add mulch over the water basin to make it sturdier.

For a **container-grown tree**, follow the same directions for digging and loosening the soil. Shovel about one-third of the soil into the hole. Pour in 2 quarts of transplant solution. While it's still in its container, soak the tree in a bucket of transplant solution for several minutes. Remove the tree from the container. If it is packed in tightly, which indicates it may be rootbound, cut the container from around the root mass with scissors and, if necessary, unwind any roots. If it's very rootbound, with roots spreading all over the sides, use a knife to make four ½-inch-deep vertical slits equidistant around the rootball. This loosens the roots, allowing them to grow into the surrounding soil. Place the tree in the hole, adjusting the amount of soil underneath so it is at the same soil level it was in the pot. Hint: lay a ruler or board across the hole to check the levels. Fill the hole following the directions above, including making a water basin and mulching.

Planting a **balled-and-burlapped tree** is similar, but do *not* soak it in transplant solution. It is hard to tell real burlap from the plastic type, so remove it. Real burlap decays in the soil, but the plastic type inhibits root growth. Trees that are balled and burlapped can be large and heavy, so you may need help. Once you have dug the hole, move the tree next to it. Add soil to the hole so the tree will be at the proper height when planted. Loosen the tie around the top of the burlap. Place the tree in the hole,

It's probably not necessary to stake, but if you do, then remove the wires and stakes after one year.

and by angling and lifting it (this is where the assistance comes in), remove all the burlap. Sometimes there's a surprise under the burlap—a metal or plastic mesh basket. Remove that too. Once the tree is positioned at the proper height, water with several gallons of transplant solution. Fill in with the remaining soil, firm the soil with your hands, make a water basin, and water with another gallon or two—depending on the size of the tree. Mulch as described previously.

Staking

Staking isn't necessary unless the tree is in a windy site or its rootball is too small to keep it upright until it has established a good root system. Researchers have discovered that small amounts of movement of a tree actually *help* strengthen the trunk and root system.

If staking is necessary, you will need three metal tree stakes that are looped (or eyed) at the top; a hammer or mallet; heavy wire and wire cutters; and some old hose. Drive the stakes into the ground about 3 feet away from the center of the tree (or just outside the water basin)—angled slightly outward—equidistant from each other. Measure the wire. For each stake, the wire needs to be twice the distance from the stake to the trunk (just above the lowest sturdy branch) plus 12 inches. Attach one end of the wire to the stake, looping it around the eye. Slide a 12-inch length of hose onto the wire. Loop the hose-covered wire around the trunk, not too tight. Attach the other end of the wire to the stake, wrapping it several times. Cut off any excess wire. Repeat for each stake. Check the stakes monthly to be sure they aren't too tight around the trunk. Do not leave the tree staked for more than six to eight months.

Unless otherwise noted in the "Regional Advice and Care" section, the featured tree has no major pest or disease problems. Many trees, evergreens and deciduous, are container grown. Now you can sit back, relax, and watch your trees grow.

Other Choice Trees

Here are some more trees that would make a great addition to your home and garden.

Balm of Gilead	*Populus balsamifera (P. candicans)*
Black cherry	*Prunus serotina*
Boxelder	*Acer negundo*
Catalpa	*Catalpa speciosa*
Eastern cottonwood	*Populus deltoides*
Honeylocust	*Gleditsia triacanthos*
Japanese yew	*Taxus cuspidata*
Norway spruce	*Picea abies*
Quaking aspen	*Populus tremuloides*
Southern catalpa	*Catalpa bignonioides*

Allegheny Serviceberry

Amelanchier laevis

Botanical Pronunciation
am-ul-LANK-ee-ur LEE-viss

Other Name Smooth serviceberry

Bloom Period and Seasonal Colors
Spring, white; fall, orange or red foliage

Mature Height × Spread 25 to 30 ft. × 20 to 25 ft.

Zones 4 to 8

Native to woodland creek banks, this suckering tree gets its common name from the settlers' tradition of holding memorial services when the tree flowered for those who died during winter. Shadblow, another common name, refers to its flowering when shad fish begin swimming up creeks. It's grown for its hanging clusters of white or pink-flushed flowers and for the sweet, blueberry-looking, pie-quality summer fruit to which birds race gardeners in June—hence its other common name, Juneberry. These berries formed the basis of pemmican, a Native American trail food; the tree's stems were made into arrows. Dark green leaves are bronzy purple when new and turn a fine orange or red in autumn. Its grayish bark is attractive, and the winter silhouette is airy and graceful.

When, Where, and How to Plant
Allegheny serviceberry is available locally, however, the choice varieties can be found through online and mail-order sources. It prefers wet woodsy sites, so grow it in acidic, fertile, and moist but well-drained soil in sun to part shade. Create a naturalistic woodland soil by digging a wide area of native soil at least a foot deep around where the tree will go. Thoroughly mix in a 2- or 3-inch layer of a mixture of compost and peat moss. Plant as described on page 159, and then cover with a thick mulch of natural leaf litter (shred oak leaves by running them over with a lawn mower).

Growing Tips
Feed the newly planted tree very lightly and keep it moist through its first summer. Mulch with leaf litter, which breaks down to feed the tree, and water during drought.

Regional Advice and Care
Many gardeners prefer pruning it up as a specimen tree, removing any suckers every year or two. Bees are attracted to the fragrant flowers in spring. It can be a race against the birds to pick the berries (delicious cooked in pies and jams, and yummy fresh in smoothies, with breakfast cereal, or as a topping on ice cream). It has no serious pest or disease problems.

Companion Planting and Design
Grow Allegheny serviceberry in a small grouping at the edge of a woodland or as a specimen tree in a shrub border, preferably with a dark background to highlight its bright show of flowers, fall colors, and winter form. Its noninvasive roots and light shade make this a good tree under to underplant with ferns, trillium (*Trillium* spp.), and other woodland perennials. It makes an interesting background addition to a wildlife garden.

Try These
'Cumulus' (to 30 feet tall) is a vigorous, upright-growing tree with orange-red fall color. 'Prince Charles' (to 25 feet) has an upright, oval form; emerging leaves are bronzy red; fruit is almost as tasty as the species. 'Snowcloud' (to 25 feet) has a fastigiate form and large white flowers; blue-green leaves turn orange in autumn; excellent fruit.

American Arborvitae

Thuja occidentalis

Botanical Pronunciation
THOO-yah oks-ee-den-TAL-is

Other Name Northern white cedar

Bloom Period and Seasonal Colors
Late summer, reddish cones; evergreen foliage

Mature Height × Spread 20 to 30 ft. × 10 to 15 ft.

Zones 3 to 7

American arborvitae, also known as Eastern white cedar, is a mighty tree, with a compact, conical form. An evergreen conifer, it has unique, flattened branchlets of overlapping, yellowish green, fragrant small scales—each pair of branchlets at right angles to the pair above and below. Oblong cones, about ½-inch-long, are erect on the branchlets. Handsome, furrowed, ridged bark is somewhat fibrous, ranging from reddish brown to gray. Separate male and female cones are borne in spring. The small ½-inch, fertilized female cones mature in late summer and are lovely shades of light yellow to cinnamon red. They are fragile and stand erect on the branchlets. Numerous cultivars are available ranging from 20-inch-high dwarf conifers to others 20 feet or taller. All are slow growing.

When, Where, and How to Plant
American arborvitae is available locally as well as from online and mail-order sources. It grows well in limey, moist, or boggy soil. It thrives in full sun protected from the wind, but will also grow in part sun or part shade. Plant following the directions on page 159.

Growing Tips
Water lightly until it is established; water deeply during drought. Do not fertilize for the first two years. After that, use fertilizer stakes in spring, following package directions. There are different types for all kinds of trees and shrubs. Be sure to use one for evergreen trees. Pound the stake(s) into the ground, and the fertilizer gradually releases into the soil.

Regional Advice and Care
This is a very low-maintenance plant. It is slow growing—about 8 to 10 inches a year. It will tolerate pruning and shearing, but let it keep its natural shape. I like to cut off the lower branches to expose its handsome trunk. On a 15-foot tree, allow about 3 feet of trunk to show. You can transplant it in spring, summer, or fall.

Companion Planting and Design
American arborvitae makes a beautiful specimen tree all by itself on the lawn. In a grouping, it makes an excellent windbreak or hedge. It is even handsome when kept pruned back at the back of a mixed border. Plant it where its foliage, which turns bronze in winter, can be enjoyed during the cold months.

Try These
'Danica (to 20 inches) has upright, emerald-green branchlets that turn blue-green in winter. 'Filiformis' (to 8 feet) is a weeping form with branches that sweep the ground. 'Gold Drop' (to 6 feet) has a dwarf pyramidal form with golden foliage. North Pole® ('Art Boe', to 15 feet), a patented variety that's illegal to propagate, has a narrow columnar form. 'Smaragd' (also sold as 'Emerald' or 'Emerald Green', to 15 feet) has glossy green foliage in a narrow pyramidal form. 'Techny' (sometimes sold as 'Mission', to 15 feet) has a perfectly pyramidal shape; dark green foliage doesn't change color in winter.

Crabapple

Malus spp. and cultivars

Botanical Pronunciation MAL-us

Other Name Flowering crabapple

Bloom Period and Seasonal Colors
Mid-spring, shades of white, pink, red; late summer into winter, wine-red fruits

Mature Height × Spread 10 to 25 ft. × 15 to 20 ft.

Zones 4 to 8

We had a crabapple in our garden when I was a child. I wish I knew the variety, as its fruits were large, deep wine red, and *delicious*. I was discouraged from eating them, even though we did eat jarred spiced crabapples. I remember what a beautiful tree it was—year-round. In spring, it had clusters of pretty pink flowers followed by bright green leaves. We didn't even notice the fruit, with so many other things going on in the garden, until it colored up in early fall. Some years—depending on how hungry the birds and I were—the fruit persisted into winter. Even the shape of a bare tree, with its horizontal branches, gave architectural interest in winter, especially with snow-covered branches.

When, Where, and How to Plant
Many crabapples are available in spring at nurseries, garden centers, and home-improvement stores. But superior varieties are only found through online and mail-order sources. Crabapples grow and produce fruit best in full sun in slightly moist, well-drained, average to rich, slightly acidic loamy soil. Plant dormant crabapples as soon as the ground can be worked in spring, following the instructions on page 159.

Growing Tips
Keep soil lightly watered until the plant is established (the first year and a half). Water deeply if the top inch of soil is dry. Do not fertilize the first year, but fertilize yearly thereafter with fertilizer stakes, following package instructions for flowering deciduous trees. Before you eat the fruit, check the fertilizer label to be sure it is safe for edible plants.

Regional Advice and Care
Prune any crossed or rubbing branches to open the center of the tree to sunlight and air circulation, and to promote fruit production. Promptly prune branches damaged by wind or winter storms. Crabapple is susceptible to apple scab and apple canker, both of which can damage leaves and fruit. Remove and destroy any infested branches. Bees are attracted to the fragrant flowers and birds feast on the fruit. Fruits are good pickled or made into preserves.

Companion Planting and Design
Crabapples are beautiful planted with spring bulbs, such as daffodils (*Narcissus* spp.), tulips (*Tulipa* spp.), or Siberian squill (*Scilla siberica*), beneath them or with a groundcover "skirt" of periwinkle (*Vinca minor*).

Try These
'Cardinal' (to 15 feet) has bright red flowers, purple-tinged leaves, and ½-inch, deep red fruit. 'Donald Wyman' (to 20 feet) has white blooms, ⅜-inch bright red fruit, and dark green leaves that turn gold in fall. 'Leprechaun' (to 8 feet) has pink flowers that mature white and ¼-inch, cherry-red fruit. 'Prairifire' (to 20 feet) yields deep pinkish red blossoms, ½-inch purplish red fruit, and leaves with red-tinged veins that turn orange in fall. 'Red Jade' (to 15 feet) is an heirloom weeping variety with white flowers and bright red ⅝-inch fruit.

Dwarf Alberta Spruce

Picea glauca 'Conica'

Botanical Pronunciation pye-SEE-uh GLAW-kuh

Other Name Dwarf white spruce

Bloom Period and Seasonal Colors
Evergreen foliage

Mature Height × Spread
6 to 15 ft. × 3 to 8 ft.

Zones 3 to 6

Very few plants give the instant eye-appeal of dwarf conifers. As accents, companions to perennials, or as tough container plants, they're great. And talk about tough—they can be found growing unattended in cemeteries. Dwarf Alberta spruce (formerly *Picea glauca* var. *albertiana* 'Conica'), a natural miniature form of white spruce (discovered in the wild in Alberta, Canada, in 1904), is a bluntly conical bush, very dense yet soft to the touch—almost huggable. Its light green needles are densely set, radiating around the stem. It is noted for its naturally formal, semi-dwarf, evergreen, and stately pyramidal appearance. Because it's extremely slow growing (only 2 to 4 inches yearly), taking many years to grow from a small plant, buy one close to your ideal size.

When, Where, and How to Plant
Dwarf Alberta spruce is available at nurseries, garden centers, and home-improvement stores as well as through online and mail-order sources. It grows best in full sun in well-drained, slightly acidic soil. Choose a site a few feet away from any other plant, wall, or irrigation to allow sunshine and good air circulation. Shelter it from strong winds. Don't plant near roadways or walkways where winter salt is used. Plant as described on page 159.

Growing Tips
Water deeply but infrequently the first summer—just enough to keep deeper roots moist. Dwarf Alberta spruce does not tolerate long dry spells or being irrigated frequently. Little or no water or fertilizer is necessary after the first year, unless there is drought.

Regional Advice and Care
Lightly shear stem tips to improve its look, encourage new growth, and promote thickness. Hard pruning often kills conifers. If you prune a stem back to where no needles remain, it will usually die all the way back to its point of origin. Dwarf Alberta spruce is susceptible to spider mites.

Companion Planting and Design
Dwarf Alberta spruce is often used in pairs at foundation entranceways or singly as a dramatic lawn focal point. It can provide year-round interest for perennial beds, acting like a sentry around which seasonal bulbs, such as daffodils (*Narcissus* spp.), tulips (*Tulipa* spp.), and iris (*Iris* spp.), come and go. It works well as a long-lived, low-maintenance container plant as long as it's watered during dry spells and the container is large enough so it doesn't freeze solid in winter.

Try These
'Cecilia' (to 2 feet tall and wide) forms a bluish green, flat-topped globe. 'Jean's Dilly' (to 5 feet) is a shorter variety, with light green needles that are concentrated at the ends of each season's short stem growth; it has a wonderful distinctive twist to the needles; its perfect cone shape never needs shearing. 'Sander's Blue' (4 to 20 feet tall) is a sport of dwarf Alberta spruce with soft blue-green needles.

Eastern Redbud

Cercis canadensis

Botanical Pronunciation
SIR-sis kan-ah-DEN-sis

Bloom Period and Seasonal Colors
Spring, pink; fall, yellow foliage

Mature Height × Spread
15 to 30 ft. × 15 to 35 ft.

Zones 4 to 8

Growing up on the East Coast, I always had a particular fondness for redbud, which grew there as a shrub, usually in the 5- to 8-foot range and rarely more than 12 to 15 feet high. It was kind of scraggly and scruffy looking. Part of what endeared me to it was the pink flowers, borne in clusters right *on* the branches. Redbud is in the pea family. Its flowers are edible (as long as you don't spray the tree with chemicals), with a surprising crunch and a pea-like flavor. Moving to Iowa, where redbuds are full-blown big, beautiful, full trees, I was dazzled—and overjoyed. Charming heart-shaped, blue-green leaves emerge after the flowers fade and turn a lovely shade of yellow in autumn.

When, Where, and How to Plant
Redbuds are available locally. A good choice of varieties, however, is only found through online and mail-order sources. In the wild, redbuds are understory trees, growing in filtered shade from taller trees; however, if you really want to see a redbud show its stuff, plant it in full sun. It will grow in any well-drained soil, acidic or alkaline; however, wet soil is a death knell. Plant as described on page 159.

Growing Tips
Keep the tree very lightly watered until it is established—for the first two years. After that, it requires deep watering only when the top 2 inches of soil become dry. It will not tolerate constantly wet soil. Do not fertilize the first year. After that, fertilize yearly using tree spikes following

package instructions for the size of the tree. If you want to eat the flowers, read the fertilizer label carefully. Use a fertilizer that is specifically for edible plants.

Regional Advice and Care
Each spring, add a fresh 3-inch layer of organic mulch. There are some pests and diseases to watch out for, such as scale, aphids, leafhoppers, downy mildew, canker, and blight. If the tree is healthy, has good air circulation, is well fed but not overfed, and is not stressed from drought, any of the pests may be present but not in numbers to damage the tree.

Companion Planting and Design
A redbud is a lovely specimen tree that is also at home at the edge of a woodland, mixed border, or cottage garden with other spring bloomers like forsythia (*Forsythia* spp.), star magnolia (*Magnolia stellata*), and wildflowers. If you want to eat the flowers, don't plant under the tree; you want access to the branches.

Try These
'Alba' (to 20 feet tall) bears white flowers, as does 'Royal'. 'Forest Pansy' (to 25 feet), pictured above, bears beautiful dark purple leaves; it is slightly less hardy than the species. Lavender Twist® ('Covey', to 8 feet) is a patented variety (it is illegal to propagate it), which has a unique weeping form.

Japanese Maple

Acer palmatum

Botanical Pronunciation
AY-sir pal-MAY-tum

Bloom Period and Seasonal Colors
Spring, purplish red (inconspicuous); fall,
colorful foliage

Mature Height × Spread
10 to 25 ft. × 10 to 25 ft.

Zones 5 to 8

Every day of the year, even in winter, Japanese maples are stunningly graceful and colorful and come in such huge array of forms and hues of red or green there should be at least one in every landscape. The small- to medium-sized trees, native to Asian forests, have been selected for the most exotic forms, even including shrublike dwarfs. Their sinuous, dark trunks and branches are exciting in the winter; however, their deeply divided leaves are the attention-grabbers. Foliage colors range from light yellow or green to red-tinged, to blood red or deep burgundy, even variegated. Flowers are not showy—just purplish red clusters in the spring. However, they are followed by classic red winged maple seedpods (called samaras) that can be fairly splendid.

When, Where, and How to Plant

Many Japanese maples are available locally, but the range of varieties is found through online and mail-order sources. These plants tolerate full sun, but in hot windy summers they hold their color better and suffer less leaf-tip burn when planted in light afternoon shade. Avoid root damage by providing deep, well-drained soil. Mix organic matter, such as compost or rotted manure, with the native soil, or grow in slightly raised mounds for extra drainage in the wet seasons. Add just a little fertilizer to get new plants started. Don't overdo it, or rampant leaf growth, unsupported by a struggling new root system, will result. For detailed planting information, see page 159.

Growing Tips

Keep soil lightly moist with occasional deep soakings. Fertilize once a year.

Regional Advice and Care

Prune only to remove or direct branches and limbs, leaving no stubs that can rot into the trunk. This can be done any time of the year. It has no major pests. Water during dry spells to prevent leaf-tip burn.

Companion Planting and Design

Large Japanese maples are used as street trees or specimens beside houses, where their leaves are attractive even as they drop in autumn and become colorful additions to leaf piles and compost bins. Small Japanese maples are perfect eye-catchers in flowerbeds, as accents by entries or turns in garden paths, or as container-grown specimens. They are doubly stunted when grown in pots, looking all the world like natural but oversized bonsai plants.

Try These

'Bloodgood' (to 20 feet tall) has 2- to 5-inch-long, dark red-purple leaves in summer that turn crimson red in fall. 'Dissectum' (to 12 feet), known as cutleaf Japanese maple, has very finely divided leaves on cascading branches; there are many colorful varieties. 'Oshio-beni' (to 18 feet) has 3-inch leaves that emerge bright orange-red, mature to bronze-green in summer, and turn scarlet in fall. 'Sango Kaku' (also known as coral bark maple, to 25 feet) has an electric combination of 2-inch leaves (emerging red-edged, yellow-green, maturing to light green, and turning yellow-gold in autumn) with showy new pink bark.

Littleleaf Linden

Tilia cordata

Botanical Pronunciation
TILL-ee-uh kore-DAY-tuh

Other Name Small-leaved lime

Bloom Period and Seasonal Colors
Early summer, pale yellow; fall, yellow leaves

Mature Height × Spread
35 to 70 ft. × 15 to 40 ft.

Zones 3 to 7

Littleleaf linden, as its name implies, has the same typical heart-shaped leaves as other lindens but is more diminutive. The deep green, lustrous leaves are 3 inches wide, with blue-green undersides. In fall, it turns a lovely shade of yellow. For centuries, Europeans have used tea made from the fragrant linden flowers (if tree is grown organically) as a calmative. It has a sweet floral flavor; make the tea from fresh or dried blooms. The flowers are quite unique—small clusters, highly fragrant, pale yellow, with a large bract attached. When the linden is blooming, it's abuzz with bees. The tree is quite handsome and has the pyramidal shape typical of all lindens. It is tough enough to be a street tree and beautiful enough to be a specimen plant.

When, Where, and How to Plant
In general, it is easier to find a littleleaf linden through online and mail-order sources than locally. It grows best in loose, average, well-drained soil; otherwise, the roots will girdle. Plant as described on page 159. Do not fertilize the first year.

Growing Tips
Keep lightly watered until the plant is established, for the first two years. After that, it requires deep watering only when the top 2 to 3 inches of soil become dry. Fertilize using tree spikes yearly; follow directions for the number of spikes for the size of the tree. If you plan to use the flowers for tea, make sure to use a fertilizer that is specifically for edible plants. Add a fresh layer of organic mulch each spring; it will break down and also feed the tree.

Regional Advice and Care
If given ample space for its roots and kept well watered and fertilized, it is relatively pest free; however, it is susceptible to fungal problems such as anthracnose and powdery mildew. Usually these problems are unsightly, but they don't affect much of the tree. A professional arborist or tree company can examine an infested tree. Choose the least-toxic treatment. Watering at the base of the tree (not spraying the leaves) can help avoid fungal problems. Japanese beetles can be a scourge.

Companion Planting and Design
If you have a large lawn, littleleaf linden is a splendid specimen tree. It is tough and makes a great street tree as well as a shade tree to keep the house cool in summer. Plant it far enough away from the house that it doesn't grow too close as it matures. An allée of lindens is beautiful and wonderfully scented in early summer.

Try These
'Chancellor' (to 50 feet) has a narrow, upright habit when young, becoming pyramidal as it matures; good yellow fall foliage. 'Greenspire' (to 50 feet) is handsome with its dark green leaves and spire shape. 'Rancho' (to 50 feet) has a narrow, upright growth habit and very small leaves.

Sargent Cherry

Prunus sargentii

Botanical Pronunciation
PROO-nus sar-GEN-tee-eye

Other Name North Japanese hill cherry

Bloom Period and Seasonal Colors
Spring, pink; fall, orange-red foliage

Mature Height × Spread
20 to 30 ft. × 20 to 30 ft.

Zones 4 to 7

Sargent cherry is an elegantly beautiful tree and the finest ornamental cherry for our region. It is the first showy tree to flower in the spring. This spreading tree is initially vase-shaped but becomes more rounded with age, eventually getting as wide as it is tall. The copper- or cinnamon-tinted, shiny bark is studded with prominent light-colored bumps (lenticels). Glossy leaves up to 5 inches long are red when young, expanding to dark green by late spring then turning an exquisite orange-red in early autumn. Bowl-shaped, pale pink flowers up to 1½ inches across are produced in clusters in spring and can even tolerate late snow. In early summer, pea-sized, bitter fruits turn from red to purple-black and are easily found and devoured by birds.

When, Where, and How to Plant
Sargent cherry is available locally. The superior varieties can be found through online and mail-order sources. Plant in full sun and slightly acidic, moderately fertile, very well-drained soil where water never stands, or on a slight slope to create surface drainage away from the trunk. Plant as described on page 159. Feed lightly at planting and water to get it established.

Growing Tips
Water deeply during dry summers. Fertilize lightly every spring.

Regional Advice and Care
Some horticulturists recommend cutting a skinny new, young Sargent cherry back to about 3 feet tall, even if it removes all the branches, to force the development of strong multiple trunks that will make it sturdier later. Prune in winter or as needed to remove cluttered, crossing, and wayward branches. Most diseases are aggravated by poor growing conditions, including overfeeding. Remember that feeding the lawn also feeds trees, so if the cherry is planted in the lawn, additional fertilizer is not necessary. Trunk wounds from mowers or string trimmers also lead to decay. Japanese beetles *love* the foliage but rarely seriously damage the tree. Sargent cherry can live longer than other flowering cherries. Bees and other pollinators are drawn to the flowers.

Companion Planting and Design
A magnificent specimen tree because of its early flowers and stunning fall colors, Sargent cherry also serves well as a street tree (and parking lot tree) for its toughness, and because its small fruits are not very messy. The canopy is too dense for grass to grow very well underneath; plant groundcovers like periwinkle (*Vinca minor*) or spotted deadnettle (*Lamium maculatum* 'Nancy') or simply spread a neat mulch to dramatically set off its trunk and surface roots.

Try These
'Columnaris' (to 30 × 15 feet) has a lovely upright form, growing tall and narrow. 'Rancho' (to 30 × 10 feet) is another narrowly upright form. Pink Flair® ('JFS-KW58', to 15 × 15 feet) is a patented variety (it is illegal to propagate) that blooms a week or two later than the species, avoiding frost damage that can occur in colder areas.

Sugar Maple

Acer saccharum

Botanical Pronunciation
AY-sir SAK-har-um

Bloom Period and Seasonal Colors
Spring, yellowish green; fall, yellow, orange, red, scarlet leaves

Mature Height × Spread
40 to 70 ft. × 30 to 40 ft.

Zones 3 to 8

The main source for maple syrup and countless children's leaf rubbings, this "Canada flag" leaf tree has *spectacular* fall colors, which contribute mightily to tourism everywhere. Summer leaves are dull green, 3 to 7 inches wide with three to five rounded lobes, but they really fire up in autumn with brilliant yellows, oranges, reds, and scarlets. Twin seeds arranged in the typical maple helicopter samara are not very showy. The tree is intolerant of road salt or urban pollution, so it should be used mostly in large urban woodland settings, away from roads and traffic. When looking for a good maple for your part of the region, visit local garden centers, nurseries, or home-improvement stores in fall when foliage of container-grown trees is changing hue.

When, Where, and How to Plant
Sugar maples are readily available locally. Find interesting varieties through online and mail-order sources. Sugar maples need full sun and slightly acidic, well-drained soil; they also need ample moisture for their shallow roots. Prepare a wide planting hole, amended with organic matter (compost, rotted manure, leaf mold) ideally on a slope. (The bottom of a hill has more moisture in summer than the top.) Plant as described on page 159. Cover the planting area with leaf mulch to protect roots its first summer.

Growing Tips
No fertilizer is needed the first year. After that, fertilize lightly in spring. Water as needed to prevent drying out—especially during a drought.

Regional Advice and Care
Mulch the root area every spring. The far-ranging, competitive roots of sugar maples will find fertilizer under any nearby lawn. Feed the lawn, and you feed the tree. Water deeply during hot, dry summers. Prune lower and cluttered limbs and branches to shape the tree, but don't leave stubs. Protect the trunk from the lawn mower and string trimmer. You can tap the tree and make maple syrup.

Companion Planting and Design
Sugar maple is not the best choice for a street tree because of its intolerance of road salt, its attractive but bulky leaf litter, and the nuisance of brittle branches dropping on parked cars and sidewalks. That said, it's great as a specimen or in groupings. Little or no grass can be grown under sugar maple. Edge the lawn in a wide area under the outer reach of maple limbs, cover with mulch, and naturalize bulbs such as snowdrops (*Galanthus nivalis*), grape hyacinth (*Muscari armeniacum*), and autumn crocus (*Colchicum autumnale*).

Try These
'Caddo' (to 30 feet tall) is native to Oklahoma; it's more tolerant of alkaline soils and moderately drought tolerant. Fall Fiesta® ('Bailsta', to 75 feet) is patented (it is illegal to propagate) and has good heat and drought tolerance; more oranges and reds in fall foliage. 'Green Mountain' (to 60 feet) tolerates heat and drought; it has yellow to orange-red fall color.

Tuliptree

Liriodendron tulipifera

Botanical Pronunciation
leer-ee-oh-DEN-drun too-lip-IFF-ur-uh

Other Name Tulip poplar

Bloom Period and Seasonal Colors
Early summer, greenish-cream with orange

Mature Height × Spread
60 to 90 ft. × 30 to 50 ft.

Zones 4 to 8

A full-grown tuliptree is a truly awesome sight. With the ability to reach 100 feet in height in the wild, it is our tallest native tree. For Native Americans, its size made it the wood of choice for the best and most watertight canoes. Tuliptree is named for the flowers, which, if you can see them, are usually borne fairly high up in the tree on the ends of branches. The flowers look like—and are the size of—a viridiflora tulip (greenish cream, and striped with orange.) Bright green, the leaves are also tulip shaped. I was fortunate to stay at a bed and breakfast with a second story window (complete with window seat) that looked out into a tuliptree in bloom.

When, Where, and How to Plant
Tuliptree is readily available at nurseries, garden centers, and home-improvement stores. Look to online and mail-order sources for the cultivars. To help it achieve its true potential, plant a tuliptree in moderately rich, slightly acidic, moist, well-drained soil in full sun. Plant following the directions on page 159. Do not fertilize the first year.

Growing Tips
Keep the tree lightly watered for the first two years until it is established. After that, give it a deep watering every three weeks during the growing season. During dry spells, water more frequently. Fertilize yearly using tree spikes, following package instructions. Use spikes that are labeled for flowering trees. Each spring, add a fresh 5-inch layer of organic mulch. Over time, the mulch breaks down, forming humus, which enriches the soil, thus feeding the tree further. Mulch out to the drip line (where the ends of branches reach).

Regional Advice and Care
Be patient; a tuliptree is often slow to get started growing and may seem to malinger for several years. The flowers do not appear until the tree is at least ten years old. Tuliptree is generally free of pests and diseases.

Companion Planting and Design
As it has a large network of fleshy, shallow roots that are easily damaged, do not try to grow anything under or near the edge of your tuliptree; just keep it well mulched. A tuliptree is a magnificent specimen tree that also looks handsome planted in front of a mixture of evergreens.

Try These
'Ardis' (to 15 feet tall and wide) has all the beauty of the species, but in a manageable size for small yards. 'Aureomarginatum' (also listed as 'Aurea-marginata' and 'Majestic Beauty', to 80 feet) has gorgeous leaves with broad creamy greenish yellow margins; it's considered one of the most beautiful variegated trees. 'Fastigiatum' ('Arnold', to 60 × 20 feet) has a columnar (fastigiate) form with the same beautiful color and flowers as the species; it's somewhat rare but worth finding as its size is more suitable for a typical yard.

LAWN CARE

lthough there is always a great debate on chemical versus organic lawn care, experts on both sides agree on one thing: Lawn care should be made to be as simple as possible. It may require some extra work initially to get your lawn in good shape with healthy soil. But after that, you can follow a regular regimen.

Spring

After the snow melts and warmer weather starts to settle in, it is time to get out the rake and give the lawn a good cleanup. Use a lawn/leaf rake (the kind with splayed-out tines) to clean up leaves and other debris that may have accumulated over winter. Add the organic matter (toss any trash) to your compost pile. Raking raises the mat of the lawn, allowing it to breathe.

Do you lime or sulfur your lawn every year? *Before* adding anything, get your soil tested. Many nurseries and garden centers do soil tests; there are simple at-home testing kits, too. For a modest fee, most Cooperative Extension Services will perform a soil pH test. It is important to take a sample that is representative of the lawn area, coming from beneath the sod, in the top 2 to 6 inches of soil. If you have extensive lawn areas it is a good idea to take samples from several locations, such as front and back lawns and other areas. You'll need about ½ cup of soil in a plastic sandwich bag, labeled so you know what area it came from.

John Doyle, noted turfgrass expert, recommends core aeration in spring to reduce thatch, promote better root development, and improve compacted soil. Experts agree that compaction is a major lawn problem. People don't think about the soil under the lawn the same way they do about regular garden soil. Gardeners, who wouldn't step in their flowerbeds for fear of compacting the soil, lithely walk across lawns. That's not to say that lawns should be off-limits, but you should recognize the effects of foot traffic. Aeration machines punch out 2- to 3-inch plugs of soil every 4 to 6 inches. De-thatching machines, however, can be detrimental to the lawn. Some experts recommend adding organic matter to help reduce compaction and improve soil structure. Spread a ¼-inch layer of compost, well-rotted manure, or humus across the lawn and lightly rake it in. If you do this after aeration, it will sink into the ground quicker.

Any lawn, especially an old lawn, benefits from overseeding in the spring. Many lawn experts suggest blending grasses (even different types of grasses); unfortunately there is no perfect grass. For example, mix fine fescue with ryegrass for shady areas. Using a variety of grasses cuts down on the incidence of disease and insect problems. Even an all-ryegrass lawn, for example, should a blend of two or three kinds of ryegrass.

Bluegrasses are still the backbone of the lawn industry. They have the advantage of being able to repair themselves and fill in areas. When overseeding, calibrate your drop spreader to distribute about fifteen to eighteen seeds per square inch.

Fall

In most cases, *fall* is the best time to fertilize. Otherwise, (contrary to what most lawn care companies, and lawn fertilizer brands would have you believe) you create *more* work for yourself by fertilizing (especially with a high-nitrogen fertilizer) in spring. This is why: Cool-season grasses have a bimodal growth curve. That is, they have a strong vertical growth period in spring, go dormant in summer heat (without watering), and have a moderate growth period in fall. When you fertilize in spring, the plant puts out top growth at the expense of root growth, requiring earlier and more frequenting mowing—a waste of time and natural resources. Then in summer, when drought conditions are likely, the roots don't reach down very far into the soil. As a result, more frequent watering is necessary to maintain a green lawn—another waste of resources.

When you fertilize in the fall, the plant puts energy into its roots and stores carbohydrates. Doyle makes an analogy of the lawn to a car. When a car runs, the alternator charges the battery so that when it is turned off, there is energy to start the car back up. Fertilize a lawn with slow-release fertilizer in fall, and it stores energy as carbohydrates, ready to get the lawn off to a green start in the spring. I always fertilized my lawn on Thanksgiving Day (even if there was snow). It is a good way to work off that big dinner, feed another life form, and be thankful for the beauty it provides through the growing season. In a case of a lawn that is not in good shape, however, fertilize in spring *and* fall, preferably with a slow-release, organic fertilizer.

Mowing

All the experts recommend cutting lawns high—between 3 to 3¾ inches—especially in hot weather. The longer blade shades the roots, helps conserve moisture, and shades out any weed seeds that might want to germinate. When mowing, do not cut off more than one-third of the height of the grass. If you have let the lawn go and the clippings are too long and look like windrows, rake them up and add them to your compost pile. Otherwise, leave the clippings. They break down and help feed the soil—thus in turn, feed the lawn.

Lawn Weeds

As for lawn weeds, if you are concerned about the environment, it is best to accept them. As your lawn becomes thicker and healthier, there is less chance of weeds having a place to take hold. For now, if it is green, enjoy it. Those young dandelion greens are great in salads or stir-fries—and since you're not using chemicals on the lawn, you can enjoy the greens as well as the dandelion flowers (see page 177).

PEST & DISEASE CONTROL

Take my advice and don't get caught up in all the problems that *might* befall your garden. In all my years of gardening, I have taken St. Francis' prayer to heart (note: he isn't the patron saint of gardening, that honor goes to St. Fiacre). "God grant me the serenity to accept the things I cannot change, the courage to change the things I can, and the wisdom, to know the difference"—especially when it comes to garden pests and diseases.

I have always had a varied garden, with a mix of plants—evergreen, deciduous, edible, and ornamental—and a great diversity. I believe I have had far fewer pest problems than other folks because there is a balance between "good bugs" and "bad bugs." There are places for praying mantis to pupate. Certain plants (trees, shrubs, and many perennials) have permanent homes, while other plants move around from year to year (like vegetables and annuals that can invite problems). This rotation help keeps soil-borne diseases at bay. Keeping plants healthy minimizes the damage caused by insects and disease.

Insects and Diseases

Caterpillars of different kinds can roll up in a leaf and eat it from inside out, skeletonize leaves, or even feast on flowers. Aphids can suck on some particularly succulent stems and buds, and a pair of Japanese beetles could eat, sleep, and breed all on a single rose blossom. Blackspot can kill a rose after a few years. Don't let naysayers spook you with tales of all the pests and diseases to which plants succumb. Nor should you let them try to convince you that lots of sprays and powders and noxious chemicals are the only lines of defense. Have an armament of good bugs at the ready to seek and destroy any bad guys. Encourage beneficial insects—ladybugs, lacewings, praying mantises—that eat aphids and other troublesome pests. Also watch for bees, butterflies, and hummingbirds that visit your garden.

You cannot control the environment, but you can work with nature to keep pest problems under control. Everything does not have to look picture perfect. If you see a few caterpillars, beetles, cabbage moths, or other pests, it's important to remember that not every insect is bad. Armed with a good insect identification book, identify the bug and find out what they will evolve into—some caterpillars turn into monarchs, other beautiful butterflies, or moths, while others are definitely bad guys. Then decide how much damage you can tolerate.

Check plants frequently for signs of pests. Attack insect pests early, while they are young, to avoid an infestation. Pick off infected leaves and insects as soon as they appear. Minimize your use of pesticides; the fewer pesticides used, the greater number of beneficial insects you will find.

Japanese beetles: These are small, shiny beetles that eat holes in plant leaves. Lacy leaves are often the first clue that the beetles are present. Insecticides can be used, but they are harmful to beneficial insects. Do not use commercially available traps; these tend to bring more Japanese beetles into your garden. Remove and destroy the beetles. Japanese beetles are not early risers, so you can shake the insects off the flower or leaf into a zippered plastic bag.

Aphids and mites: Check upper and lower leaf surfaces and stems for aphids and mites. Aphids are small insects (green, black, brown, or orange) that suck the juice out of buds, stems, and leaves. Mites also suck out plant juices; both cause leaves to yellow and brown. Before you do anything, be sure that you know what you have. Once identified, try hosing them off the plant with a strong stream of water. Repeat every other day for a week. If they persist, use insecticidal soap to treat damaging populations. Insecticidal soap is formulated to kill soft-bodied insects; it is not harmful to plants or the environment. It is available commercially as a concentrate or in a ready-to-use squirt bottle (or use the formula below).

Leafhoppers: Check plantings for signs of leafhoppers. These wedge-shaped insects hop off a plant when disturbed. Their feeding can cause stunting and tip burn on the leaves. Leafhoppers also carry the aster yellows disease that causes a sudden wilting, yellowing, and death of susceptible plants. Prevent the spread of this disease by treating problem leafhoppers with insecticidal soap; several applications may be needed for control.

Baking Soda Solution

One persistent problem is fungal disease, including downy mildew, powdery mildew (common on zinnias and lilacs—a white powdery coating on the leaves). It rarely kills the plants; in fact, I'll have silver-leaved zinnias in full bloom, but it does take its toll. This homemade mixture works wonders (especially when spraying starts early in the season, before the disease takes hold). Use it for blackspot on roses too.

Mix a solution of 1 gallon water, 1 tablespoon baking soda, several drops Ivory® dish soap, and several drops vegetable oil; shake well before using. It keeps for weeks at room temperature. Spray the tops and bottoms of the leaves in the early morning, every seven to ten days. Never spray if the temperature is above 80 degrees Fahrenheit. Good hygiene is important as well. Pick up affected leaves from the ground, and cut them off the plant. When cutting zinnia flowers, dip the pruners in alcohol between each cut to avoid spreading the problem.

Insecticidal Soap Spray

Insecticidal soap works well for whiteflies, aphids, caterpillars of many kinds, and Japanese beetles. You can purchase the concentrate or "ready-to-spray" solution (more expensive concentrate lasts for a long time), or you can make your own. Mix equal parts vegetable oil and Ivory dish soap. Shake well to mix. Cap and store the concentrate in a cool, dry place. To use, combine 1 to 2 teaspoons concentrate in 1 cup of water or mix ¼ to ½ cup concentrate in 1 gallon of water. Spray on affected plants, making sure to spray all surfaces. Spray early in the day, once the dew has dried. Never spray if the temperature is rising forecast to go 80 degrees Fahrenheit.

First, Do No Harm

When choosing plant material for the garden, I looked for plants that are resistant to some of the more common diseases, or more often, rely on old standbys like heirloom varieties. I may have some tomato hornworms, but I can tolerate a few (especially as they turn into wonderful hummingbirdlike sphinx moths). When there are too many and the leaves are being eaten quickly, I use tweezers or latex gloves to handpick them and drop them in a zipper-type plastic bag. Sometimes I drop them on the ground and stomp them (good for getting out aggressions). Another caterpillar eats the leaves of the members of the carrot family, including dill, parsley, fennel, and carrots. I plant lots of parsley (both curly and flat leaf make good edgings) and plenty of the other plants. The caterpillars munch away for a few days, but I leave them alone as they turn into swallowtail butterflies.

Sanitation is usually sufficient to keep flower diseases under control. Pick off spotted leaves as soon as they appear. Deadhead flowers during rainy periods to reduce the risk of botrytis blight. Thin out plantings infected with powdery mildew. This increases air circulation and light penetration to help slow the spread of the disease.

I try to live peacefully with the other creatures in the garden. However, I do have a good book that identifies the critters, so I know what is good and what is bad. Remember that if you spray an insecticide (even an organic one like insecticidal soap), it kills both good and bad bugs. If you find things out of control, choose the least-toxic remedy. What I have described are the tenets of IPM (Integrated Pest Management). Learn to accept the less-than-perfect apple, lettuce, or dahlia. And rejoice when the butterflies flock to the Autumn Joy sedum in late summer and early fall.

First and foremost, remember that a healthy plant is not a lure for diseases and pests; a weak, malnourished, or stressed plant attracts them. If you follow the principles described above, your plants should be happy and vigorous.

EDIBLE FLOWERS

Edible flowers are dual-purpose plants—beautiful in the garden and flavorful in the kitchen.

Although it may seem like the idea of eating flowers is a recent culinary development, the fact is that flowers have been eaten for millennia. In ancient China, both daylilies and chrysanthemums were prized for their culinary qualities. Daylilies are a standard ingredient in Chinese hot and sour soup. Roses, too, have a long culinary history. Ancient Romans used roses as savory accompaniments to meat. Today we are rediscovering our floral culinary heritage.

Besides flavor, flowers add a dimension to food that few spices can: Color. Just think of it; flowers come in every color of the rainbow. Flowers make food fun and beautiful. You can even turn family fare, such as homemade tuna salad or macaroni salad from the deli, into food fit for company simply by tossing in some chopped tulip petals, thyme, rosemary, or pansies. To make the dish truly memorable, serve it in a large edible flower such as a tulip, daylily, hollyhock or hibiscus. One of the best ways to introduce friends and family to flowers is to chop them finely and toss them into a mixed greens salad dressed with extra virgin olive oil and wine vinegar, then garnish the salad with several whole flowers. Most people won't eat the whole flowers, but will love the flavor of the salad. Tell them the flavor came from the flowers, they'll become part of the ever-growing number of people who appreciate flowers for their beauty *and* flavor.

But don't just go out to the garden and start nibbling. Here are some guidelines and a list flowers that are safe to eat (vetted by Dr. Jim Duke, author of *The Green Pharmacy*) and delicious.

The 10 Commandments of Edible Flowers

1. Eat only those flowers you can positively identify as safe and edible. Learn the Latin or botanical names, which are universally accepted (common names may vary from region to region).
2. Do not assume that restaurants and caterers always know which flowers are edible. Just because it is on your plate does not mean it is edible (see Rule #1).
3. Eat only those flowers that have been grown organically.
4. Do not eat flowers from florists, nurseries, garden centers or public gardens (see Rule #3).
5. Do not eat flowers if you have hay fever, asthma, or allergies.
6. Do not eat flowers picked from the side of heavily trafficked roads.

7. Eat only the petals of flowers; always remove and discard the pistils and stamens before eating (except for the tiny flowers like thyme where it would be like performing microsurgery to remove the pistils and stamens).

8. Not all sweet-smelling flowers are edible; some are poisonous.

9. Eat only the flowers of the recommended plants; other parts may be toxic or inedible, even though the flower may be delicious.

10. Gradually introduce flowers into your diet—one at a time and in small quantities, the way you would introduce a new food to a baby.

Common Name	Botanic Name	Flavor
Anise hyssop	*Agastache foeniculum*	Licorice
Apple	*Malus* spp.	Floral
Arugula	*Eruca vesicaria sativa*	Peppery
Banana	*Musa* spp.	Sweet
Basil	*Ocimum basilicum*	Herbal
Bean	*Phaseolus vulgaris*	Beanlike
Beebalm	*Monarda didyma*	Spicy/sweet
Borage	*Borago officinalis*	Cucumber
Broccoli	*Brassica oleracea* var. *italica*	Spicy
Calendula	*Calendula officinalis*	Slightly bitter
Canary creeper	*Tropaeolum peregrinum*	Peppery
Chamomile	*Chamaemelum nobile*	Apple
Chicory	*Cichorium intybus*	Slightly bitter
Chives	*Allium schoenoprasum*	Oniony
Chrysanthemum	*Dendranthema grandiflorum*	Mild to slightly bitter
Coriander (Cilantro)	*Coriandrum sativum*	Herbal
Dandelion	*Taraxacum officinale*	Sweet to slightly bitter
Daylily	*Hemerocallis* spp.	Sweet to vegetal
Dianthus	*Dianthus caryophyllus*	Sweet, clove
Dill	*Anethum graveolens*	Herbal
Elderberry	*Sambucus canadensis*	Sweet
English daisy	*Bellis perennis*	Slightly bitter
Fennel	*Foeniculum vulgare*	Herbal
Garlic chives	*Allium tuberosum*	Garlicky
Hibiscus	*Hibiscus rosa-sinensis*	Mild citrus
Hollyhock	*Alcea rosea*	Mild nutty
Honeysuckle	*Lonicera japonica*	Sweet floral
Hyssop	*Hyssopus officinalis*	Strong herbal
Japanese plum	*Prunus* 'Mume'	Sweet almond
Jasmine	*Jasminum sambac* and *J. officinale*	Sweet floral
Johnny-jump-up	*Viola tricolor*	Slightly minty
Kale	*Brassica oleracea*, Acephala group	Spicy
Lavender	*Lavandula* spp.	Strong floral
Lemon	*Citrus limon*	Sweet citrus
Lemon verbena	*Aloysia triphylla*	Sweet citrus
Lilac	*Syringa* spp.	Floral

Common Name	Botanic Name	Flavor
Linden	*Tilia* spp.	Sweet
Marjoram	*Origanum vulgare*	Herbal
Mint	*Mentha* spp.	Minty
Mustard	*Brassica juncea*	Spicy
Nasturtium	*Tropaeolum majus*	Peppery
Nodding onion	*Allium cernuum*	Oniony
Ocotillo	*Fouquieria splendens*	Sweet cranberry
Okra	*Abelmoschus aesculentus*	Mild, sweet
Orange	*Citrus sinensis*	Sweet citrus
Oregano	*Origanum* spp.	Herbal
Pansy	*Viola × wittrockiana*	Slight minty
Pea	*Pisum sativum*	Pea-like
Pineapple guava	*Acca (Feijoa) sellowiana*	Sweet tropical
Pineapple sage	*Salvia elegans*	Spicy sweet
Radish	*Raphanus sativus*	Peppery
Red clover	*Trifolium pratense*	Sweet
Redbud	*Cercis canadensis*	Pea-like
Rose	*Rosa* spp.	Floral
Rose of Sharon	*Hibiscus syriacus*	Mild
Roselle (Jamaica)	*Hibiscus sabdariffa*	Cranberry-citrus
Rosemary	*Rosmarinus officinalis*	Herbal
Runner bean	*Phaseolus coccineus*	Beanlike
Safflower	*Carthamus tinctorius*	Bitter
Sage	*Salvia officinalis*	Herbal
Scented geranium	*Pelargonium* spp.	Floral
Signet marigold	*Tagetes tenuifolia*	Citrusy tarragon
Shungiku	*Chrysanthemum coronarium*	Slightly bitter
Society garlic	*Tulbaghia violacea*	Sweet garlicky
Squash	*Curcubita pepo* spp.	Vegetal
Summer savory	*Satureja hortensis*	Herbal
Sunflower	*Helianthus annuus*	Bittersweet
Sweet woodruff	*Galium odoratum*	Fresh, sweet
Thyme	*Thymus* spp.	Herbal
Tuberous begonia	*Begonia × tuberhybrida*	Citrus
Tulip	*Tulipa* spp.	Bean- or pealike
Violet	*Viola odorata*	Sweet floral
Winter savory	*Satureja montana*	Herbal
Yucca	*Yucca* spp.	Sweet (must be cooked)

Find additional information in *Edible Flowers from Garden to Palate* by Cathy Wilkinson Barash, which contains 280 recipes for sixty-seven different flowers.

GLOSSARY

AARS: (All-America Rose Selections) from 1938 to 2013, winners of 2-year trials in more than twenty test gardens across America. A great honor to be bestowed on a rose.

AAS: (All-America Selections) since 1933, a network of industry-based trial gardens throughout the country that test new introductions of flowers and vegetables. Winners are top-notch plants that are sure to be around for a long time.

Acid soil: soil with a pH less than 7.0. This is often found in regions with high rainfall. Most garden plants thrive in a slightly acidic soil with a pH between 6.0 and 7.0.

Alkaline soil: soil with a pH greater than 7.0. Sometimes called sweet soil. Limestone or concrete leaching from a house foundation can contribute to alkalinity.

All-purpose fertilizer: powdered, liquid, or granular fertilizer with a balanced proportion of the three key nutrients—nitrogen (N), phosphorus (P), and potassium (K). It is suitable for maintenance nutrition for most plants. 10-10-10 is an all-purpose, balanced fertilizer.

Amend: the addition of organic matter (compost, peat moss, well-rotted manure, etc.) or minerals to improve the soil.

Annual: a plant that lives its entire life in one season. It is genetically determined to germinate, grow, flower, set seed, and die the same year. In our region, there are numerous plants that are perennial in warmer climates that we grow as annuals.

Bacillus thuringiensis: (*Bt*) a biological insecticide (which can kill good and bad insects) that, when sprayed at the right stage of an insect's growth, can control caterpillars, cabbageworms, and mosquito larvae. Another species (*B. popillae*), more commonly known as milky spore disease, is used to treat Japanese beetles and other grubs.

Backfill: the soil that is put back into a planting hole after the plant has been positioned. This soil may be native (as is) or amended.

Balled and burlapped: (B&B) a tree or shrub grown in the field whose rootball was wrapped with protective burlap and twine when the plant was dug up to be sold or transplanted.

Bare root: a dormant plant that has been packaged without any soil around its roots. (Shrubs, trees, and perennials purchased through online or mail-order sources arrive with their exposed roots covered with moist peat or sphagnum moss, sawdust, newspaper, or similar material, and wrapped in plastic.)

Beneficial insects: insects or their larvae that prey on pest organisms and/or their eggs. They may be flying insects (like ladybugs, parasitic wasps, praying mantis, and soldier bugs) or soil dwellers (like predatory nematodes, earthworms, spiders, and ants).

Bicolor: a flower or leaf that has more than one color; in leaves this is often called *variegation*.

Biennial: a plant that takes two years to complete its life cycle; sprouting and leafing out the first year, flowering, setting seed and dying the second. Some—such as foxglove and hollyhock—reseed so may seem perennial.

Blackspot: a fungal disease of roses that manifests itself as small black spots on the leaves and stems. Leaves eventually turn yellow and fall off.

Bog: a waterlogged area of land, which is usually acidic.

Bones: the hardscape of a garden; the background that provides the structure; all non-plant material in the garden.

Bolt: to grow quickly and go to flower or set seed, often as a result of warmer weather.

Bract: a modified leaf structure on a plant stem near its flower that resembles a petal. Often it is more colorful and visible than the actual flower, as in dogwood.

Bt: see *Bacillus thuringiensis*.

Bud: a small swelling or nub on a plant that will develop into a flower, leaf, or stem.

Bud union: the place where the top variety of a plant (usually a rose) was grafted to the rootstock; on roses this is seen as a rounded area near the bottom of the stem. With roses in Zones 3 to 7, the bud union should be planted at least 2 inches below soil level.

Bush: a small shrub with many branches and no main stem.

Cane: a long pliable stem, such as a grape, but most commonly one of the main stems of a rose.

Canopy: the overhead branching area of a tree, usually referring to its extent including foliage.

Catkin: a dense spike of small flowers without petals, such as on a birch tree or Harry Lauder's walking stick.

Climber: a plant with the ability to wend its way upward and attach itself, whether by tendrils, rootlets, adhesive pads, or twining stems; needs to be planted near a support. Climbing roses, however, have no physical way to climb.

Cold hardiness: the ability of a plant to survive the winter cold in a particular area.

Composite: a flower that is actually composed of many tiny flowers. Typically, it is a flat cluster of tiny, tight florets, sometimes surrounded by wider-petaled florets. Composite flowers like daisies, black-eyed Susans, and purple coneflowers are highly attractive to bees and beneficial insects.

Compost: decomposed organic material that is used as a fertilizer and soil amendment. Every gardener should be making his or her own compost, no matter how small the garden.

Compost tea: liquid fertilizer made by steeping compost in water—several days is ideal; good for general watering or foliar feeding.

Conifer: a tree or shrub with needlelike leaves that forms a cone that holds the seeds. Most (hemlocks, pines, cedars) are evergreen, but a few (larch, dawn redwood, bald cypress) are deciduous.

Container grown: a plant that has been grown from seed or cutting in a container, usually at a nursery, as opposed to a plant that is dug up from the ground and put into a container with soil.

Corm: the swollen energy-storing structure, analogous to a bulb, under the soil at the base of the stem of plants such as crocus and gladiolus.

Corymb: a cluster of flowers or florets that starts blooming on the outer edges and works its way in.

Crotch: the place where a major stem or branch of a shrub or tree joins the trunk.

Crown: the base of a plant at, or just beneath, the surface of the soil where the roots meet the stems.

Cultivar: a hybrid plant variety (cultivated variety), selected for particular desirable qualities, which can only be reproduced vegetatively (from cuttings) or from the original cross of its parent seeds. It will not grow true from its own seed. In a plant name, the cultivar name is always denoted within single quotes, such as a specific lilac—*Syringa vulgaris* 'Scentsation'.

Cutting: 1) a method of propagation in which a portion of the stem is cut from the plant and induced to produce roots, eventually growing into a plant on its own. 2) The part of a plant cut off from the parent plant that is treated so it produces roots and becomes a plant itself.

Cyme: a cluster of flowers or florets that is branched; flowers start opening from the center outward.

Dappled shade: the pattern of light cast by trees with branches open enough to let light pass through their leaves, branches, or needles.

Deadhead: to remove faded flowerheads from plants to improve their appearance, prevent seed production, and stimulate further flowering. May be done manually or by pruning. Deadheading, however, will remove seeds that some birds and other animals use as a food source.

Deciduous: trees and shrubs that drop their leaves in fall and send out new leaves in spring. Plants may also drop their leaves in order to survive a prolonged drought.

Desiccation: drying out of foliage tissues, usually due to drought or wind.

Die back: a stem that has died, beginning at its tip and continuing inward, most often from cold temperatures, but may also be a result of insufficient water, insect attack, nutrient deficiency, or injury.

Dioecious: male or female flowers are on separate plants. A plant of each sex is necessary for fruiting.

Disk flower: the center of a composite flower, composed of tightly packed florets. This is the center of a daisy, black-eyed Susan, purple coneflower, and others.

Division: the practice of splitting apart perennial plants to create several smaller-rooted segments. The practice is useful for controlling the plant's size and for acquiring more plants; it is also essential to the health and continued flowering of certain perennials.

Dormant: the state in which a plant, although alive, is not actively growing. For many plants, especially deciduous ones, this is in winter—a survival method for cold or drought. Spring-blooming bulbs are dormant from summer through winter.

Double-flowered: a flower that has more than the usual number of petals, usually arranged in extra rows.

Drip line: the area underneath the farthest-reaching branches of a tree that receives water from rain dripping down the leaves and branches.

Dwarf: a naturally occurring smaller version of a plant, such as a dwarf conifer. The dwarf is small in relation to the original plant, but is not necessarily diminutive in stature.

Established: the point at which a newly planted tree, shrub, or flower begins to produce new growth, either leaves, flowers, or stems. This is an indication that the transplantation was successful and the roots have begun to grow and spread.

Evergreen: perennial plants (woody or herbaceous) that do not lose their foliage annually with the onset of winter. Needled or broadleaf foliage will persist and continue to function on a plant through one or more winters, aging and dropping unobtrusively in cycles of three or four years or more.

Fastigiate: narrowly upright. A term used to describe the shape of trees or shrubs.

Fertilizer: a substance that is used to feed a plant—may be liquid, granular, or solid form.

Firm: to gently press (by hand) the soil down around a plant after planting in order to eliminate air pockets.

First frost date: the date in fall before which it is unlikely that the temperature will drop below 32 degrees Fahrenheit.

Floret: a small individual flower, usually part of a cluster that comprises the larger flower.

Foliar: of or about foliage.

Foliar feeding: spraying the leaves with liquid fertilizer (often kelp or fish emulsion, but may be a other liquid fertilizer diluted according to package directions); leaf tissues absorb liquid directly for fast results, and the soil is not affected.

Genus: (plural genera) a group of species that have certain traits in common. When written, the genus is capitalized, and both genus and species are italicized (*Rosa rugosa*).

Germinate: to sprout. Germination is a fertile seed's first stage of development.

Glaucous: a whitish powdery or waxy coating, usually on a leaf. If it is rubbed off or removed by snow and ice, it will come back in time.

Graft: the area on a woody plant where a plant with hardy roots was joined with the stem of another plant. Roses are commonly grafted. Some plants, such as members of the apple family, may be grafted onto a different plant, such as an apricot onto a peach. This technique is often used to produce dwarf plants.

Hardscape: the permanent, structural, nonplant part of a landscape, such as walls, the house, sheds, pools, patios, arbors, and walkways.

Herbaceous: plants having fleshy or soft stems that die back with frost; the opposite of woody.

Hybrid: a plant that is the result of intentional or natural cross-pollination between two or more plants of the same species, variety, or genus.

Last frost date: the date in spring after which it is unlikely that the temperature will go below 32 degrees Fahrenheit.

Leaflet: the leaflike parts that make up a compound leaf.

Mulch: a layer of material over bare soil to protect it from erosion, slow evaporation of water, modulate soil temperature, prevent the soil from heaving due to thawing and freezing in winter, and discourage weeds. It may be inorganic (gravel, fabric) or organic (wood chips, bark, pine needles, chopped leaves). Mulch is usually put around plants.

Naturalize: 1) to plant seeds, bulbs, or plants in a random, informal pattern as they would appear in their natural habitat; 2) to adapt to and spread throughout adopted habitats (a tendency of some nonnative plants).

Nectar: the sweet fluid produced by glands on flowers that attract pollinators, such as hummingbirds and honeybees, for whom it is a source of energy.

Neutral soil: soil with a pH of 7.0. It is neither acidic nor alkaline.

Organic material, organic matter: any material or debris that is derived from plants. It is carbon-based material capable of undergoing decomposition and decay.

Peat moss: organic matter from peat sedges (United States) or sphagnum mosses (Canada), often used to improve soil texture. The acidity of sphagnum peat moss makes it ideal for boosting or maintaining soil acidity while also improving its drainage. It also helps hold moisture.

Perennial: a flowering plant that lives over two or more seasons. Many die back with frost, but its roots survive the winter and generate new shoots in spring.

pH: a measurement of the relative acidity (low pH) or alkalinity (high pH) of soil or water based on a scale of 1 to 14, 7 being neutral. Individual plants require soil to be within a certain range so that dissolved nutrients are available to them.

Pinch: to remove tender stems and/or leaves by pressing them between thumb and forefinger. This pruning technique encourages branching, compactness, and flowering in plants, or it removes aphids clustered at growing tips.

Pollen: the yellow, powdery grains in the center of a flower. A plant's male sex cells, they are transferred to the female plant parts by means of wind, insect, or animal pollinators to fertilize them and create seeds.

Potbound: see rootbound.

®: the registered symbol denotes a patented or trademarked plant. It is illegal to propagate these plants.

Raceme: an arrangement of single stalked flowers along an elongated, unbranched axis.

Ray flower: a flat petal-like floret in a composite flower. Ray flowers surround the central disk flower.

Rhizome: a swollen energy-storing stem structure, similar to a bulb, that lies horizontally in the soil, with roots emerging from its lower surface and growth shoots from a growing point at or near its tip, as in iris.

Rootbound: the condition of a plant that has been confined in a container too long, its roots having been forced to wrap around themselves and even swell out of the container. Successful transplanting or repotting requires untangling and trimming away of some of the matted roots.

Root flare: the transition at the base of a tree trunk where the bark tissue begins to differentiate and roots begin to form just before entering the soil. When planting a tree, avoid covering this area with soil.

Self-seeding: the tendency of some plants, often annuals and biennials, to drop their seeds, which sprout the following spring, producing new plants.

Self-sowing: another term for self-seeding.

Semievergreen: a plant that remains evergreen in a mild climate but looses some or all of its leaves in a colder one.

Shearing: a pruning technique whereby plant stems and branches are cut uniformly with long-bladed pruning shears (hedge shears) or powered hedge trimmers. It is used when creating and maintaining hedges and topiary.

Slow-acting fertilizer: fertilizer that is water insoluble and therefore releases its nutrients gradually as a function of soil temperature, moisture, and related microbial activity. Typically granular, it may be organic or synthetic.

Sport: a natural mutation (usually a variegation) on the stem of a plant. This may be cut from the parent plant, propagated, and sold as a new variety.

Subshrub: a plant that has a woody base and herbaceous (soft) growth, such as sage, English lavender, and Russian sage. Usually classified as a perennial.

Succulent growth: the sometimes-undesirable production of fleshy, water-storing leaves or stems that results from overfertilization.

Sucker: a new growing shoot. Underground plant roots produce suckers to form new stems and spread by means of these suckering roots to form large plantings, or colonies. Some plants produce root suckers or branch suckers as a result of pruning or wounding.

Tamp: when sowing a seed or putting a plant in the ground, the act of gently pressing on the soil with the palms of your hands to make contact of seed and soil, and to help eliminate air pockets.

Topdress: apply fertilizer on a lawn or on top of the soil.

Tuber: a type of underground storage structure in a plant stem, analogous to a bulb. It generates roots below and stems above ground (example: dahlia).

Variegated: having various colors or color patterns. The term usually refers to plant foliage that is streaked, edged, blotched, or mottled with a contrasting color, often green with yellow, cream, or white.

INDEX

Photo Credits

André Viette: pp. 108, 121
Bill Adams: p. 100
Bill Kersey: pp. 16 (all), 17 (all)
Candace Edwards: pp. 13 (all), 21, 41, 90, 105, 106 (both), 131, 142, 159 (all)
Cathy Wilkinson Barash: pp. 22, 28, 33, 43, 47, 53, 57, 71, 73, 77, 79, 96, 118, 120, 134, 135, 137, 151, 153, 162
Cool Springs Press: pp. 10, 11 (all), 12, 93, 144 (all), 160
Dave MacKenzie: p. 101
George Weigel: pp. 63, 170
Getty Images: pp. 24, 37, 65, 98, 99
Jerry Pavia: pp. 14, 32, 35, 36, 44, 66, 69, 80, 94, 103, 104, 112, 114, 119, 122, 128, 130, 138, 139, 141, 147, 152, 167
Liz Ball: p. 169
Monrovia Nursery: pp. 97, 155
Monrovia Nursery, Sandra Nyeholt: p. 123
National Garden Bureau: pp. 8, 87, 109
Proven Winners® Wine & Roses®: p. 157
Ralph Snodsmith: p. 46
Shutterstock: pp. 6, 19, 25, 26, 31, 38, 39, 40, 45, 49, 50, 51, 55, 58, 59, 67, 68, 78, 81, 83, 84, 92, 95, 110, 111, 117, 146, 148, 150, 154, 164
Tom Eltzroth: pp. 18, 23, 27, 29, 30, 34, 42, 48, 52, 54, 56, 60, 61, 62, 64, 70, 72, 74, 75, 76, 82, 85, 86, 88, 89, 91, 102, 113, 115, 116, 124, 125, 126, 127, 129, 136, 140, 145, 156, 163, 165, 166, 168, 171
Troy Marden: p. 149

MEET CATHY WILKINSON BARASH

Cathy Wilkinson Barash is a life-long organic gardener. She has been active in the Garden Writers Association (a group of more than 1,800 professional garden communicators) since 1988, served as president for two years, and in 2010 was honored as a Fellow.

From childhood, Cathy has held a firm belief in economy of space and time in the garden by planting edibles ("beautiful and tasty") among ornamentals. A garden designer whose designs have been published nationally, Cathy specializes in low-maintenance and edible landscapes. Anne Raver of the *New York Times* was the first to give her the appellation "gourmet horticulturist."

Cathy is author of twelve books, and is a successful photographer, nationally acclaimed speaker, and avid cat lover. She is best known as the author of *Edible Flowers from Garden to Palate*, which Martha Stewart described on her television show as "very excellent." The book, published in 1993 and still considered the best resource on the subject, was nominated for a Julia Child Cookbook Award and garnered an Award of Excellence from the Garden Writers Association.

Cathy's other books include *Edible Flowers: Desserts & Drinks*; *Evening Gardens*; *Choosing Plant Combinations*; *Month-by-Month Gardening in the Prairie Lands States*; *Prairie Lands Gardeners' Guide*; *Roses*; *Taylor's Weekend Gardening Guide to Kitchen Gardens*; *The Climbing Garden*; *The Cultivated Gardener* (co-authored with Jim Wilson); and *Vines & Climbers*. Her writing and photographs have appeared in hundreds of books, magazines, and newspapers, including *Foodscaping*, *My Mother's Garden*, *Garden Gate*, *Horticulture*, *Woman's Day*, and the *New York Times*.

A life-long New Yorker (Long Islander), she moved to Des Moines in 1997. After moving to her second Des Moines home, she transformed the front lawn into a showplace garden in four months. Her garden combined edible landscaping with container plantings, and innumerable tough plants. She is about to move again and is eager to create a new garden, this time with lots of containers and a "manageable space." Writing this book is inspiring her to try new plants, as well as include old favorites. Of her experiences, she says, "It is like learning to garden all over again." Cathy is continuing to learn and grow, while in awe of the Prairie and Plains states plants, gardens, and most of all, the gardeners.